NEVER FORGOTTEN

NEVER FORGOTTEN

the search for and discovery of Israel's lost submarine *DAKAR*

david w. jourdan

NAVAL INSTITUTE PRESS
Annapolis, Maryland

Naval Institute Press
291 Wood Road
Annapolis, MD 21402

Library of Congress Cataloging-in-Publication Data

Jourdan, David W.
  Never forgotten : the search and discovery of Israel's lost submarine Dakar / David W. Jourdan.
     p. cm.
  Includes bibliographical references and index.
  ISBN 978-1-59114-418-2 (alk. paper)
   1. Dakar (Submarine) 2. Submarine disasters—Israel. 3. Submarine disasters—Mediterranean Sea. 4. Submarines (Ships)—Israel. 5. Israel Hel ha-yam—Search and rescue operations. I. Title. II. Title: Search and discovery of Israel's lost submarine Dakar.
  VK1265.J68 2009
  359.9'3834—dc22

                                                                                        2009006333

Printed in the United States of America on acid-free paper

14 13 12 11 10 09   9 8 7 6 5 4 3 2
First printing

Book layout and composition: David Alcorn, Alcorn Publication Design

Contents

Foreword: The Story of the Israeli Submarine *DAKAR*

The lost Israeli submarine *Dakar* was found! This outstanding achievement was the result of thirty-one years of continuous effort by the Israeli Navy, with help from the U.S. Navy and other entities. During most of these years, searches had been conducted along the coastal shelf of the eastern Mediterranean, inspired by the discovery of *Dakar's* escape buoy on the beach of Chan-Junes (in the Gaza Strip) in 1969, about a year after the *Dakar* disappeared. Yet, in spite of three decades of research and work, no evidence of the ship was found.

In 1995, a new committee was appointed by the Israeli Navy commander to reevaluate the data collected concerning the *Dakar* and make recommendations on new areas where search efforts should be concentrated. I was given the privilege of leading that committee. The mutual efforts of the Israeli Navy committee, a delegation of the U.S. Navy led by Rear Admiral J. J. Krol, and a team from the U.S. company Meridian Sciences (Nauticos), managed by David Jourdan and Tom Dettweiler, culminated in May 1999 in the location of the sunken *Dakar* off the southeastern coast of Crete at a depth of three thousand meters.

The discovery of the *Dakar* brought to an end thirty-one years of suffering for the relatives of the *Dakar's* crew members and refuted all manner of baseless and wicked rumors that haunted the young sailors and officers of the submarine flotilla, the Israeli Navy, and the whole of the nation. The efforts invested by the Israeli Navy and the Israeli government to continue the search for the *Dakar* are without precedent compared to the responses of other nations to similar events. The tradition of the Israeli Defense Forces to honor the dead and to bring them home for burial, when possible, is one we in Israel believe we owe to the dead and to their relatives.

Solving the mystery of the whereabouts of the *Dakar* left many unresolved questions about the cause of the disaster. Was it a technical failure?

A human error? A collision with a passing surface vessel? Or a combination of failures? David's book does not have all the answers, but it brings to the reader the complete story. *Never Forgotten* is a reliable source that provides us with all that is known of the mystery of the *Dakar*. I believe that we owe a lot to David for bringing it to the world's public.

Gideon Raz, Rear Admiral (Ret.), Israeli Navy
December 2008

Preface and Acknowledgments

I am in the storage room of my home on the coast of Maine, in front of several dozen steel shelves loaded with boxes, bins, and file drawers, all packed carefully with material saved from the last eighteen years of my career in underwater exploration. The containers are marked with handwritten labels telling of exciting and successful deep-ocean expeditions: our 1995 discovery of the I-52, a Japanese submarine that was sunk during World War II while carrying critical war materials to Germany; our work on the live broadcast from the wreck of the *Titanic* in 1998; the discovery in 1999 of the aircraft carrier *Kaga*, a part of the Japanese Imperial Fleet that was defeated at the Battle of Midway in 1942; our role in the construction of a replica of the ancient Greek ship *Kyrenia*, which sailed into Greece as part of the 2004 Olympics; and the 1999 discovery of an ancient Hellenistic vessel that was carrying a cargo of wine to Egypt around 200 BC. These rank among the oldest, deepest, and most challenging ocean discoveries ever made, and each is a fascinating story of history, tragedy, technology, and achievement.

This time, though, I am focused on an unforgettable adventure, a true-life drama that could never have been imagined. I have pulled out all the boxes of information, reports, publications, photos, videos, and other documentation about the discovery of the Israeli submarine INS *Dakar*, and I'm struggling with the sheer weight of the collection. I am also very grateful that I was able to keep it all together, and even reasonably well cataloged, over the years. Although I am the rightful owner of this material by contract with the government of Israel, its legacy belongs to the people of Israel, and I intend to continue to preserve it so the story of the ship, its crew, and their families can be fully told. *Never Forgotten* is my contribution to that story.

The finding of the *Dakar* changed the course of more than one history. There is the history of the Israeli Navy, which had been searching for the submarine since it disappeared in January 1968; the histories of the families left behind, haunted by the mystery and unresolved tragedy; and the history of Nauticos, my company that made the discovery in 1999 and went on to raise part of the ship in 2000. That search and discovery came after thirty-two years of mystery and speculation about the ship's whereabouts—in spite of more than a dozen separate search operations. It was a heart-stirring saga in 1968, as well as in 1999. As Yechiel Ga'ash, lieutenant commander of the Israeli Navy and chief *Dakar* project officer, said, "You have a perfect story, like a Hollywood movie."

How did Nauticos come to solve the mystery of the missing ship? The story begins in three places at once. It begins in Israel, where the submarine community and the families remained confounded by the immense and unexpected loss; with the U.S. Navy, which had assisted on more than one occasion with the search; and with the people of Nauticos, veterans of deep-ocean discovery, who helped me fulfill my own youthful dreams of searching the unknown.

To tell this story, I drew heavily on my personal experiences, beginning with the 1996 investigations in Israel and subsequent activities leading to the discovery of the wreck in 1999, along with the documented experiences of my Nauticos staff and subcontractors while conducting operations at sea. Principal among these were the accounts of Tom Dettweiler, my operations manager, who was later invited to participate on Nauticos' behalf in memorial ceremonies at sea with family members. I worked closely with Israeli Navy personnel during the events of 1996 to 1999, and later consulted with experienced Israeli submariners to gather background information, to coordinate interviews, and ensure my account of the ship and its history was accurate. I visited Israel twice and Cyprus (our base of search operations) several times. I was able to retain all of the formal documentation of our investigations and search operations, including detailed logs, narratives, reports, interviews, and analytical studies. The quotes from family members and accounts of their histories were drawn primarily from transcripts of eleven filmed interviews, conducted shortly after *Dakar's* discovery, in support of the National Geographic documentary *Mystery of the Dakar*, which first aired in 2002. These were supplemented by additional interviews and follow-on discussions I conducted with the help of editor Michele Cooper while writing the book.

I'd like to give my thanks to the incredible *Dakar* search operations team led by Tom Dettweiler; to the staff at Nauticos, for their unflagging support and management of this complicated business during the mission; to Mike Williamson, Mike Kutzleb, and Darios Melas, our dedicated and expert subcontractors; to Yechiel Ga'ash, Gideon Raz, and the Israeli Navy staff, for their faith in and cooperation with Nauticos; to Abe Ariel, for support and friendship over the years; to Ken Lee, Pat Dugan, John Shilling, and Jim Stavridis, who gave me encouragement, as well as constructive criticism on the text; to Lynn Jourdan, for encouragement, support, and occasional prodding through it all;

to Bethany Jourdan for artwork; to Michele Cooper, patient editor and faithful friend; and to Dick Boyd, director of the Mission Planning and Analysis Center, who was kind enough to make that first call looking for our help.

Special thanks to Commander Yoram Bar-Yam (Ret.), who cheerfully answered many questions about Israeli submarine operations, read the entire text (more than once), and helped coordinate with contacts in Israel; and to Oded Ra'anan, Michael Marcovici, and Chava Barkay, for their heartfelt accounts and family photographs. It is wonderful to have so many friends in Israel!

It could not have happened without any of you.

Above all, I dedicate this book to the men of the *Dakar*, never to be forgotten.

Prologue: The Great Expectation

The following has been adapted from pages 138–41 in Uri Oren, *The Commander's Wife* (Tel Aviv: Bitan Publishers, 1968), translated from the Hebrew by Yoram Bar-Yam. Quotes attributed to Oren elsewhere in this book have been taken from this work.

A t 8 AM sharp the city held its breath. As if an alarm was sounded, as if a signal was given, pedestrians and drivers slowed to a stop and gazed at the ocean.

At 8 AM sharp the submarine was due to arrive.

All of a sudden, like a clock, like a wish, like a solved riddle, it will emerge from the sea, exactly according to plan, and dock in its appointed spot at the port of hopes. The entire seaside at Carmel became an arena; the ocean became a stage, and the multitudes became the audience. Only the curtain was not raised.

The *Dakar* did not arrive.

Haifa is a sailor's town. If someone doesn't have a seaman in his own family, he definitely has one in his home or street.

These families.

They were standing there by the breakwater, gathering together like chicks in an incubator with their feet at the water. It seemed as if they wouldn't let go of one inch of the immeasurable and impassable distance between them and the submarine.

Sixty or seventy desperate people.

The wind strikes the faces of the women, with kerchiefs on their heads, and the unshaven cheeks of the men; a crowd of strangers brought together by desperation that exceeds hope. We've seen this all before; we've seen this in the pictures and movies telling the stories of mining disasters, those people gathering by the pit and wishing for a miracle. The same desperate waiting by the sea's abyss, the same eyes that cannot hide any longer what the voice cannot express.

The same faces of pain.

There were two brothers there, perhaps twins, very thin, long and ageless. They held each other's hand and ran all over like a pair of frightened birds. Their grip was so strong that their fingernails were white.

And there another man, a small person with a hearing aid stuck in his ear, who felt as if the only thing preventing the news from reaching him was his deafness. "What do they say? What do they say?" he kept on asking repeatedly.

And on the side, away from the crowd, sat a grandmother and her ten-year-old granddaughter. They sat one by the other on a rock, as two images of agony, facing the ocean.

But the ocean still kept its secret.

Hanover, Maryland, December 1996

T he phone call came out of the blue. Christmas was on the way, the year was winding down, and I was focused on preparing for a flight to London that afternoon. My cryptic notes of the conversation said:

11 Dec 96
Ed Giambastiani . . . Adm. Krol's boss
Netanyahu brought 3 admirals over
Plan to use NR-1, piggy back on Ballard op (4 weeks).

The caller was Richard (Dick) Boyd, director of a government lab known obscurely as the Mission Planning and Analysis Center (MPAC), our biggest and best customer. Admiral Joseph Krol was in charge of the Navy program that included MPAC—essentially, Krol was our boss. Admiral Ed Giambastiani was his boss, commanding the Submarine Warfare Division for the chief of naval operations. And, of course, Benjamin Netanyahu was the new prime minister of Israel.

These were not the kind of names dropped on me as a rule, so Dick had my attention. What he told me was even more interesting: the U.S. Navy was planning to support a search for the lost Israeli submarine the INS *Dakar*, and they wanted our help. Trying not to let on that I had never heard of the *Dakar*, I took in the few bits of information that Dick was willing to share over the phone; not much, but I would certainly hear more, as soon as we could meet. Of course, anything having to do with sunken submarines was a top priority for my company, Nauticos.

Details unfolded in the weeks to follow. Our role in the story began with the former chief of naval operations, Admiral Mike Boorda, who made a goodwill offer to Israel to spend some time searching for the *Dakar* with the U.S. Navy research submarine *NR-1*, which would be operating in the Mediterranean the following year. Tragically, the popular Boorda committed suicide in May of 1996, distraught over questions about the legitimacy of some of his combat medals. His promise to Israel was not forgotten, however, and plans were hatched by the Navy to devote a few weeks of ship time in the summer of 1997 to the effort.

My first question was, "What's the *Dakar*?" quickly followed by, "When was it lost?" and "Who wants to find it?"

✡ ✡ ✡

It was a bad year for submarines.

In January 1968, the French submarine *Minerve* lost contact with the French Navy during exercises in the Mediterranean off Toulon. The entire crew of fifty-two sailors was lost. The wreck has never been found and the cause remains unknown, although it is speculated that a leak in the snorkel mast flooded the ship as it dove.

In May of the same year, the U.S. Navy deep-ocean sonar listening array (known as the Sound Surveillance System, or SOSUS) detected some very unusual sounds coming from somewhere in the eastern Atlantic. When the nuclear attack submarine USS *Scorpion* failed to return from a Mediterranean cruise, it became all too clear that the SOSUS detected its explosively violent demise. Readings from widely spaced arrays were able to locate the event about four hundred miles southwest of the Azores, in water depths of around ten thousand feet. This was the second U.S. nuclear submarine to be lost at sea; the first (and only other to date) was the USS *Thresher*, which sank in a training accident off the U.S. east coast in 1963. The *Scorpion* was on patrol; could it have been sunk by enemy action? By accident? Commander Francis A. Slattery and ninety-eight fellow crewmen were lost at sea. It was imperative to learn what had happened.

The question fell to John Craven, chief scientist for the Navy Deep Submergence Program. With little to go on but the sketchy sonar data from SOSUS, Craven applied a systematic approach to develop plausible theories of the loss. Then he led the development of deep-ocean search techniques that revealed the wreckage of the *Scorpion* on the sea floor in October 1968. Photographic surveys showed catastrophic damage to the submarine as a result of implosion of the hull as it exceeded crush depth, which added to (and disguised) any damage suffered that directly caused the sinking.

Although controversy remains over this tragedy, Craven believes the *Scorpion* was sunk by one of her own torpedoes. One of the most fearsome events a submariner can contemplate is a "hot run" of one of his own weapons while in its torpedo tube or, even worse, still in the torpedo room. Besides the deadly gasses that would be released in the confines of the living spaces, contaminating precious breathing air, a running torpedo can do what it is made to do—explode. Detonation of a torpedo warhead inside a submarine is guaranteed to be fatal; in fact, this appears to be exactly what happened to the Russian submarine *Kursk* in August 2000.

Craven interpreted the SOSUS signals as showing the *Scorpion* had reversed course just before the first explosion. This is one of the actions prescribed to be taken in an attempt to shut down a hot-running torpedo, since they are designed to disable themselves if they endanger their own ship by turning around immediately after launch. Evidence in the wreckage was not completely conclusive because of the damage due to implosion, but the scenario seems to fit well. Of course, there are those who still insist that the *Scorpion* was sunk by a Soviet sub, but there is certainly no evidence to support that intriguing claim.

Although the book is closed on the *Scorpion* tragedy, the site continues to be monitored for environmental effects, and many lessons were learned in the investigation of submarine disasters. How well they were learned would be seen when, thirty years later, the case of the mysterious disappearance of the INS *Dakar* was reopened.

Gosport, England, 1968

T he Israeli sailors, in dress uniform befitting the ceremony of the occasion, marched in ranks along the Gosport pier to man their remade warship and begin the long-awaited journey home. They looked proud and eager, maintaining an easy discipline that comes from competence and confidence. A British liaison officer, a Scotsman, stood in traditional kilted uniform with bagpipes and played a haunting farewell. As the sailors reached the brow, they strode single file onto the black deck, along the rail, and disappeared one by one into the small hatch fitted into the side of the bridge fin. Many were sad to leave, having made friends and found loves in England, but all were eager to return to Israel.

Soon, First Officer Abraham "Boomie" Barkay made his way to the bridge, smiling as he appeared at the rail. He waved to the gathering, and as the ship slid away he gestured thumbs up. The *Dakar* was underway. It was January 9, 1968, a gray, cold Tuesday on the English Channel. The procession was captured on film, and the scene could not have been better staged. Every newsreel or documentary made about the *Dakar* includes the image of Boomie Barkay, his thumb in the air, confident, and proud of Israel's newest ship.

✡ ✡ ✡

It was a day of joy and inspiration at the naval submarine base in Gosport on the southern coast of England, near the Portsmouth naval shipyard. After months of planning, refurbishment, training, and outfitting, the Israeli Navy ship INS *Dakar*, one of Israel's very first submarines, left England for home. With sixty-nine men on board, she would cruise down the Spanish and Portuguese coasts to the Port of Gibraltar, a six-day transit. There, she would refuel and proceed submerged across the full length of the Mediterranean Sea to the Israeli naval base at Haifa, where a jubilant Israeli Navy would gather with colleagues, families, and friends of those on board to welcome ship and crew with ceremony and celebration. It would be a historic day for the Navy—indeed, for the entire nation—moving Israel into the world of modern submarine warfare, using some of the most advanced undersea technology.

Israel was at war. Although the Six-Day War had recently ended with a truce declared on June 10, 1967, the small country's enemies were positioned all around its precarious borders, and they were hardly mollified by the terms of surrender. Egypt still possessed a substantial navy, at least in numbers, and together with their Soviet allies patrolled the eastern Mediterranean with as many as ten hostile submarines. Soviet intelligence trawlers, sub-hunting aircraft, and patrol gunboats equipped with deadly Soviet-made Styx missiles compounded the marine threat. The *Dakar* and her sisters, the *Leviathan* and the *Dolphin*, would assume a pivotal position in the critical planning for Israeli maritime defense.

And it couldn't come at a better time. Hostile fallout from the war that had ended only months before was raging across the Middle East, and Israel felt the impact of intense Arab anger and frustration expressed in violent skirmishes, in newspapers, and at the United Nations. The military situation was tense. The population felt shaky. All of Israel needed this boost in morale and sense of security from the arrival of the newly refurbished submarines.

✡ ✡ ✡

Three new submarines—it was a beautiful strategy and was finally coming true. Before that time, the Israeli Navy had only two subs, the *Tanin* and the *Rahav*. These were ancient British S-class boats (the former HMS *Springer* and the HMS *Sanguine*), reclaimed from World War II mothballs. During the period of the state of tension before the Six-Day War, the INS *Rahav* under the command of Michael (Yomi) Barkay conducted antisubmarine patrols (as a surface vessel), using its lower sonar and depth charges. "The *Rahav* was not able to dive," Michael Marcovici, brother of Isaac Marcovici, a mechanic on the *Dakar*, recalled. "They put some guns on top of the submarine and she was out like a small [gunboat]—they didn't do too much but they were doing some patrols. She was not really able to do too much."

The three ships would make Israeli defenses a significant presence on the sea. The government and the military were not the only ones who believed this was the prudent path. Everyone recognized the need for these ships, especially at the time of the *Dakar*'s acquisition. The Six-Day War was fought when the *Leviathan*, the first of the three, was almost ready for service and the *Dakar*, the second, was undergoing refitting. The *Leviathan* was ordered to race for home, but couldn't make it in only six days.

"We did our best," said Gideon Raz, the first officer who eventually rose to become vice-admiral and retire as second-in-command of the Israeli Navy, "but . . . it was a Six-Day War, and you couldn't beat it. Our passage was mainly on the surface because we wanted to make it as fast as possible, so we managed to do eleven or twelve knots on the surface, which was not the plan. Normally, a submarine should do submerged voyages. We did not find any technical problems with the *Leviathan.*"

It had been a long road getting the three submarines into service. World opinion of Israel was at best guarded and at worst hostile toward the young nation. The support of the Western world was balanced between countering a Soviet military buildup in the region while simultaneously trying to soften Soviet influence in the Arab world. Strong public support for Israel in the Jewish community abroad helped create opportunities for Israel to import technology or find the money to develop it on their own. Israel built capable planes and tanks, but warships were beyond their industrial capabilities. Submarines were needed, and they had to be bought.

Israel petitioned Britain to sell her new submarines, but the proposal was shouted down by the international community, fearful that the maritime balance of power in the Mediterranean would be disturbed. Finally, the sympathetic English, still burdened by the legacy of the prewar Mandate to establish an Israeli state in Palestine, agreed to sell three more World War II veteran subs, this time the more modern T-class boats. Negotiations took place from 1963 to 1965, and sub reconstruction began in 1966, with delivery to take place beginning in 1967.

One of these three submarines had started its service with the British Royal Navy in September 1943 as the HMS *Totem*, renamed the INS *Dakar* for the Israeli Navy. Two others, the *Turpin* and the *Truncheon*, became the INS *Leviathan* and the INS *Dolphin*, respectively. The reason for the choice of the name *Dakar* is a bit obscure. Presumably, in some ancient language the "dakar" was a fierce and dramatic creature. In some sources it has been translated, incorrectly, as "swordfish" or "spinefish." However, in modern Hebrew *dakar* is the epinephelus, a subfamily of the sea bass, otherwise known as the lowly grouper. I doubt this is what the officials who named the submarine had in mind.

All T-class boats were christened with names beginning with the letter T, including historical names such as *Thermopylae* and fanciful ones like *Tallyho* and *Tiptoe*. Over fifty of these vessels were built starting in 1938, and many served gallantly during World War II. Of the twenty-six that saw action, according to *Jane's Fighting Ships of World War II*, fourteen were lost during the conflict.

Back in 1945, the ship was presented with an Indian totem pole by the Cowichan tribe in British Columbia, Canada. The gift, a talisman or good luck charm, came with a blessing: as long as the totem pole sails with the HMS *Totem*, she will come to no harm. Over twenty years, the pole, with its figures representing the thunderbird, the grizzly bear, the killer whale, and the fire god, was proudly displayed on the bridge when the *Totem* entered or left harbor. But when the ship was sold and renamed, the totem pole was saved and taken to the Royal Navy Submarine Museum in Gosport, England, where it can be seen to this day. The *Totem*'s good luck charm was not on board the ship when she set out to sea for the last time as the INS *Dakar*.

✡ ✡ ✡

Officers and staff submariners had months to plan for the acquisition and refitting of the *Totem*. Members of the team started moving to Portsmouth, England, to oversee the refitting, crew training, and takeover. Among the first was the young captain, Yaacov Ra'anan, who was barely in his thirties yet already an expert in submarines. His wife and three sons moved with him to Portsmouth in 1966; the youngest was four-year-old Oded (called Odie), who remembers not seeing very much of his father while captain and crew prepared for the cruise to Israel.

Seaman Isaac Marcovici joined the *Dakar* in 1967, leaving his parents and younger brother Michael (Micha) behind. "We were not a rich family," Michael Marcovici recalled in a 2002 interview, "but all the needs were fully given to us by our parents. But always, we knew that we have to be better, we have to study, we have to do things better, and to try to achieve things that our parents didn't achieve. This is why he went to the Navy. This is why he went to the submarine. . . . As an Israeli I can tell you, always, that there is a huge fight for the elite groups in the Navy, that you always have more than one candidate for any job and if you succeed, you are already one of the best. By being chosen to go to the U.K. and to bring home the *Dakar* put him definitely in a different league."

The Six-Day War couldn't have emphasized the critical work more. In Portsmouth, the sailors rejoiced in Israel's victory and its capture of Jerusalem. They all wanted to be home in solidarity with their country.

✡ ✡ ✡

The *Totem* was already a capable and proven instrument of war when Israeli and British naval engineers began its transformation into the deadly *Dakar*. Technology had improved substantially as British Cold Warriors had worked to keep up in the race to develop better deterrents and more sophisticated means to wage battle under the sea. The submarine's role had blossomed from being simply a stealthy weapons carrier to becoming also an instrument of intelligence gathering and means of delivering commandoes to foreign shores. But the *Totem*'s main weapon, as reincarnated in the *Dakar*, would remain the old-fashioned torpedo. The *Dakar* was equipped with six 21-inch diameter tubes, and could carry modern British weapons, which were much more reliable, accurate, and deadly than their World War II predecessors.

To be effective in countering the fleet of Egyptian warships and even Russian nuclear subs, the *Dakar* needed more range and underwater endurance than was afforded by the pre–World War II design. The only solution was a drastic one. As part of a British "T-Conversion" program in 1955, the ship was cut in half and made bigger, and a new section with an additional battery compartment was added in the middle. Together with better batteries, the *Dakar* could go faster and spend a longer time underwater.

Still, like all non-nuclear submarines, the *Dakar* could spend only short periods of time completely submerged, and even then not far below the surface. Because her main propulsion and source of power was a diesel engine, the power plant needed to breathe air to work. With a "snorkel" mast, the ship could submerge just below the waves with air supplied to the engines through that breathing pipe; the Brits referred to this as "snorting" and the Israelis adopted the term. However, the snorkel could be detected by radar or even visually, and would leave a wake that could be seen by a sharp-eyed sailor or pilot. So the only way for the sub to become completely stealthy was to secure the diesel, lower the snorkel (snort) mast, and run on electric motors, with all power for propulsion and equipment coming from the battery. On battery power alone, the *Dakar* could dive deeper and creep along at a few knots speed, for as long as twenty-four hours if necessary. Higher submerged speeds were possible, but only in short bursts, and at the expense of draining the precious battery charge.

Even then, the boat could not dive very deep. The hull was originally designed to operate no deeper than about 360 feet. If through accident, malfunction, or enemy attack any part of the ship descended to more than half again as deep, the hull would be in danger of collapse. So, the ship would rarely dive as far as it could. Most of the time, the *Dakar* traveled just below the surface, snorkel mast up, trying to hold depth to keep the minimum amount of mast exposed to eyes and radar, while avoiding dunking the breathing pipe underwater. In rough seas, this required constant attention and depended on people and equipment operating in smooth coordination.

Of course, no person or system is perfect, and sometimes the snorkel would dip below the waves. To keep from drowning the vital diesel, and to keep water out of the "people place," the mast included a float valve that would slam shut if dunked. Now, the diesel must have air, and there was only one other place to get it: inside the ship. Many a submariner felt the pain in his ears as the diesel gulped precious air from the living spaces and the pressure dropped.

Even worse, if the mast did not pop right back up, the engine had to be shut down before the air pressure dropped too far. Then, propulsion was shifted to the electric motors, depth control regained, diesel restarted, and the diving officer of the watch upbraided.

Operating completely submerged is also tricky for submarines in general, and depends on a delicate balance of many factors. The key is to keep the ship as near to "neutrally buoyant" as possible, so it tends neither to sink or float. Then the diving planes (control surfaces, known as "hydroplanes" in British and Israeli jargon) can be used to adjust and maintain depth as desired, essentially flying underwater.

The buoyancy of the ship is very simple to understand. The submerged hull displaces a certain volume of water. If the weight of this water exceeds the weight of the ship, the ship will float; otherwise, it will tend to sink. If the weight of the displaced water exactly equals the weight of the ship, the buoyancy is neutral. The trick is to adjust the weight of the ship by filling or pumping seawater to or from ballast tanks in the ship. The complication is that the weight of the displaced water can change, depending on the temperature, pressure, and salinity. These things can, in turn, change with depth, so diving the ship can be especially difficult.

I can attest to the challenge of controlling submarine buoyancy from painful personal experience, in 1980 as a young naval officer on board the ballistic missile submarine USS *Kamehameha*. One of the many critical events in submarine operation is making the first dive after a period of time in port. The ship's weight can change considerably during this time, as the weapons load changes, food and supplies are brought on board, tank levels change, and even as crewmen come on board and leave. The trick is to make the ship as neutrally buoyant as possible before entering port, then keep track of all changes in weight while there. When you head back to sea, before your first dive, you fill out a long and complicated form to calculate all of the changes in weights, and make the appropriate adjustments by filling or draining various ballast tanks. This includes adjusting for "moments" or unevenly distributed weights that would cause the ship to list.

The ship's diving officer (in this case, yours truly) is responsible for calculating these changes and adjusting for them. It was my first dive in this new position of responsibility, and even though I had a couple of years' submarine experience by then and was becoming a senior member of the officer cadre, I was, of course, anxious. Still, I did all measurements and calculations meticulously, had them checked, and expected nothing to go wrong. Expecting nothing to go wrong is, of course, the worst mistake.

Leaving the port of Charleston, South Carolina, we headed out to sea, seeking deep water for our dive. It was winter, and the water was cold, just under

40 degrees. I knew this because changes in water temperature cause changes in water density; warm water expands somewhat, and the volume displaced by the ship will weigh less, so in warmer water the ship will be heavier, all other things being equal. In our case, that amounted to over two thousand pounds (a ton!) for every 1-degree change. Among many other measurements going into the ballast calculations, water temperature was included.

Reaching our dive point, with the ship at general quarters and all stations manned, the captain gave the order to the officer of the deck to dive the ship to periscope depth, which was, in our case, sixty-eight feet. A well-choreographed series of commands, responses, and actions that are fundamental to all submarine operations began . . . sinking the boat in such as way as to be able to control its depth and, at some future time, bring it back to the surface.

"Diving Officer, dive the ship. Make your depth six-eight feet."

"Aye, aye, Sir, dive the ship, make my depth six-eight feet. Chief of the watch: on the 1MC, 'Dive, dive,' sound the diving alarm. Open all main ballast tank vents."

"Aye, aye, Sir!" The chief of the watch repeats back the command to be sure it is understood, then turns to his complicated ballast control panel with its dozens of switches and indicators allowing him to manage the valves, hatches, pipes, and pumps that keep the seawater out and the ship's weight under control. He reports "Straight board!" when he sees that all major hull openings, such as entry hatches and the diesel intakes, are secured, as evidenced by all green bars on his panel. He picks up the microphone for the ship's general announcing system, the "1MC," and says, "Dive, dive," then triggers two blasts of the ship's diving alarm. In the unfathomable wisdom of modern U.S. submarine builders, the traditional foghorn alarm, with the "ah-OOOO-gah" sound everyone has heard in the movies, has been replaced by a blaring, blatting sort of sound that brings to mind an electronic goat in distress. But no matter—every submariner knows the sound and what it means.

The ballet continues.

"Main ballast tank vents indicate open, Sir, . . . full dive on the fairwater planes, 5 degrees down on the stern planes."

"Aye, aye, Sir," the helmsman and stern planesman acknowledge, repeating the order and moving their airplane-like control sticks as directed.

Massive hydraulic accumulators send high-pressure oil to move pistons in hydraulic rams pushing the heavy control surfaces to the right angle, as directed by valves controlled by the sticks. Hundreds of tons of seawater flow into grates at the bottom of the main ballast tanks, as air is allowed to escape from the open vents at the top. The officer of the deck, looking through the attack periscope, verifies that all vents are open by seeing the geyser of spray bursting from each one.

"Helmsman, make your depth, six-eight feet." Sixty-eight feet was "periscope depth" to us, the depth of the keel of the ship that would have all of the ship underwater but close enough to the surface to allow the periscopes to peer over the wave-tops.

The ship began to descend, as the main ballast tanks filled, making us near neutrally buoyant, and the down-angle of the ship, controlled by the planes, forced us slowly down. We moved along at one-third power, a sedate four knots. Everything was proceeding deliberately and cautiously. The helmsman reported the depth as we descended: "Six-zero feet . . . six-five feet. . . ."

But something was amiss. All of a sudden, we had passed our mark and were still descending smartly. The fairwater planes were on full rise; 10 degrees rise on the stern planes was ordered, forcing an up-angle on the ship. Still, we sank.

"Eight-zero feet . . . nine-zero feet . . . one hundred feet, Sir, still descending!"

My anxiety was proceeding to embarrassed confusion as we kept going down . . . the officer of the deck was livid. His periscope was underwater, and he was barking, "Diving officer, get me up!" I ordered the chief of the boat to pump auxiliary tanks to sea. At 250 gallons per minute, the trim pump could get a ton of water out of the ship in sixty seconds. But still we sank! Two hundred feet. Two-fifty. Two tons of water out, and we're still going down. Finally, the officer of the deck orders "Ahead two-thirds!" We are doubling our speed to eight knots, counting on the up-angle of the ship and the lifting force from our increased speed to "fly" us back to periscope depth. I had miserably failed. The entire watch station was upset, and the captain had a serious, frowning face, enough for me to know I was in deep trouble.

But lectures were for later; we still had to regain control of our ship. We finally resorted to engines "ahead full" and we pumped 60,000 pounds of seawater out of our tanks before we arrested the descent at four hundred feet. Now, I can't tell you how close this was to our maximum depth, as some things are still classified. But it was certainly a scary event, and it was deep enough to have crushed the *Dakar*.

As soon as we were under control, I was dismissed to find out "What the hell happened, Mr. Jourdan!" and report back. I had every tank level and storeroom rechecked. I recalculated the form three more times, and had another officer check my work . . . again. Still no difference. Finally, I had only one thing left to check—the seawater temperature. Remember, it was winter in the mid-Atlantic; before diving, we measured under 40 degrees. The answer came back . . . 68 degrees! Almost 30 degrees higher than my original number! At over two thousand pounds per degree, that explained the thirty tons we had to pump out. But what accounted for the rise in temperature? Suddenly, it hit me. I ran to the control room and looked at the chart on the plotting table. Sure enough

. . . during the fifteen minutes between the last time I checked the temperature and the time we dove, we had entered the Gulf Stream. A river of tropical Caribbean water was coursing up the eastern seaboard, and we unwittingly crossed its wandering boundary at just the wrong time.

So, diving a submarine is a tricky business, even for an experienced crew and a modern ship. There was much less margin for error on the *Dakar*. Many a World War II diesel boat succumbed to a diving accident; flooding from the snorkel induction; failure of hydraulics at the wrong time; collision, fire—lots could go wrong, not even counting enemy attack.

✡ ✡ ✡

Modifications to the *Dakar* proceeded as the ship was rebuilt to new specifications in the Portsmouth dry dock. This included a secret weapon—a diving chamber that could hold ten commando "frogmen," allowing them to leave or enter the ship while submerged. This chamber was located at the base of the forward part of the "conning tower" or what was known to the Brits as the "bridge fin." Today in the U.S. Navy we call it the "sail," and it is the familiar tower that sits atop the submarine hull. Another major improvement to the *Dakar* was an up-to-date suite of electronic surveillance gear known as "Tavlit," with special antennas housed in the modified bridge fin, to allow the ship to eavesdrop on enemy communications.

In the fall of 1967, the *Dakar* conducted six weeks of sea trials, testing the ship's power and seaworthiness in the cold North Sea, where the usual minor malfunctions were noted. Captain Yaacov Ra'anan reported problems with the large batteries for the electric motors and noted some leaks that needed dependable repair. (Although these sorts of sea trial problems were not uncommon, even today, their significance was subsequently questioned when the *Dakar* disappeared.) When the malfunctions were carefully taken care of and checked, the *Dakar* was tested again, this time successfully, and stamped ready to leave. She was not fully armed and would sail without torpedoes, but by January of 1968 she was fit for the long sea voyage and operational duty.

Departure day was January 15. The ship would sail south to Gibraltar and, after a short stop for supplies, proceed due east across the Mediterranean for Haifa, where dignitaries representing all of Israel and its military hierarchy would be waiting to honor them. With this in mind, Captain Yaacov Ra'anan took his place at the helm, supported by Boomie Barkay, the first officer (also known as the deputy commander). Arriving in Haifa, they knew, would be a major milestone in their careers—and the history of the Navy as a whole.

At Captain Ra'anan's behest, the ship would ride part of the time on the surface and part of the time underwater during the Atlantic leg. After Gibraltar, the plan was to remain submerged for the remaining transit. It was likely in the captain's mind to beat the record time for a submerged transit of the Mediterranean Sea; such was the competitive drive of these men. The first lap between Portsmouth, England, and Gibraltar was flawless, and the *Dakar* team was excited beyond words. This was a prized assignment, history in the making, the crew made up of the best in the country.

And so were the crew's families excited—wives and brothers and sisters and parents and a handful of very young children of those on board—full of pride and respect for their submariners and their Navy.

Chapter 3

"I find submarines."

T om Dettweiler is a quiet man, full of strong convictions, beliefs, and opinions, which he usually keeps to himself. He is also good at what he does; actually, he is quite good. He finds shipwrecks, particularly sunken subs. Tom and I teamed up for a dozen years as leaders of Nauticos, and together we never failed to find our quarry. Quiet competence and a track record have been Tom's ingredients for leadership.

Tom grew up in Indiana, far from the ocean, but became interested in things marine as a young boy. When you can get him to talk, he'll tell you of quarry-diving with scrounged equipment in water as cold as "liquid ice," dark as "the inside of a cow." Once he described a harrowing experience of being caught on the wrong side of a reef and being dragged across the coral by a buddy, near death. But you don't get enough detail to paint a clear picture, and you always feel that there's more to the story. Tom usually gives you the impression he knows more than he is saying, and often enough you discover later that he really does.

Tom is also smart. He went off to Purdue University in the early 1970s to study electrical engineering, one of the hardest majors out there. After graduating from Purdue, he decided to pursue his love of the ocean in earnest, and he aimed high from the start. Leaving his childhood Midwest home, he headed to the University of Miami and the prestigious Rosenstiel School of Marine and Atmospheric Science. Two years later, in 1976, he had a master's degree in ocean engineering and was ready to learn the trade.

Tom was never an egghead; he believed in doing, and valued practical knowledge and hard-won experience as a companion to book learning. His first job out of school was perfect. Sun Shipbuilding and Drydock Company hired him as an instrumentation engineer. In this capacity, he got to design cutting-edge electronic technology for advanced ship systems, and build his designs, take them to sea, and see how they worked. There are excellent design engineers who spend all of their time in a lab or office, but Tom demonstrated the value of taking your designs in the field and learning directly from your mistakes.

The late 1970s was a great time to be a budding ocean engineer. The Apollo space program had recently set standards for exploration, and the deep sea was becoming recognized as the newest final frontier. Key technologies for deep-water diving had been demonstrated by French and American engineers with the *Trieste's* dive to Challenger Deep in the Mariana's Trench, far deeper than Everest is high. Spinoffs from space technology held commercial promise and encouraged marine explorers to consider the market value of deep-water resources.

But exploration of the ocean was not a natural extension of the space program, despite similarities in the technology and challenge. The Vietnam War was just over, and the Cold War was in full swing. Unknown to the American public, a far-reaching national policy was being crafted. The oceans were deemed too important to national defense to be left to civilian industry. There would be no equivalent to NASA for the oceans, and relatively little government support of deep-ocean exploration outside of classified military projects. Commercial ocean technology development and most ocean scientific research were left to fund and fend for themselves. (To a large extent, this situation persists more than a decade after the end of the Cold War, as the U.S. arsenal of manned scientific deep-ocean exploration vehicles is limited to a single deep-diving sub, the venerable and aging *Alvin*, which, in the twilight of its career, can dive only to about 12,000 feet, 60 percent of its original design depth, and only one-third of the way to Challenger Deep.) Tom's career path was dramatically influenced by this circumstance, as he worked in, with, and around commercial, scientific, and military ocean endeavors.

Although the U.S. military undersea program was veiled in secrecy, its existence had a profound influence on civilian projects. In the late 1970s, industrialist Howard Hughes announced the launching of an ambitious program to recover nuggets of manganese and other metals from the deep-sea floor. Large swaths of the deep abyssal plains are sprinkled with these black, golf-ball sized nodules like pepper on paper. Other companies quickly joined the race to stake out virgin territory in far offshore realms owned by no nation. Treaties were proposed and discussed to consider the existence of natural resources in international waters. And new technologies for undersea mining were designed, built, and tested to try to keep up with Hughes and his new mining ship, the *Glomar Explorer*. In this heady climate, Tom joined Deepsea Ventures, Inc., and became a member of an elite group of engineering and operational pioneers, trying to figure out how to mine the oceans four miles below the surface.

But the *Glomar* was not built for manganese nodule mining; that was only the cover story. Hughes was out to mine a secret treasure. As we now know, the *Glomar* was really a tool of the Cold War, designed to secretly lift and recover a sunken Soviet submarine, an intelligence coup beyond reckoning. But it didn't work as planned, and the billion-dollar project was canceled as suddenly as it had begun. While Tom and his compatriots were designing deep-sea sonars, robots, and sensors, making real progress, and beginning to map some of the ocean bottom in real detail for the first time, the bottom fell out. The *Glomar* was put in mothballs, the race was over before it was finished, and it became clear that it was still cheaper to dig manganese out of the ground than to pick it up from the ocean. The fledgling deep-ocean mining industry wound quickly down, leaving a few small businesses eking out a living supporting undersea cable route mapping and surveying for offshore oil.

But lessons were learned that could be applied elsewhere, and Tom quickly turned with his newfound skills to science. During his six years in the ocean mining business, he took a year off to work with the Cousteau Society and served aboard the famous R/V *Calypso* as electronics engineer and science officer. He speaks very fondly of his time with the Cousteaus, and maintains a friendship to this day with Jacques' son Jean Michel. (Felipe Cousteau, Jean Michel's brother, tragically died in a diving accident during one of the Society's missions.) Along the way, Tom married Hélène, a fiery French Canadian, as outspoken as Tom is quiet. They enjoyed several years in Belgium with the Cousteaus and subsequently working with the Université de Louvain. Tom found ocean science to be as compelling as engineering and technology. So when it was time to move on, he found the Woods Hole Oceanographic Institution (WHOI) on Cape Cod, Massachusetts.

Tom's five years at WHOI were remarkable, and were a chance to solidify his place in the ocean industry. Working under Dr. Robert Ballard at the Deep Submergence Laboratory, he helped develop and operate some of the Institution's cornerstone 20,000-foot capabilities, including the Argo/Jason submersible systems and the SeaMARC sonar system. He used these tools and managed at-sea operations for Ballard in the historic discovery of the RMS *Titanic*, and even got to dive to the deck of the fated liner, 12,600 feet deep, in the submersible *Alvin*.

Tom's work was again bound to Cold War military programs through WHOI. Although WHOI is a nonprofit, private research foundation, many of its projects were at least partly funded by the Navy, as our undersea defense and intelligence programs depended on working with the best and brightest. Also, projects like the *Titanic* provided means to test Navy-developed technology under cover of scientific research. So Tom, in time, became a key contributor to the military community, rounding out his commercial and scientific experience. It is rare to find someone with such a broad range of expertise. Coupled with his blend of analytical skills, practical, hands-on technical ability, and accomplished seamanship, he had become a "triple threat" ocean explorer.

Through these connections, Tom had a chance to explore the wreck sites of the USS *Thresher* and the USS *Scorpion*, the Navy's lost nuclear attack subs. After honing his skills on deep-water operations and underwater forensics, Tom added other targets of military and national security interest to his resume. But Tom was never an effective self-promoter, and after years of working under Ballard's shadow he began to seek more direct opportunities to ply his craft and work with the Navy boys, who had the biggest and best toys in the playhouse.

It was around the time of the *Titanic* discovery that I co-founded Meridian Sciences, Inc. (later renamed Nauticos), helping the Navy to apply fledgling computer workstation technology to problems of underwater navigation, databasing, and sensor analysis, essentially to help locate, position, and map things in the ocean for the Cold War military. Although we already had operational experience as submariners, and had a successful track record of finding small objects in big oceans, we recognized the value of field experience and wanted to build our own at-sea operations team. So when our customer Dick Boyd suggested that we meet this fellow Tom Dettweiler, who was looking for a job, we were intrigued.

My partner Joe Crabtree and I were on a business trip to San Diego, where Tom was temporarily working. Tom had left WHOI for a small company that promised to get him a position working with the Naval Intelligence Command in Washington. After moving his family to Maryland, Tom was shipped out to the San Diego home office after the company failed to get the contract, leaving him with nothing to do. When he asked for an assignment, his supervisor suggested that he go out and wash the company vehicle. This was not a good use of Tom's talents. Joe and I met Tom at our room on Hotel Circle and heard his story. When we shook hands and he left, I said to Joe, "I know we don't have a job for Tom, but we have to figure out a way to hire him!"

This was no small risk to our three-year-old company, with a staff of fewer than ten and cash-flow demands gnawing at what was left of our IRAs. We were about to hire one of the best in the business to start a new division for which we lacked staff, equipment, and customers. Somehow, we convinced our other partner, Dan Schoenberger, that this was a good idea, and so in the summer of 1989, Tom came out to Maryland and joined Meridian Sciences.

Over the ensuing years, Tom helped us build a topnotch operations team, as well as supporting our Navy customers with operations and analysis. He was equally comfortable directing a vehicle recovery, splicing a line, identifying a nematode, repairing a power supply, or briefing an admiral. Although always more comfortable at sea, where his leadership skills would blossom, he was also a visionary who helped develop long-range company strategies, eventually becoming my vice president and Nauticos' second largest shareholder.

Meridian's vision to become a full-service commercial ocean exploration firm was realized in 1995 with the discovery of the Japanese World War II submarine, the I-52. This cargo-carrying sub was built by Japan to exchange critical war materials and technology with Germany when Allied blockades precluded any other form of commerce. On its maiden voyage, the ship was carrying vital metals, raw rubber from Malaysia, three tons of opium (used to make morphine), and two tons of gold bullion. The gold was to pay for German bombsights, radars, and other high-tech products to be shipped on the return voyage. Through a combination of code-breaking, weapons technology, and brave, competent piloting, the I-52 was sunk in the mid-Atlantic in June 1944 by an Avenger torpedo bomber launched from a converted Liberty ship carrier.

Meridian was hired by historical researcher Paul Tidwell and a group of investors led by Arkansas engineer Fred Neal who were interested in recovering the valuable cargo. Tom led our operations team at sea, which included using an advanced sonar computer processing system developed by our own software group. Back home, we analyzed data from the war patrol logs of the ships and aircraft involved in the attack. Using a system we developed for the Navy called "Renav" (short for " renavigation"), we reconstructed the events of the engagement and redirected the search to a point nearly twenty miles from the position recorded by the U.S. Navy at the time of the sinking. We found the wreckage of the I-52 barely one-half mile from the position we computed with Renav. Resting at over 17,000 feet, the I-52 is one of the deepest shipwrecks ever discovered.

The I-52 discovery was a dramatic proof of principle of Meridian's skill, business plan, and Renav technology. Our success was widely publicized, including spots on Dan Rather's *CBS Evening News* and in *The New York Times*. A later trip to the site was featured in a *National Geographic* magazine article and television documentary. (As of this time, nearly a decade later, Tidwell and his investors have not launched a mission to attempt salvage, or even determined if they have the legal rights to do so. This circumstance has little to do with technology, and a lot to do with business.)

So when our qualifications for being selected as the company to search for the *Dakar* were being examined, and members of our staff were questioned about their credentials, Tom was able to give a simple answer:

"I find submarines."

"For him, the ship was more than a piece of iron."

I never met the men of the *Dakar*. I only saw their portraits, sixty-nine of them, in a solemn row at the memorial in Haifa. The pictures themselves are not solemn; they show the men as in life, in a variety of poses, dress, and demeanor. Some seem to be posing for a school yearbook, some are in formal military attire, some in casual dress. Some are grinning, some are serious and intense, some have a rakish look, like action-adventure movie stars. I think this reflects the tradition of the Israeli Navy service: hard work and discipline are expected, but a man can perform better if he is recognized as an individual and can make a personal contribution to the cause. I'm sure their personalities and eccentricities were tolerated and even embraced by their captain, confident still that he could depend on their dedication and performance at any time.

Michael Marcovici is the brother of Isaac Marcovici, a mechanic on the *Dakar*. Isaac, also known by his Hebrew name, Yitzhack Ogen, was born in France on December 3, 1948, and immigrated to Israel as a toddler in 1951, before Michael was born. The chosen Hebrew name reflects the family's strong connection to the sea, as *ogen* means "ship's anchor." Their father, Carol, was also in the Navy, and he taught the boys about dedication and striving to be better than others, including doing better than their parents. Being a submariner qualified as better; it meant being among the elite.

Isaac was just twenty years old when he went down with the *Dakar*. Michael was a boy of sixteen, and remembers his brother in a 2002 interview:

> I think that my elder brother was someone who I wanted always to follow. We were two kids, and because my father was also a seaman and used to be a lot of time on the sea, my brother was the dominating person for me. So I remember him as my clever big brother, for the good fights that we had (and we had a lot at the time), until the moment that he went to the Navy, when he was around seventeen years old. I was

thirteen, and starting to share some youth, secrets about girls, cigarettes, and all this stuff. But for me, he was somebody who I wanted to follow, and I loved him, of course. We had very, very good connection.

I am still living with the memories—although I have my family, I have my wife with children, he is still with me.

You have to understand why he joined the Navy. As I told you, my father was a seaman. For him, joining the Navy was to go in the same way that my father did. To volunteer for submarines was to do the same, but a little bit better, and he wanted always to be a little bit better. But this is a part of what we received from our parents. Always, we knew that we have to be better, we have to study, and to try to achieve things that our parents didn't achieve. This is why he went to the Navy. This is why he went to the submarine.

When you go to the Navy, first you have to do the military training like all the soldiers, which is very difficult. He told me what they were doing, how they were shooting, all this stuff. And then they came to Haifa for training. Then we had the Six-Day War, and one day, I went to see him and my father was there with him. This I will remember. They were standing and smoking cigarettes, and I said, oh, gosh, he is a vet, because we were not allowed to smoke in front of our father. Suddenly, he is smoking in front of my father. He is a man.

At that time, Israeli Navy had two submarines, the *Tanin* and the *Rahav*. He served aboard the *Rahav*. It was not able to dive. So they put some guns on top of the submarine and she was out like a small [gunboat]—they didn't do too much but they were doing some patrols. She was not really able to do too much.

His assignment to the *Dakar* was the first time for him to leave Israel. So suddenly to go to Portsmouth in the U.K., to see a different world, to be in a very modern submarine, to be a part of the best one, was a kind of a dream. And it was a kind of recognition from his friends and family, that he was chosen to go there.

We received all the time letters from him. Only letters. He told me a lot of things about the submarine. In one of the letters, he said that they even have a shower on the submarine, because at that time on the old one, there was no shower. He said that he bought some things for me. I wrote to him, he wrote to me. He had a girlfriend at that time who wrote to him, also. I knew exactly what was going on between him and her; as I told you, we were very, very close.

I remember in one of his letters, he said that they just finished a very tough time, they were six weeks in the North Sea, to check everything, that everything was going well before the long journey to Israel.

And when you are on the sea you have to fight with the sea. When you are diving, you have to fight with the sea, and also with the diving itself, which is not so easy. But this is what you are trained to do, and if you're doing this well, then everything goes well.

He said that they have a very nice submarine, a big one, and it looked good. I felt that he believed in this creature, the *Dakar*. For him, the ship was more than a piece of iron, and being a part of the group with the people on board, made him feel very proud.

These are volunteers, and there is a huge fight for the elite groups in the Navy, you always have more than one candidate for any job, and if you succeed, you are already one of the best. By being chosen to go to the U.K. and to bring home the *Dakar* put him definitely in a different league.

Michael Marcovici knew his brother as an honored submariner, one of the elite *Dakar* crew and someone to admire as they were growing up.

Oded (Odie) Ra'anan had a different perspective entirely, as he is the youngest son of the *Dakar*'s captain, and was only four when the ship departed Gibraltar with his father at the helm.

What could a boy of that age remember? It's all in the details and, in a telling in 2002, Odie reveals a little of what life was like for the families of submariners who came to Portsmouth, England, while the ship was being outfitted, and how their children might feel.

I don't have a lot of memories of the *Dakar* itself because I was three or four years old. We'd been in Portsmouth something like one year; in the end of the period, I think the last weeks, I remember the Hanukkah ceremony that all of the families and the crew made in the submarine. I remember it was evening, and there were a lot of lights because it's Hanukkah, and a big Hannukeyah on the bridge of the submarine. We got inside, had some drinks, and all of the children got some toys for the holiday.

I liked it in England; it was nice to be there. We lived all of the family together, and in the end of the period, another family of the *Dakar* lived with us in our house because they already had to give back their home. So it was nice. We used to travel a lot. In the end of the period, we actually didn't have a lot of time together because my father was with the *Dakar* all of the time.

It was the period that they were preparing for the cruise to Israel. So my father was not at home, and if he was, it was for a couple of hours. So it was busy for him, maybe pressure for him.

I have memories of my father, but they are not related to the *Dakar*. They are related to things that happened at the house with the family. One of them was that one day I am chewing some gum, and I get it stuck in my mouth, and I began to turn blue. My father took me and punched me in the back and turned me upside down, and it came out.

And one thing I remember before even we went to England. It was in Israel. It was Saturday, I think, and all of the family was prepared to go out, and I was playing with my brother and chasing him. He ran away and closed the door, which was a glass door, and as I get inside the door it cut my hand. And I remember my father taking me to the bath and washing me and then to the hospital to fix the cutting. And I think these are the only two times that I remember him, in a visual way.

✡ ✡ ✡

It's just two or three weeks before *Dakar* leaves Portsmouth for home. The crew is saying good-bye to their British hosts in the Navy and at the shipyards, good-bye to the remaining Israeli submariners still at work on the *Dolphin*, and good-bye to their families who would fly back to Israel and await their arrival— including couples like Chava and First Officer Boomie Barkay who had brought their kindergarten-age son Guy to live in Portsmouth for two years.

Chava was very supportive, and so much in the spirit of her husband's work that she eagerly went to Portsmouth at the end of 1966 and stayed in a small hotel with their young son until they could find housing. She witnessed every step of the refitting and shared every trial, challenge, and success with Boomie. "They started to build it in the harbor," she recalled in 2002, "piece by piece. It was very exciting, and he shared it all with me. I loved the submarine like it was my house. . . . I think she was a beautiful lady."

Like the others, Chava and her husband were separated for six long weeks while *Dakar* was being tested and undergoing repairs and modifications in Scotland. After they reunited in Portsmouth in December, they had the Hanukkah party and spent a few days together, including outings to buy gifts and things for home. On January 7, 1968, they drove to the airport together, and she and their son left for Israel. "He took Guy and he hugged him," she said, "and me, too. And then we separated. In a few minutes, we just looked around, and he was going on his way." It was their last moment together.

In a few hours, Chava and Guy were back in Israel. In her words:

We all came to Portsmouth about the end of 1966, and we stayed in a small hotel, bed and breakfast, until we found a place to live. We rented flats and houses, and most of the Israelis lived in the same neighborhood. But we were only fifteen people from the submarine that were married, and the other people were young, so they leave the family in Israel. I know that some of the mothers didn't see their sons for two years before this terrible thing happened.

But I was with them until the last minute, and we were sending our children to kindergarten, and we enjoyed the city. It was a small, very, very nice place. The Jewish community was in touch with us and this was the base of the Royal Navy, so we were in touch also with British officers. We were making barbecue together and we went to visit each other.

But they were working very hard. We were all young couples, and all the wives met in the morning to send our children to kindergarten. I especially liked the College of Art, spending six months taking courses there. It was very interesting, because in '66 not many people from Israel went to England to live. The streets and the big shops were very nice.

Boomie, my husband, was the first officer, and had a lot of responsibility. They started to build it in the harbor, piece by piece. It was very exciting, and he shared it all with me. I loved the submarine like it was my house. I didn't understand all the secret electric [equipment] they put inside. But I saw what kind of a curtain or what kind of furniture they had. With this glass they drink the wine; with these, they drink the whiskey. They had not very much, but what they had was the real thing. I think she was a beautiful lady. She was beautiful on the inside also, all the mahogany. . . . I love him. I love the submarine. I don't know which is first. You can see why they go to the sea . . . it's really beautiful.

My husband had volunteered for this duty. He wanted to do it very much. When I met him, before we got married, he wanted to go to the submarine because it was like being in the Air Force, you must be a pilot, so it's the same in the Navy. You must be in the submarine, because this was the dream. But it took one year before he went to serve in the submarine, because his older brother was already there, and the commander of the Navy didn't want two brothers to be in the same unit.

He knew that he wanted to be in the most interesting and the necessary place. That's why he wanted to go there. I was very proud, and all the way through the whole year, I heard only one thing, that we have a good crew, good people, and a very special submarine. They were very happy; nothing was going through anybody's mind that something could happen.

We were excited; this was—don't forget—after the Six-Day War in Israel and we have Jerusalem! We can go to Jerusalem! We were in England when the Six-Day War was in Israel, so everybody dreamed of coming back, to be in Jerusalem. We always looked far to the east, and Boomie, especially, and he said, "Believe me, I'm waiting to come home, and we're going directly to Jerusalem." To go through the streets, to smell the smells, the food . . . very exciting.

Before we came to the *Dakar*, my husband was seven or eight years in submarines. Now it's war, we're in England. He wanted to be in the action, to serve. He says, "They pay me every month. I need to be there. This is my job; not to be in England." But they couldn't do anything because one of the submarines—the *Leviathan*—was already ready to go home, so she left during the war.

But the *Dakar* was the middle of the rebuild, and they couldn't go there. They wanted to finish everything, but they had to go to Scotland for six weeks. He called me from Scotland, and said that he's feeling so good because the crew is in its place, everybody knows his job, and the submarine has behaved very good. They were waiting to come home to Portsmouth.

We had six weeks to wait in Portsmouth. I talked with him maybe one or two times, once on our anniversary day. Eighth of December. So I get a flower, which I get every year. He didn't forget.

It was very cold over there. We had a very nice small house. I liked it. It was not easy, I mean six weeks, but it was okay. But all the time, we watch BBC and we see what happens in Israel. So everybody wants to go home, me, too, and all the Israelis.

And then they came back Christmastime, and it was very nice. The harbor was full of Christmas. All the ships were with Christmas lights, so the harbor was full of light. We six wives knew they were coming in the evening. So we took one babysitter for all the children and we went over to the harbor.

Suddenly, it's very quiet. [The submarine arrives] without engine. I don't understand it. And [then we see] a big light of Hannukeyah! It was exactly the Jewish holiday of Hanukkah, and they decided to put the Hannukeyah [on the ship], and it was very exciting. They invited all the wives to have a drink in the submarine. After six weeks, that we didn't see each other—for me, it was too much. But, you know, when you are married to a seaman, this is the price.

It was Hanukkah, and we had a party for the children inside the submarine. We made them cakes and everything, and we sang songs. We had parties, a good-bye from the Jewish community, a few evenings with [friends], and then, on the sixth of January, it was his birthday. So we took a day off and we went to buy presents for each other, and some stuff for the house. We had a nice dinner, and then on the seventh or on the eighth of January, we took a big bus, all six families that stayed in Portsmouth, and we went to London, to the airport.

And in the airport, we sit all together, all the six families, and suddenly Boomie says, "Let's go to the bar, and have a drink, alone." So we took Guy and we had a drink, and then we went to the airplane. He took Guy and he hugged him, and me, too. And then we separated. In a few minutes, we just looked around, and he was going on his way.

But he was jealous, because in four or five hours we are in Israel, and he was going to take two weeks. Yeah.

This was the last time I saw him.

✡ ✡ ✡

Sons, brothers, wives . . . and also mothers, fathers, sisters . . . families and friends. All shared the same pride in their *Dakar* sailors and were anxious for them to return home after many months in a foreign land. They were eager to share the exhilaration of Israel's Six-Day War victory, and the anxiety of the uncertain future to come. They just wanted to be together again.

Young Odie remembered the excitement of returning to Israel, and to family he hardly knew: "After the Hanukkah party, the families all came home. My mother and my two brothers went to Paris, I think, or to Vienna, and I went back to Israel with the other families of the crew, but not with my family. And in the airport, my grandfather was waiting for me. My mother and brothers joined me in Israel after a couple of days."

Everyone anticipated a joyous gathering to honor the arrival of *Dakar*. Details of the welcoming ceremony were carefully arranged, the guest list checked, and proclamations printed. Every day the ship got closer to its destination, and every few hours she checked in as scheduled to make contact and give her daily position in Morse code.

And then the unthinkable happened.

Well, really, stopped happening. After ten days of routine and uneventful radio reports the messages suddenly stopped coming. At first, this was known only to the military, and was hoped to be some kind of technical problem with the communications system. The Navy deployed to search the sea for the *Dakar* and offer assistance if needed. Then the day of arrival came . . . and no *Dakar*.

What happened? How could it happen? Action must be taken immediately. Could the ship be somehow found and, if necessary, rescued? Haifa was stunned, and word spread across Israel within hours. The ship had seemed to evaporate! The Navy at home hoped she wasn't lost, couldn't conceive that she could be lost. They hoped a simple communications problem could easily be solved when they reached the ship. An immediate mobilization was ordered and the first of many land, air, and sea searches began. People stayed by their phones, watched TV, and waited for good news—and then for any news.

How did four-year-old Odie learn of the loss of his father who was meant to arrive in a couple of weeks to a hero's welcome?

I think it came, you know, from time to time. It developed. It wasn't an exact moment that someone realized that something happened. In the beginning it was kind of a rumor. We are going there to the sea to look out, and then, the loss developed to something that you are growing with.

Exact point, I don't remember. I don't think there is exact point.

I remember that people used to come to our house, which was a kind of a headquarters of the families or the relatives from the Navy because we used to live in a neighborhood that most of the people were from the Navy. Some people came, and journalists, and friends, and the friends from the neighborhood. So it's kind of a thing that you are growing with. It wasn't something that one day you know that something happened.

The atmosphere, for me, was kind of a party. You know, people come, and stay, and talk, and listen to the BBC, and trying to get some information or conclusions or something.

My mother was the wife of the captain, and in the *Dakar* crew I think there were seven or eight families. Most of the crew were sailors without wives and kids. Since she was the oldest of the wives, I think she was the one that you talk to if you want some details from the Navy, and the Navy will talk with her if they want to say something to the families.

In the Israeli daily life, the *Dakar* is a very big story. It's a mystery. And everyone is inside the story, not just the families. It's not a story that belongs to the Navy or the families. It belongs to all of the community.

That was the first day of the loss of the *Dakar*.

The Pros from Dover

January 1997, was a whirlwind. After the Christmas holidays, we began to realize that we really would be going to Israel and have the opportunity to solve another long-standing mystery of the sea. We met with Dick Boyd on January 14 at his offices in Washington, and took the assignment to prepare a letter for Captain Meshita, the Israeli naval attaché at the embassy. We were to offer a briefing about our company and a presentation about our latest undersea discoveries. On January 29, we were given a schedule (leaving in barely two weeks!) and began to make all preparations for a three-week absence from home and business. We scrambled to obtain visas, update vaccinations, gather equipment and software, and think of everything we could possibly need, knowing little of what to expect.

We met Captain Meshita at the Israeli Embassy in Washington on February 12, three days from departure, and learned a bit more. We planned to spend two weeks learning all we could, performing any analyses we deemed relevant, and preparing our conclusions. On March 3, we would present our findings to a gathering that would include Admiral Krol and the officer-in-charge of the *NR-1*. Then we would spend a day touring, followed by a couple of days of follow-up discussions, and return home.

We were given the name of our POC (point of contact, or escort officer) in Israel, Lieutenant Commander Barry Grinker, who would introduce us to Lieutenant Commander Ga'ash, the project officer. We would be working at Navy Headquarters in Tel Aviv. Our flights were arranged: Baltimore to Kennedy then straight to Tel Aviv, seven time zones away. We had lots of questions: Will we have access to phones? What is the address? Can we bring computers and software? We were warned that we should not go to Jerusalem in the company of an Israeli citizen, to lessen our exposure to a terrorist attack. This did not comfort our wives, as can be imagined. My hastily scribbled notes of the day reminded me to pack the essentials: a camera and a three-week supply of Snyder's pretzels!

We tried to imagine exactly what we would be doing, and how we would go about our task. We could not assume that there would be time to get anything we needed once we discovered the need, so we prepared for everything. We brought two laptop computers with extra disk drives, modems, connectors, and software in the hopes that we could apply some of our techniques that had helped in past successes. Today, laptops are pretty common, but in 1997, for a growing small business of thirty people, laptops were a precious and expensive commodity, and somewhat less rugged than today's models. We were very worried that they would become damaged or be confiscated by customs. But we were assured it was okay to bring them, so we just did our best to pack well and think of everything we could. The collection of luggage was quite impressive, most of which, in hindsight, we could have dispensed with.

On the evening of March 15, after a most exhausting day of final preparations, Tom and I departed for Washington National Airport. We had no idea at the time that our journey would last four years.

✡ ✡ ✡

I believe in the idea of "good luck." I think it happens to almost everybody. But to be "lucky" one has to notice the circumstance and do something about it. It also helps to be prepared, thereby increasing exposure to promising circumstances. We at Nauticos were fortunate to be invited to join the quest for the *Dakar*. How did we get to be so lucky?

Unlike Tom Dettweiler, I did not begin life with the ambition of exploring the oceans, but I think the idea of exploring was always there. When I was young, second or third grade, I was tremendously inspired by the Mercury space launches. They took place in the wee hours of the morning, and I remember television coverage beginning at 4 or 5 AM. My mother woke me up, and we sat together and watched every minute of the countdowns. Long holds for technical or weather problems brought exciting tension. She always said a prayer at the moment of ignition, which made my heart pound. We loved those times—they got me interested in space exploration, which I've always been drawn to, and science in general. I always thought I would strive to be an astronaut, but opportunity and circumstance led me to explore a different frontier.

When I was in third grade, about eight years old, my family moved to Venezuela, where we lived most of the time until I finished ninth grade, about six years altogether. My years in South America as a grade-school kid were a wonderful experience, as I learned to live in a different culture, communicate in a foreign language, and meet people from all around the world. Venezuela is a beautiful country, with fabulous Caribbean beaches, dark rain forests, and breathtaking Andes peaks, and we took many trips around the region. Through it all, I came to better appreciate the beauty, freedom, and opportunity of my own country, where government is effective, the living standard is high, and public safety is taken for granted. It also exposed some of the weaknesses of our society, especially our cultural friction and self-absorption with our own ways and interests. In later years, I was drawn to international travel, and have enjoyed working with people from other places and cultures.

One of my many memories of Venezuela is stargazing. We lived in the small town of Maracay, located about fifty miles west of Caracas on the shores of Lake Valencia. Because of circumstances of population, industry, and geography, there was little smog or light pollution, and the skies were crystal clear. The nights were pleasantly warm, year round. Our houses had flat roofs, accessible by ladders. And since we were near the equator, we could see both the northern and southern skies. My friend Ken Hastings and I would spend many nighttime hours on our backs, with binoculars or small telescope, tracing out constellations, star clusters, and nebulae with the aid of hand-copied star charts and a red-lens penlight. My interest in space and astronomy grew; later, in college, I took every astronomy course offered, and eventually learned the art of celestial navigation. Today, with dozens of global positioning satellites whizzing about, electronic charting, and automated piloting accessible to the smallest of craft, celestial navigation is never used. But it is a key to solving past mysteries, when ships and aircraft depended on the stars to find their way. This arcane skill has been very valuable to me, and was nurtured during those pleasant hours on equatorial rooftops.

My mother was a very disciplined person. She taught me a lot about being organized and persevering. On the other hand, my father liked to go places and do things. We were always traveling, including cross-country car trips in Venezuela, always looking for new experiences. From them I learned how to "do things according to the book," while at the same time to "go out and have fun, learn more, and explore." Part of this was the idea of cultivating opportunity, exposing oneself to lucky circumstances. Whenever I am faced with an uncertain decision, I try to pick the route that will lead to more choices later, more chances to "get lucky."

After finishing high school near Philadelphia, the issue of college loomed large. My parents divorced when I was a senior, and under those circumstances finding money for college was a problem. Of course, I wanted to attend a high-priced engineering school, but there was no way to afford anything like that. Somewhere along the way my mother said, "Why don't you consider the Naval Academy?" and I said, okay, why not? I had no direct experience with the service, and had never even met anyone in the Navy. We filled out the paperwork and started the process. One thing led to another and I was accepted. I saw this as a great opportunity, an adventure, and a challenge, and gladly took advantage of it.

It was 1972 and while the Vietnam War was winding down, it was still intense—and the idea of joining the war was pretty unpopular at that time among my peers. As it turned out, we left Vietnam during my college years, so I never went there, but it was a prospect when I was considering the Naval Academy. I remember one of my acquaintances at school looking at me with pity, shaking her head, and wondering how I could "just throw my life away." I wasn't always in step with the people around me.

So, all of a sudden I had a free education and a guaranteed job upon graduation. This solved a lot of problems, and allowed me to think about my future, with many choices ahead. It was quite a luxury, and it has taken me a long time to fully appreciate the opportunity I was afforded. My dear mother, with hardly any money and my younger sister, Susan, to care for, paid my uniform fees, drove me down to Annapolis, and did everything that she could possibly do to get me going. (She did okay with Susan, too. Six years my junior, Sue made her way through an entirely different path to become an ocean explorer, as well. As an underwater robotic vehicle technician, Sue has joined me on expeditions and runs an offshore survey business with her husband, Jeff Morris. It has been a pleasure to go to sea with Sue, and one of my fondest memories was a surprise radiophone call we made together to Mom from the middle of the Pacific Ocean. You can only imagine her excitement!)

When I went into the Navy, I decided at that point I wasn't cut out to be a pilot, which was part of the natural process of becoming an astronaut. Other opportunities interested me, and somewhere along the way I decided to enter the Navy Nuclear Power Program. This led to the idea of submarines, which appealed to me as a more technical and scientific kind of job than some of the other options.

Two days after graduation, I married Lynn, who was finishing a nursing degree at West Chester State in Pennsylvania. Although many midshipmen married at the Naval Academy Chapel with lots of fanfare and pageantry, complete with full-dress uniforms and sword bearers, I have never cared much for ceremony. We married at Lynn's house in the Pennsylvania countryside, in casual, homemade dress, with only about twenty family members in attendance. As I said, I wasn't always in step with the people around me. Fortunately, Lynn and I have always been in step!

My five submarine patrols on the USS *Kamahameha* were interesting, exciting, challenging, and boring in various combinations. I visited many ports in Europe and the Caribbean, learned to operate the ship's nuclear power plant and, ultimately, the ship itself. Standing watches as officer of the deck was a fantastic experience. At age twenty-five, having the responsibility to be the senior watch officer of a billion-dollar nuclear ship, while underway submerged, with weapons capable of destroying a country, was a very maturing experience.

I ended my tour as assistant to the ship's engineer, with the vessel in overhaul in Portsmouth, New Hampshire. In the summer of 1981, I joined the staff of the Johns Hopkins University Applied Physics Laboratory (APL) in suburban Maryland as a physicist. I worked in the Navy Ocean Engineering Program, where I had the opportunity to learn more about underwater systems and operations. All of the work was highly classified, so even though I had fairly high-level security clearance in the Navy, I still had to wait about five months to get the clearances I needed to do the job I was hired to do.

Here, I was lucky again. They had a brand new computer lab in the facility (it was 1981, so there were no personal computers as yet), a big rack-mounted machine with disk drives that looked like hat boxes, in cabinets the size of furniture. I was allowed in that room, and they gave me software to install on the system, to keep me busy. One of the programs involved submarine navigation, and I took a real interest in it. I don't think they expected very much from me, but when I was allowed to come in and work with everyone, I was the expert in the use of this tool.

I got to work with some of the important submarine missions and became accomplished at reconstructing the events of the mission and underwater locations, to good accuracy. We learned how to re-create the paths subs had followed, and help other ships repeat them and find the underwater targets again with sonar and other sensors. This success got some recognition for our group, so when the Navy wanted to find something they began to call on us at Johns Hopkins. We helped find lost Navy equipment, downed aircraft, shipwrecks of military interest, and wreckage from failed missile tests. Among other things, we got some experience working with the *NR-1*, the Navy's nuclear-powered research submersible that would later figure in the search for the *Dakar*.

During this time, I owed a lot to my bosses, George Starken and Dave Ellis, as well as to my mentors in underwater navigation and analysis, Mike Cruz, Jerry Scanlon, and Duncan Crawford. Along with the rest of the team and others at the laboratory, they taught me a lot about the craft, as well as teamwork, management, and leadership. This all helped tremendously in later years when developing my own business. I couldn't have asked for a more supportive organization, and I remain grateful for the experience.

✡ ✡ ✡

So Tom and I were on our way to Israel. Neither of us were strangers to international travel or extended absences from home. But it never gets easier to say good-bye to family, and it's impossible to ignore the anxiety of unknown days ahead or concern of obligations left behind. As usual, Lynn did her best to allay any worries, assuring me that she and the kids would be fine. I knew she would make it so, even though life with fifteen-year-old Bethany and her younger brother Eric could be complicated at times. Tom's wife, Hélène, would manage as well with their two boys, David and Johann.

The beginning of our voyage was inauspicious. For reasons unknown, our schedule had us flying to Kennedy Airport at 4:30 PM, even though our flight to Tel Aviv didn't leave until 9:30 PM. Everyone has sad tales of unpleasant flights, and I am normally not one to complain, but I couldn't avoid putting a discouraging word in my journal of the trip:

2/16, Sunday, Tel Aviv: What a flight! I am not one to complain as a rule (am I?), but that was the worst plane flight I can remember. Everyone from the ticket agent through the flight attendants ranged from harried to surly, and even the passengers were argumentative (either because of, or the cause of, the crew attitude). We had the two middle seats in the middle section on the 747, and the seats were clustered more like you would expect on a commuter plane than a transoceanic liner. The salad was cooked, the cold water was hot, the coffee was weak, and Tom and I were both missing items from our meals. The sound system didn't work. I sat next to a sullen young woman who didn't crack a single smile or get up to go to the bathroom once for the entire flight. We sat on the runway for over an hour in Kennedy because they were slow to load passengers and baggage. They were disorganized and inefficient, and I promise not to complain about anything else anymore! There, I got it out of my system!

Thankfully, aircraft cannot stay in the air forever, and we had to come down one way or the other eventually. As luck would have it, we landed safely in Tel Aviv and were relieved from our misery before any permanent damage was done. Things began to improve immediately.

2/16, Sunday, Tel Aviv: We arrived in Tel Aviv's Ben-Gurion Airport at 4:30 PM local (+7-hour time zone) after 10 1/2 hours of flying or waiting on runways. We were met by El (he said we couldn't pronounce his name) Ga'ash, a Navy lieutenant commander who is the project officer and our main escort for the week. Along was Commander Baruch (Bar) Perezmann, a paratrooper who must have seen his share of action, with a hook for a left hand and a badly disfigured left side of his face. Both are wonderfully friendly, and seem to be very happy to have us visit. They whisked us through customs (since we had "called ahead" through the Israeli Embassy) and drove us to our hotel.

The day was beautiful and sunny, cool and dry. The palm trees and something about the air reminded me of Venezuela. Most of the road signs are in English in addition to Hebrew. Seat belts are mandatory (front and rear), and they have a great law: cell phones must be turned off while driving! Since this appears to be the world capital of cell phones, I think it's a great idea and one we should adopt in the U.S.!

"El" was Yechiel Ga'ash, who was to become our inspirational leader, constant companion, and loyal friend over the course of the *Dakar* project. We did learn how to pronounce his name, at least passably. Baruch, as a commander, was technically Yechiel's superior officer, but in all ways deferred to the project officer's leadership. As we later learned, Yechiel had been pursuing the *Dakar* for eighteen years, most of his career. It became clear in time that Yechiel's dedication to solving the mystery sometimes swelled to obsession. Promotions and career-enhancing postings were turned down over the years in pursuit of this goal. Although Yechiel got his paychecks from the Navy, he served no one, only the *Dakar.*

Although Yechiel and Baruch were surprised at the volume of baggage we brought, they were prepared to see us through customs without waiting in line, inspections, or other delays. They were also kind enough to recognize that we were exhausted from a combination of the prior day's work, jet lag, and time-zone change, and took us directly to our hotel. Our lot continued to improve as we took advantage of our first evening in Israel. My journal continues:

Our home for the next three weeks, the Carlton Hotel, couldn't be better. We have individual rooms with bath, a balcony on the ninth floor overlooking the beach, cable TV with channels from everywhere (forty-six, including Russia, Egypt, Jordan, Morocco, Luxembourg, Turkey, and Italy, along with the customary CNN, BBC, NBC, MTV, EuroSport, and Home Shopping). We also get chocolates on our pillows every day. Otherwise, life is rough for us.

We took an evening walk along the promenade to keep from falling asleep too early, noticing there is a McDonald's, Burger King, and Planet Hollywood nearby. Then we checked out the Melodies Bar and claimed our free Welcome Drink (something with grapefruit and liquors), then sampled the local beer. We met some Brits who are here working for Air Products, and I told them the joke about the Irishman who drank three pints at a time (they loved it, I think).

We accidentally left the bartender a tip 1/100 of what we intended, owing to a misinterpretation of the coinage. We plan to go back and rectify the situation tomorrow, assuming he will let us in.

On Monday, we were met at the hotel by Barry Grinker (our escort officer) and taken to the Navy Headquarters complex, about a twenty-minute drive from our hotel. Barry was very likable, and told us he went to the Navy Postgraduate School in Monterey, California, earning a master's degree in hydrography. We tried to absorb the sights and sounds of the city as we drove through business districts, parks, and neighborhoods. Tel Aviv is a modern city, with the normal abundance of cement, steel, and asphalt, thickly sprinkled with autos, buses, motorcycles, and pedestrians. There were a few buildings, especially along the waterfront area, which featured a more rounded architecture that looked clearly Middle Eastern.

Most of the people were in typical Western city dress. However, it was impossible to overlook the occasional armed soldier everywhere. As we neared Navy Headquarters, their numbers grew, and each street corner sported a pair of soldiers clearly standing guard. Although this was intimidating at first, at the same time it felt very casual, as it seemed to be the accepted way of things. It was interesting to us to see young girls in fatigues with automatic weapons, not something we were used to seeing in the 1997-vintage U.S. Army. Every soldier carried a weapon very visibly, whether they were actually on guard duty or just walking to a lunch spot. If Tom and I had harbored any doubts, we could now be sure: we were in Israel, and there was a war going on, and Navy Headquarters was a target.

We were ushered through the security gates into a nondescript building and then a large room. We faced a rectangular ring of tables with eighteen officials who were seated, waiting for us. I had this image later of the scene from the movie *M*A*S*H* when the characters Hawkeye and B.J. walk in and announce that the "pros from Dover" had arrived, and start giving orders. The look in the assembled faces made me think of that; they seemed to expect us to be the ones who would make everything right. But we hardly felt that way. At that point, we were mainly hoping we wouldn't embarrass ourselves, our company, or the U.S. Navy. I suppose we had a dim hope that maybe we could even contribute in some small way.

Fortunately, we didn't have to conduct surgery on anybody, and we could begin to get our bearings as introductions were made. We learned that the assembled group was the Search Committee, the most recent incarnation formed to address the U.S. Navy's offer to help with the *Dakar* search. Led by retired Admiral Gideon Raz, the group included submariners, intelligence specialists, hydrographers, naval engineers, communications specialists, meteorologists, marine biologists—every discipline relevant to the problem. Naval officers, engineers, academicians and businessmen, were represented. As we later discovered, if a question was raised that could not be completely addressed by the expertise present, the Committee would send for the best expert available anywhere in the country. Within hours, someone would appear, whisked from Haifa or Eilat or wherever, just to answer one question and return to resume whatever business he was engaged in before our interruption. It is a small country, but I was impressed.

Admiral Raz did his best to make Tom and me feel comfortable and respected from the start, while at the same time making it clear that much was expected from us. Raz had served as submarine squadron commander from 1971 to 1973 and retired in 1985 as deputy commander of the Israeli Navy. He also had been the deputy commander of the *Leviathan*, the *Dakar's* sister ship. His commanding officer was Mike (Yomi) Barkay, the brother of Boomie Barkay, who was the deputy commander of the *Dakar*. When the ship was lost, Raz had to inform Mike Barkay. He told us later, "We both, as experienced submariners, understood something—that most probably the submarine is lost, that his brother is gone." So Raz had a deep personal connection with the *Dakar*.

When I met Gideon Raz, he immediately reminded me of the actor Sir Sean Connery. I later compared photos of the two of them, and could see the same eyes and a few common facial features; but mainly it was the knowing smile Raz flashes often that reminds me of Connery. As it turned out, Raz was lucky to have us, and he took advantage of the situation by making us feel at ease and setting the tone for the Committee. We did, indeed, feel a little like the "pros from Dover," and this gave us a bit of confidence that made all the difference. Such is the stuff of leadership, and Raz had it.

By 1997, Tom and I and our team at Nauticos had certainly earned the respect Admiral Raz afforded us. That part of the story started ten years earlier, in the fall of 1986. I was enjoying a rewarding and interesting job at the APL, and starting to establish some real expertise in the arcane field of underwater navigation.

In that time, I decided to try to go for a master's degree in applied physics, which they offered as a part-time program at the Johns Hopkins University. The APL paid for the courses, and I could go in the evenings. It took a couple of years, but meanwhile I was working in my regular job, which included use of a special kind of underwater navigation device called a Doppler sonar system. A Doppler sonar bounces a sound pulse of a single tone (or frequency) off the ocean bottom and listens for the echo. If the device is moving with respect to the bottom, this echo will have a different tone than the original pulse. Everyone is familiar with this phenomenon: as one can hear the change in pitch of the sound of a train whistle as it passes, the pitch is high as it approaches, and suddenly drops as the train passes and recedes. The Doppler sonar device measures the change in the echo frequency and relates this to the speed. (This is also the same principle used in Doppler radar, except in that case the radar device is stationary, and the pulses are echoed off moving masses of air, thus revealing wind speeds. And of course, the Doppler radar uses radio frequency signals, not sound.) The Doppler sonar is very useful in lots of underwater applications, but back in the early 1980s it was pretty experimental and used as a military application for research.

We were using this device but, like any other system, it was not perfect. The principle of operation was very simple but the practical implementation was fraught with difficulties in making the measurements, knowing how the device was pointed, the behavior of the electronic devices, and even the physics of the sound traveling through the water. At the time, I was casting about for my master's thesis, and I felt we could really afford to learn more about how the errors were behaving in this system. So I proposed that I study the Doppler sonar and accomplish two things at once. The tricky part was that all the data I had to work with was classified and I needed to study it in an unclassified way. Fortunately, with the support of my boss, George Starken, and others at the APL, including Allan Bjerkaas, as well as our Navy sponsors, I made my case and succeeded in the study. What I learned was subsequently used by the Navy, as well as in future Nauticos commercial applications. To carry it one step further, the paper I wrote for my master's project was published in the *Journal of the Institute of Navigation* and even won an award at the APL for the "Best First Paper." I got $250 for that!

I was not smarter or more capable than many others in my field, but I was able to take advantage of a lucky opportunity with the support of my coworkers and associates, and it led to unforeseen good fortune. Without this recognition, my work probably would have remained unknown but to a few, appreciated by a select but secret society of professionals. Maybe I would never have been asked to help with the *Dakar*.

The more immediate outcome of these events was an unexpected opportunity to start my own business. As computer workstations, software, and digital databases were becoming more capable, the Navy launched a project to build a new laboratory, able to work with digital data and conduct computer-based analysis. This would include underwater navigation, and I had something to contribute. Although life was comfortable at my current job, and advancement was open to me if I took on some new and different assignments, I was very excited about continuing the work I had started, and could not resist striking out on my own to pursue it. So, joined by coworkers Joe Crabtree and Dan Schoenberger, I left the APL after six great years and founded Meridian Sciences, Inc.

Our circumstances were typical. We had no immediate contracts and no office space. We cashed in retirement funds (at 10 percent penalty) to get started and keep things going until we could develop some business. We set up shop in my basement, used cheap doors set on file cabinets as desks, bought a couple of computers, and started making cold calls. Lynn and I had a four-year-old and a two-year-old, and she had dropped her nursing job in favor of running a day-care business. I remember discussing the idea with Lynn, and concluding that, at barely age thirty, with little to lose, we would have plenty of time to recover if we tried and failed.

Pretty soon, the jobs started to come in. We obtained contracts with two government labs, including work to help develop a submarine track reconstruction software system (which eventually became known as "Renav") for the Navy, incorporating the work in Doppler sonar I had developed. We hired a few staff, moved into a small office in Columbia, Maryland, and began to make plans for the future.

At that time, I had never heard of Tom Dettweiler, but he was busy preparing the ground for our future successes. Just one year earlier, the world was abuzz with the news of the discovery of the wreck of the RMS *Titanic*. Found in September 1985, at a depth of nearly 13,000 feet off the coast of Newfoundland, the haunting underwater images of the mammoth luxury liner captured the imagination of the public and inspired the creation of new technologies for underwater exploration. A cadre of young scientists and engineers turned to the oceans as a professional pursuit, and filmmakers began to propose TV documentaries and movie ideas based on marine history and underwater discovery. The leader of the *Titanic* expedition was Dr. Robert Ballard, soon to become the best-known ocean explorer since Jacques Cousteau. His chief operations manager was Tom Dettweiler.

The Deep Submergence Laboratory of the Woods Hole Oceanographic Institution (WHOI) followed this success with the discovery of the World War II German battleship *Bismarck* in 1989, at a depth of nearly 16,000 feet. WHOI led advances in underwater imaging, marine forensics, software applications, and robotic vehicles. The Jason Program was launched to bring these findings and the excitement of ocean exploration directly to museums and classrooms. Others tried their hand at exploration, and there were notable successes, including the discovery of the SS *Central America*, an 1857 Gold Rush–era ship, located two hundred miles off the Carolina coast in 1987, 8,500 feet deep.

Tom joined our team in 1989, as we were trying to find ways to expand our business beyond the confines of Navy contracts. He fit in very well with our government work, but also brought a base to begin building a full-service ocean exploration company, able to conduct field operations at sea, perform pre- and post-mission analysis, and develop special software and equipment to support this work. However, it would take several frustrating years to see any fruits of these efforts, and my dogged pursuit of this dream led to serious differences with my partners, Joe and Dan. Unwilling to accept the financial risk of such an endeavor, both left the partnership during this time, although Joe remained with me as a key staff member through it all. Over the ensuing years, Joe kept our government business growing and healthy, and made sure we didn't become too distracted with exciting exploration prospects and forget our roots. He remains with the company to this day, and has always been a true partner in spirit.

I am grateful to Dan and Joe for their enthusiasm and support in those uncertain early years. We were successful together, starting and growing a new and unique business without experience or capital, and none of us could have done it alone. On the other hand, our differences, especially in risk tolerance, would have led to its demise, and I don't think we could have continued on successfully together. I like to believe it worked out the best for everyone.

Shedding partners can be a good move for a business, but it is a risky one. The process is draining, it creates uncertainty, and it draws on scarce resources. As 1995 began, Lynn and I were left with a double-barreled debt: both the buyout money we promised to our former partners and a bank credit line that was financing company growth. To make matters worse, the bank would not continue to extend credit to just one partner, so we needed cash to pay off the credit line. We found part of our answer in family and friends. Lynn's parents and my reliable mother lent us what they could and, incredibly, our friends Roger and Cindy Copp lent us the net proceeds of their home sale for several crucial months while they were relocating. I was happy that we paid everybody back on time, with interest, but their generosity and faith in us were remarkable. We made up the balance of the cash need by simply accepting every credit-card offer that came in the mail, and asking for increases on every one we had. This is not generally recommended in business school . . . fortunately, I never went to that school! We amassed the amazing sum of $150,000 worth of credit-card debt, which financed the company until we proved we could survive and reapply for our more traditional bank loan.

Things were tight; things were tense. We struggled to get off the ground with our unique skills and talents, but with no major projects or ocean search equipment to employ them. I felt we had made the right decisions, and were steering the best course we could, but we needed a lucky break. That came in the form of a call from Ted Brockett in March of 1995.

✡ ✡ ✡

The Cold War was winding down. About the time we started Meridian, President Reagan called upon Mr. Gorbachev to "tear down this wall!" Over the next few years, the former Soviet Union began to look for ways to make use of their former military might in more productive endeavors. This included their little-known fleet of oceanographic research vessels, complete with deep-diving submersibles and sonars that could search the ocean floor at great depths. Led by oceanographer Dr. Anatoly Sagalevitch (soon to become world-known for his Mirs submersibles that helped Hollywood director James Cameron make his *Titanic* film) and a very capable team of scientists and engineers, the fleet was offered to commercial projects worldwide for very favorable lease terms. The U.S. agent for this venture was Sound Ocean Systems in Seattle, Washington, led by Ted Brockett.

Ted and Tom Dettweiler had worked together in the ocean mining days, two decades earlier in the 1970s. Ted had one of his first charter opportunities with his new Russian partners, but was wary of sending his customer, Paul Tidwell, out to sea without a seasoned operations manager. So he called Tom, who came to me immediately with this exciting opportunity for Meridian. My journal note of March 27, 1995, summarized what we knew at the time:

Operation Rising Sun
Germans reconfigured Japanese subs and built cargo subs (2,500 tons).
I-52 *Momi* (*Tanne* to Germans).
Rendezvous west of Cape Verde Islands.
I-52 sunk by aircraft, observed by German sub U-530. Later attacked, but escaped (we have logs).
Ship left Saturday to transit canal, 10 days → Balboa (Pacific side of canal).
Tom is the "Cruise Director." Top rep!
Paul Tidwell is customer.

Tidwell was, by avocation, a shipwreck researcher. He had played a role in a prior shipwreck discovery, the SS *John Barry*, a World War II Liberty ship carrying a cargo of Saudi silver, torpedoed en route to India in 1944. By his admission, he spent five years buried in the National Archives in Washington, D.C., researching the sinking of the I-52, another treasure mystery of World War II. According to Nigel Pickford's colorful picture book and gazetteer, *The Atlas of Shipwrecks and Treasures*, the I-52 was carrying a cargo of war materials including two tons of gold bullion from Singapore to Nazi-occupied France in the spring of 1944. In early June, after traveling all the way around Africa and crossing the equator in the mid-Atlantic, it was caught on the surface by American Avenger torpedo bombers operating from a nearby escort carrier, and was attacked with homing torpedoes. Pickford's article raised the question of whether it was actually sunk, and concluded: "What is certain is that this war shipment of gold never reached its destination and, so far, the I-52 and its cargo have not been found."

Tidwell's dogged research revealed several sources of information. The I-52 was built in Kure, Japan, designed to carry cargo to and from Germany. Since the Allied navies effectively blockaded the sea surface approaches to France and Germany, there was no other means of commerce between the Axis countries at that time. On the vessel's maiden voyage, the crew included a group of passengers, German and Japanese engineers and technicians who were on a technology exchange program. The ship stopped in Malaysia to load cargo, which included 228 tons of metals (tin, molybdenum, and tungsten) formed into ingots designed to fit into racks in the ship's ballast tanks. Besides that, they had 54 tons of raw rubber lashed to the deck, a critical material because there was no way to make synthetic rubber back then. They also had 288 tons of opium, which was (and still is) used to make morphine, and 3 tons of quinine. Of course, the cargo of interest to Tidwell was the 2 tons of gold bullion, which was to be used to purchase the bomb sights, radars, and other high-tech electronics and optics for the return trip.

The ship with this cargo departed Singapore in April, traveled across the Indian Ocean, all the way around Cape Horn at the southern tip of Africa, turned north up the South Atlantic, and crossed the Equator in mid-June. At that point, the I-52 was to rendezvous with a German U-boat, the U-530, operating out of the Caribbean. The U-530's mission was to provide the I-52 with radars and radar technicians that would help them to negotiate their way through the Allied blockade and into France.

It was approaching midnight on June 23, 1944, when the two submarines met, hundreds of miles from the nearest shore, over one thousand miles from any likely Allied patrol area. Over the course of less than an hour, the ships were in company on the surface, as equipment, supplies, and personnel (including two unlucky radar technicians, Shultze and Behrendt) were transferred to the I-52. When this work was completed, the ships separated, with the U-530 heading south to other missions.

All of this is recorded in the war diary of Commander Lange of the U-530. This document survived the war, and was found by Tidwell during his archive search. The diary goes on to report observing a spotlight or flare to the north, about an hour after the rendezvous ended, followed by the sound of approaching aircraft and the order to submerge. What is not recorded in the diary was the astonishment and frustration that Lange and his crew must have felt, that enemy aircraft had found them in the middle of the night in the vast reaches of the mid-Atlantic.

The Allies, of course, were reading the Axis mail. Having broken many of the German and Japanese codes, American intelligence staff was able to read the diplomatic messages between Tokyo and Berlin so they knew every move made by the I-52. As Tidwell read in the archived communications intelligence files of 1944, the American code breakers knew the names of the officers, the passenger list, the cargo manifest, and even the time and location of the rendezvous with the U-530. Hoping for an excellent opportunity to sink both ships at the same time, the U.S. Navy stationed a small task force, led by the escort carrier USS *Bogue*, to lie in wait for the unsuspecting submarines.

The *Bogue*, a converted Liberty ship equipped with a small flight deck and a wing of Avenger torpedo bombers, waited just over the horizon with her escort of destroyers. Tidwell's research and our subsequent studies revealed that these Avengers carried the most hi-tech weapons the Navy had, including airborne radar and acoustic homing torpedoes that could listen with sonar for the machinery noises of a submerged target. They also carried sonobuoys, which would float on the surface, listen for sounds below, and transmit them to the aircraft, and a wire recorder (an early version of a magnetic tape recorder) that used a thin wire to record sounds. The plane that made the successful attack on the I-52 was flown by a crew of three, led by pilot Lieutenant Jesse Taylor. When they made their attack, they deployed flares to light the area, and dropped sonobuoys into the water, which transmitted back the underwater sounds. Fifty years later, we listened, rapt, to cassette-tape copies of the eerie sounds of the propeller noises of the submarine, the torpedo in the water, the weapon exploding, and the noises of air escaping and metal crunching as the I-52 sank to the bottom. The recording included a voice-over of the pilot's communications with the crew, remarking as he listened to the results of the attack, "We got that son-of-a-bitch!"

The I-52, its unlucky crew, and its cargo of gold settled to the bottom of the Cape Verde Abyss, over 17,000 feet below. Later, we found in the archives copies of 78-RPM vinyl recordings that were the source of the cassette tapes, made during the war for training of other pilots and crews. Further digging, with the help of Captain Gillette of the Naval Historical Center, turned up some of the actual wires and a machine to play them back! With this information, and the help of sound engineers at the APL in Maryland, we discovered that the Navy took some artistic license when they developed the training recordings. The line, "We got that son-of-a-bitch!" was actually spoken by another pilot, Lieutenant "Flash" Gordon, who flew a subsequent mission. The producers of the training record thought it would be keen to include that line with the classic Taylor attack, and dubbed it over the I-52 attack recording. At the time, the Navy credited the sinking of the I-52 to both Gordon and Taylor, as it was uncertain whether the ship was sunk on the first attack. Our research, analysis, and subsequent discovery resolved this mystery in favor of Taylor. Of course, Gordon's efforts were no less spectacular or dangerous, and I think the entire USS *Bogue* task force deserves team credit for their many successes as premier sub hunters. It is possible to listen to these recordings on the Web site of the Historic Naval Ships Association, http://www.hnsa.org, under the heading "Historical Sound Online."

Unfortunately for the *Bogue* and the Allies, but lucky for us, the U-530 got away, and its surviving war diary proved crucial to Meridian's navigation analysis of the events. Confident in his research, which included the U.S. Navy's reported location of the sinking, Tidwell set out to raise money for a search. He eventually encountered Fred Neal, a retired mechanical engineer from Arkansas who had made some wise investments and had the means to support such an exciting endeavor. Fred and some associates invested about one million dollars. Tidwell then considered his options. By 1995, there was little left of the deep-ocean mining technology, so promising twenty years earlier. Most research off the continental shelves was being conducted in secret by the Navy, or by academic institutions like the Woods Hole Oceanographic Institution. Neither were available to Tidwell, for any price. He turned to Ted Brockett, a veteran of the ocean mining period, who in turn engaged the Russians to propose a suitable, affordable ship, and to Tom Dettweiler to help manage things at sea.

Tom proposed that we bring on board a small team from Meridian Sciences, and suggested, besides managing the operation, that we bring on board our newly developed computer software to enhance the Russian sonar information, and that we take some time to analyze the research and propose a search area. These were the cornerstones of our new company strategy: we wanted to be able to run an operation at sea, analyze the navigation data to develop search strategies, and develop the special tools to do all of those jobs. We felt that afforded us the best chance of success in any mission.

Tidwell accepted Tom as operations manager, and he accepted our software, but he said he didn't need our navigation analysis because he knew where I-52 was—he had the position of the sinking on an official 1944 Navy report. Nevertheless, Tom and Dave Wyatt, our lead computer engineer who took our software on the mission, were persuasive enough to convince him to let us take a look at it, just in case.

This proved to be a good decision, as after Tidwell had Tom search one hundred square miles surrounding the Navy datum to no avail, they placed a call from sea back to Maryland, asking if we had taken the time to study the research and could recommend a new search location to pursue in their remaining time at sea. Fortunately, we had been applying our Renav approach to the information, and soon had some answers. Redirecting the search, Tom and the Russian team detected a clear sonar image of a shipwreck, almost twenty miles from the Navy datum—but within a half-mile of the position calculated by our team in Maryland using Renav! In a few days of further work, they obtained half a dozen beautiful 70-MM camera frames of the deck of a submarine, with unmistakable features that could be matched with drawings. We had located the wreck of the I-52.

How did we do it? The simple answer is that, using the various ships' logs (including the U-boat's) unearthed by Tidwell, we did our best to reconstruct the events of the action for many days before and after the moment of the sinking. Then, we used our knowledge of navigation techniques of 1944, our understanding of the science of navigation, and our Renav statistical computer program to improve the accuracy of our reconstruction and estimate the uncertainty in the result. Then we used this new knowledge to triangulate the observations of the flare dropped by the attacking aircraft during the action. I later described this process as a combination of science, technology, and art: the science of navigation, including the physics of geodesy (the shape of the earth), acoustics, and other disciplines; the technology of Renav, a very complicated computer algorithm that involves an arcane statistical process called Kalman Filtering; and the art, or knack, of choosing the right way to set up the problem and assign all of the proper variables, including judging the uncertainty in all of them.

But how could the U.S. Navy be so far off, even in 1944? This is important. The Americans ships were busy launching and recovering aircraft, zigzagging to avoid enemy submarines, and searching for the I-52. In the process of all that, they lost track of their "geodetic" position, that is, latitude and longitude, in favor of their position "relative" to all of the things they were trying to find or avoid. After all, in the open ocean many hundreds of miles from land, how important can the latitude and longitude be?

In retrospect, it was because of this inattention to the geodetic picture that the U.S. aircraft that were flying off the carrier in search patterns failed to find the two Axis ships until after the rendezvous was complete. And it was the reliance on this information, at face value, by Tidwell that led him to search the wrong area. Our experienced navigation analysts at Meridian, using Renav and the techniques I had developed under the modern U.S. Navy umbrella, were able to reveal this inaccuracy by starting from first principles and reconstructing events patiently and objectively.

And the very important lesson of this experience is: the most unreliable information is collected at the time of a disaster. It makes sense: bombs are exploding, ships are sinking, and people are dying—it is not a situation conducive to good log-keeping. Information assimilated at the time and reported for the record is often done in a perfunctory manner, as the pieces of destruction are being reassembled and new missions are about to be undertaken. Now, we can sit in a comfortable laboratory, use the tools of far greater sophistication, and take full advantage of hindsight. We can do a better job, if we are true to our craft.

Not only was this important to the I-52 search in 1995; it would prove to be important to our study of the loss of the *Dakar*, two years later.

Tom and Meridian were proud, Tidwell was elated, and Neal's investment had paid off, or so it seemed. Unfortunately, not much good happened to Tidwell and Neal after the discovery. Fundamentally, Paul Tidwell is a treasure hunter and a loner, and he is not a businessman and didn't have a business base to work from, so it was difficult for him to convert the success into real achievement. Although a 1999 National Geographic mission to the site with the Russian Mirs submersibles collected some stunning photographs of the wreck site, no serious attempt to salvage the ship has been made so far.

✡ ✡ ✡

Our success in the discovery of the I-52 was an epiphany. It made us realize that we could apply the skills and technology developed in the course of the Cold War to projects of commercial value and of public interest. It also validated our approach to undersea discovery. If not for finding the I-52, our approach to the *Dakar* would have been very different. Or maybe we would never even have had the opportunity.

The excitement of solving a historical mystery, doing undersea detective work, and telling our stories on television forced us to think about a whole new angle to our business. We were used to protecting information, and sharing it only under carefully controlled circumstances. Now we had the challenge of talking about our work in a way that was interesting to lay people; rather than a question of security, it was a question of public relations. Dan Rather, the *CBS Evening News*, *The New York Times*, and even press in London and Japan—it was exciting and eye-opening, and we learned a lot from the exposure. I think we handled it pretty well, although the mysterious and arbitrary workings of the media world will probably always baffle me.

Over the course of the next couple of years, we rewrote our business plan and hatched the idea of relaunching the company under a new name: Nauticos. Under this aegis, we raised capital from investors, added public relations and media facets to our business, and began to develop ideas for other projects. We invested in research, scouring the archives for background on interesting opportunities, new mysteries to solve. We made appointments at the National Geographic Society and the Discovery Channel, and even made some interesting contacts in Hollywood. Around that time we hired Gary Bane, who had recently retired as director of Ocean systems at Rockwell International. Besides his remarkable background as a career ocean engineer and leader of the development of cutting-edge ocean technology, his location in Santa Barbara, California, helped nucleate a Nauticos business center on the West Coast. His proximity to Los Angeles and vast social network also afforded us many interesting opportunities to meet, brief, and sometimes get advice from some of the "beautiful people" in Hollywood (or, at least, their agents). Gary and I generally left those meetings exhausted from the adrenaline rush, shaking our heads and wondering what had just happened and why we were invited!

But we made enough progress to keep going back, and in time had some success in our remade business. Our traditional government work continued to grow as well, and capital from investors helped us add more staff and capabilities. By 1997, our team had grown to thirty on its way to fifty, and we had just celebrated our ten-year company anniversary milestone. Most of the original group that saw us through the early years were still around. In 1998, we were hired by the Discovery Channel to manage their revisit to the RMS *Titanic*, which featured a live broadcast from a manned submersible and robotic cameras at the site of the great wreck. We were busy developing a cooperative research agreement with the Naval Oceanographic Office that would lead to our discovery in 1999 of the Japanese aircraft carrier IJN *Kaga*, sunk at the Battle of Midway in World War II. We produced our own film with the Discovery Channel on that project. We envisioned a longer list of explorations, and today are still on the hunt for undersea mysteries to solve. The *Dakar* was not on our lists, but all of this preparation put us in a position to be asked.

And all of that 1994 buyout debt? Within three years we had paid everyone back and all their interest, family, friends, and former partners. Eventually, we got rid of all those credit cards; we had fun ceremoniously cutting them to pieces. I couldn't have done this without Lynn's emotional support and signing onto the loans and having confidence it would come out okay in the end. For this, I am very grateful.

✡ ✡ ✡

So that's how the "pros from Dover" found themselves in that room, facing the newly re-formed *Dakar* Committee and their high expectations.

Fortunately, the Committee was well prepared to prepare us, and we tried our best to be sponges as we spent the next couple of days learning every detail of the *Dakar* mystery. Admiral Raz had directed the preparation of a couple of volumes of documents that related to the loss of the ship, subsequent investigations, and the previous search efforts over the last thirty years. We saw many photographs of the ship prior to departure from Portsmouth and detailed pictures of the emergency buoy that washed ashore a year after the ship disappeared. Each Committee member presented some aspect of the events or background according to his expertise. All of this was news to us. Toward the end of the second day, the Committee members began to lose control of the urge to air their personal theories, and the discussions began to get animated despite Raz's best efforts. We could immediately see the value of our objectivity; since we had no prior knowledge, we could see the problem fresh, without the baggage of history and personal anguish.

2/17, Monday: No trouble sleeping last night! The ocean in the morning is beautiful, and I hope it will be warm enough to swim. Breakfast was fantastic! They have a buffet every morning laden with fruits, cheeses, smoked and pickled fish, breads, yogurts, eggs, potatoes, mushrooms, fresh juices . . . we had lunch later at the Navy Headquarters cafeteria, which is the big meal of the day here. That included cucumber salad (with a local dressing), stir-fried eggplant, peppers & onions, shredded carrots, chick peas, some kind of soup, a little roast beef, soy patties, pasta, and rice, with fruits for dessert. For someone who is trying to cut down on meats & fats and eat more veggies, legumes & fruits, I am in the right place! It is all really delicious, too.

Today was pretty easy and very interesting. We met with a new group being formed to investigate this sinking, as they have searched unsuccessfully many times over twenty-nine years and are looking for a new approach. The gathering was led by retired Admiral Gideon Raz, ex-submarine force commander. The group includes experts in submarine operations, marine biology, meteorology, communications, intelligence, geophysics, electronics . . . and then there's us! We heard all about the events back in '68, including detailed reviews of message traffic, sailing orders, weather studies, intelligence gathered, etc., etc. More of this tomorrow, then we hear about the search efforts to date. We have a thick booklet to read, with pictures, summarizing everything. They have prepared this well and are very organized, so I hope we can help in some way. It's quite a responsibility, and a wonderful opportunity.

After the workday, I took a run along the beach promenade down to Jaffa Port and back (about six miles), and watched the beautiful sunset over the sea. When I was done, I waded in the Mediterranean for my first time. The water was cool, but not as cool as Maine in August! I'll definitely go swimming on a warm day.

So ended our first full day in Israel, a good start, but with quite a challenge ahead.

Chapter 6

Crushing Boredom and
Sheer Terror

To the (admittedly) subjective eye of a modern nuclear submariner, the *Dakar* was not pretty. Of course, she was built for death, not looks. Still, in good design, form follows function, and warships can be beautiful. But the *Dakar's* functions served too many masters, and her altered design reflected a mix of purposes, technologies, and eras that, to me, didn't look quite right. Of course, to the men who labored over the ship, making it ready to fight gallantly for Israel, she was beautiful.

The *Dakar* was born as the Royal Navy ship HMS *Totem*, launched at the Devonport Dockyard on September 28, 1943. It was conceived in the mid-1930s, when the British Admiralty decided to build a new oceangoing boat to replace older submarines that had not lived up to expectations.

Requirements for this new class of patrol submarines were dictated partly by their mission and partly by the politics of the London Naval Treaty, which limited the total tonnage of new submarine construction. Born of compromise, the ships were limited in size to around one thousand tons, but still carried a strong armament and a patrol duration of at least forty-two days. The first-of-class, the *Triton*, entered service in December 1938. Fifty-three T-class submarines were eventually constructed, making it the largest class of oceangoing submarines ever built for the Royal Navy.

There were early losses, the beginning of quite a list. The first was the ill-fated *Thetis*, which was conducting a trial dive in Liverpool Bay in June 1939 when severe flooding from a forward torpedo tube sent the ship nose-diving to the bottom, 160 feet below. The boat was undiscovered for more than a day, despite her unflooded stern protruding from the surface of the bay. Of the 103 crew, shipyard technicians, and Admiralty passengers on board, only four managed to escape.

As World War II began, a new series of T-class boats was built with modifications in light of experience gained; the most significant change was a welded, rather than riveted, hull construction. This allowed deeper diving, improved the resistance to depth charge attack, and allowed hull sections to be prefabricated. The *Totem,* built in the latter days of the war, was of this modified type.

During World War II, twenty-six T-class submarines operated successfully in all Royal Navy theaters, and bore the brunt of submarine operations. As a consequence, they suffered the highest loss rate. In the 1989 edition of *Jane's Fighting Ships of World War II* fourteen boats were listed as lost during the war, thirteen in the Mediterranean alone. Remarkably, T-class boats were particularly successful against enemy submarines, credited with thirteen sinkings. In modern undersea warfare, the best weapon against a submarine is another submarine, but in World War II, antisubmarine warfare was mainly the province of destroyers and aircraft. The T-class's ability in this regard made them good candidates for evolving submarine missions; after many refits, some were still in active service with foreign navies in the early 1970s.

The HMS *Totem* was placed in operation during the latter part of the war. The boat joined the Mediterranean Fleet and began operations south of Sicily. Simon Coussell, a veteran sailor of this era, spent many months on the ship and kept a journal of his experiences. Writing under the pen name "Jolly Tar," Coussell has compiled some "sailor's yarns" that tell us something of life aboard the *Totem* in the dark days of war:

HMS *Totem* was operating in the Mediterranean and we were based in Sliema Creek on Malta at this time, and we were required to undertake patrols in the eastern Med. The intention was to intercept supply convoys to North Africa and to sink enemy shipping.

While alongside in harbour we were required to sleep ashore and frequently the boats were dived by the duty watch when air raids took place. On one occasion, we powered up the town lighting after a raid, using our generators. Three boats were lost to air raids—P36, P39, and *Pandora.* The Med was a difficult area to operate in and the clarity of the water and the bright sunlight made boat detection from the air rather easy at periscope depth. There were extensive minefields in the Med as well, and these took their toll. There were forty-one Royal Navy Boats sunk in the Mediterranean during World War II.

Our favorite treat was "Big Eats" ashore and afterward we would try and avoid paying the taxi by doing a runner on the pierhead. We usually made it, and as the first turn of the screw pays all debts ashore we had an incentive to get financially ahead. [*Author's note*: a "runner" is an escape; they ran through the security gate and escaped paying the cab fare.]

We were on patrol in the same area as United States boats that were "dry" and had no alcohol aboard. However, they had ice cream and Coca-Cola! We did a good deal of swapping food supplies! (See Simon's Web site: http://www.coussell.com/)

In time, the Nazi armies were reeling across Europe in defeat. When the crew learned the news of victory in Europe, Coussell writes, they celebrated by "splicing the mainbrace," a drink to success and victory:

In 1945, the boat was moored alongside the Depot Ship in Holy Loch [Scotland] and we set sail immediately for the Med. Shortly after, we spliced the mainbrace with a double rum ration, while off Blackpool, as "Sparks" had picked up the expected VE Day broadcast.

Despite peace in Europe, the war in the Pacific was still underway and we carried on for the Mediterranean. From Valetta Harbour in Malta we set off for Freemantle in Australia. [*Author's note*: this voyage of over five thousand miles through the Suez Canal, across the Arabian Sea, and across the Indian Ocean would have taken many weeks.] Shortly after, we were on patrol in the Malacca Straits off the East Indies. Our base and depot ship was at Trincomalee.

I was now acting 2nd Coxswain on the boat (known as "Scratch"), which was a step up, and with it came responsibility for the rum locker. Needless to say, I lost the key to this on one occasion and was not popular for this error—which I soon rectified. Rum was issued at the skipper's discretion as on all Royal Navy ships at that time. This was genuine Pusser's with a very high octane rating. The spirit was not cut with water as on surface ships and was not usually issued immediately before surfacing; as the combined effects of fresh air and alcohol made standing upright difficult. Repayment of minor debts was by "sippers" from your tot and larger ones were repaid by "gulpers."

Later on in the patrol Sparks never lived down failing to hear the first broadcast for VJ day. We spliced the mainbrace again. I was at sea in *Totem* for both VE and VJ days.

According to Coussell's compilations, of nearly 220 British submarines that served in World War II, eighty-two were lost, including over 3,000 crewmen. This was comparable to U.S. losses of fifty-two submarines and over 3,600 men, but was a low number compared to the German Kreigsmarine U-boat losses of over six hundred ships and their crews. For this added risk, submariners were paid one shilling a day above the Royal Navy rate of pay.

✡ ✡ ✡

Over the postwar years, the *Totem* was renewed and refitted on several occasions. The most drastic modification was the addition of a new twelve-foot section, added to the pressure hull, just forward of the conning tower. This allowed the ship to carry additional batteries and increase its range. It also increased underwater speed to fifteen knots, but because the pressure hull itself was cut and rewelded, the operational depth was reduced from 360 to 300 feet.

The most visible change was to the conning tower (known, as I said earlier, as the "sail" in modern parlance, or "bridge fin" to the British). And, in this respect, the changing mission of the warship was evident. The *Totem* was originally built to seek and destroy surface shipping, the traditional World War mission of the submarine. As the *Dakar*, she would be called upon to do this very rarely, if ever. As the postwar period settled into a Cold War era, the offensive power of the submarine became overshadowed by a byproduct of its stealthiness: spying. Modern submarines became ideal platforms for intelligence collection, as they could lurk unseen near enemy shores or in the vicinity of hostile fleets, looking and listening. Developments in intelligence collection and electronics in general led to sophisticated arrays of electronic intercept gear as standard issue for submarines. The *Dakar* was outfitted with the best Israel could produce at the time. Known as "Tavlit," the ESM (electronic surveillance measures) system could passively determine the direction, intensity, frequency, period, and pulse width of enemy signals in a wide range of radio and radar signal bands. Testing of this equipment showed that radars on Mount Carmel could be detected fifty miles away. The technology was so secret that even today, over three decades later, Israeli officers will not discuss technical details. This would be an excellent tool for keeping track of Egyptian and Syrian military threats, and Captain Ra'anan was certainly eager to try it out.

The ESM antenna added to a small forest of masts on the sail, including two periscopes, a radar, radio antennas of various types, and a snorkel mast. The snorkel mast allowed the ship to gulp air and discharge exhaust from the diesel engine, while keeping the ship submerged just below the waves. Because of stress on the periscopes, which must be raised while snorkeling (snorting), the ship could only maintain a speed of nine knots. However, this allowed the ship to stay underwater and reasonably stealthy while keeping its precious batteries fully charged for deeper diving when called upon.

Another important addition to the sail area included the ten-man diving chamber, installed just above the entry hatch to the pressure hull at the forward base of the sail. This feature was intended for commando egress or other covert underwater operations, another Cold War–era capability that was of great interest to Israel. The chamber was designed to withstand the same or greater sea pressure as the pressure hull, so that it would not impose any limits on operations. As designed, while the ship was lurking underwater near shore, the chamber could be sealed from sea and drained. Commandos with scuba gear could enter from inside the ship; after sealing the inner door, the chamber could be pressurized with high-pressure air to equalize sea pressure. Then it could be flooded, allowing the commandoes to swim out. The reverse process would allow them to return without the ship ever having to surface.

The deck gun (a relic of World War antiship tactics) had been removed during earlier upgrades, streamlining the hull for faster submerged cruising. Many internal features were added or modernized, including habitability upgrades. Finally, the boat was streamlined with the new fin and a new bridge.

The remade ship had swelled to a submerged displacement of 1,700 tons and almost three hundred feet in length. The ship could travel up to fifteen knots submerged or surfaced, with a cruising range of 3,600 miles. Six torpedo tubes could fire modern 21-inch diameter British weapons, and she bristled with electronics. The normal crew of sixty-seven could be supplemented with commandos for special missions, or intelligence experts for spy missions. She was quiet and capable, and could be expected to outfox Russian and Egyptian sea threats, if handled well by a competent crew. One limitation they would have to overcome: the *Dakar* could dive to only three hundred feet, barely deeper than her hull length. At full speed, in a steep dive, the *Dakar* could reach this depth in less than thirty seconds.

Thus, a thirty-year-old pre–World War II design was the basis for a 1970s Cold War mission. The hull itself had been in operation for twenty-five years, although most of the fittings and equipment had been replaced over time. The result of this cumulative effort was commissioned into the Israeli Navy on November 10, 1967, and given the Hebrew name *Dakar*.

And, in commemoration of the ship's British legacy, the Cowichan totem pole was left behind, to rest in the Royal Navy submarine museum in Gosport, not far from the submarine pier where the *Dakar* cast off on January 9, 1968.

✡ ✡ ✡

Life aboard the *Dakar* must have been similar to the British experience, as the Israeli crew was trained by the British and steeped in Royal Navy traditions. Still, the Israelis are very independent and have their own gallant military history to draw from. Social and religious customs are quite different, and the deep kinship felt by all citizens across the small country certainly influenced the *Dakar* sailor's motivations.

All submariners share a common knowledge that the risk of their job is different from other military branches. Even in the worst defeat, a wounded soldier or overboard sailor can hope for rescue; even a damaged aircraft can sometimes be landed safely, or the pilot can sometimes parachute away. Submarines, however, rarely sink without the loss of all hands. Measures to provide submarine escape or rescue are more psychological than practical. No pressure hull can survive most ocean depths, and escape from a sinking submarine is impossible. These measures are only possible for the rare case of a submarine sunk in shallow water with intact compartments in a stable condition for a long enough period of time. Although not unheard of, these cases are remarkable exceptions to a grim rule.

Retired Admiral Gideon Raz had spent enough time on submarines to develop a strong bond with the service and the sailors. To him, being a submariner was a privilege, and the added risk was not an impediment. Raz speaks of this in a 2002 interview:

> I personally believe that the submarine is not dangerous; as long as you understand it may be very dangerous. Although it's underwater, everything has its way to recover from problems, if you do things properly.
>
> People are attracted to submarines because it's a unique way of fighting together while using technology at the same time. Normally, in the Air Force and the Army, you are either a fighter or a technician. You cannot do both. In a submarine, you are fighting the same time that you are working the machines. So it's the classic man-machine interface in the submarine, and this is the reason people who are devoted to the technology like it, and cannot do without it. This is my way of thinking.

Retired Captain Doron Amir spent more than twelve years in the submarine flotilla, starting as a technical engineer and finishing as the squadron commander. He spent some months on one of the old S-class boats, then several years on the T-conversion boats, and was the second captain of the new 1976 model *Gal*-class submarine. So his experience was with three generations of submarines, starting from the beginning of World War II to the modern, Cold War designs.

As a young officer, Amir was part of the T-conversion team in Portsmouth, slated to ride home with the *Dakar*, but fate intervened. He recalls:

> The plan was that myself and one of my colleagues, will come back to Israel with the *Dakar*, but the captain of the *Dakar* decided that he's got too many people on board, sixty-nine, and they don't have space for us, and we belonged to the sister boat, the INS *Leviathan*, here in

Israel. He decided he will not take us with him, and we have to find our way back home by some other means, not with his submarine. So we flew back home, joined the *Leviathan,* and ten days later we started to look for the *Dakar.* (2002 interview)

Amir also took the risks of his craft in stride, focusing on the cause, the pride, and the camaraderie.

It's not nature for human beings to live below the water. We are used to living on the ground, and the mysteries of living in a small box below the water doing things that nobody can see what you are doing, mysteriously, it appeals to people. People who like to do something in the hidden depths.

In a submarine, you share your bunk with another two persons, which means you have a whole bunk system. And the command, the behavior below the deck is not a formal one. We never use a uniform. We used to bring our civilian clothes from home. We use sandals, if necessary, instead of shoes. We used to wear shorts instead of all of those heavy uniforms of the surface fleet.

So it's a mixture of some kind of civilian way of behavior with a naval command, and it creates a mode of operation which is very nice. Everybody knows who is the captain, although we don't wear ranks, and everybody knows who is the sailor, although he may be bigger than the captain and maybe nicer than him, but everybody knows everybody, and you live all mixed. Everything is mixed there, so it's very nice.

Retired Commander Yoram Bar-Yam spent fourteen years of active duty with submarines, and was the senior flotilla engineer in the Israeli Navy. He participated in four *Dakar* investigation committees, and wrote to me:

The very first submarines that Israeli Naval officers sailed in were French submarines. The very first literature that was available and Israeli officers read were books about the German submarines during the Second World War.

Since from the way of life, tradition and even the technical aspects there is a certain resemblance between the French and the German submarines, it was only normal that many habits, ways of "running the ship" and procedures in the Israeli boats were copied from those navies.

On the other hand, the boats that the Israeli Navy bought were British and together with the boats we received the Royal Navy processes and procedures. Most of them were later on adopted by the Israeli Navy.

Anyhow, no matter where any tradition came from, the Israeli Navy and the personnel having the Israeli character and temperament gave it an Israeli flavor.

One should also remember that the Israeli Navy is a very small navy. For a long period Israel had only two submarines. What it meant was that over the years, the few hundred submariners knew one another very well. They became so close that amongst many of them the feeling was that we are one big family. The wives became friends, we were all always in everybody's family festivities and we really became very close.

Even today, thirty-one years after I left the submarines, we meet on a regular basis and frankly, I cannot imagine my social and family life without my fellow submariners. (March 5, 2005)

Commander Bar-Yam was among the first group of twenty-seven volunteers who gathered in 1957 to form the core of the new submarine flotilla. Among the twenty-seven men, Yaacov Ra'anan (the commanding officer), Ran Shimon (the chief engineer), and Tzvi Tal (the chief electrical petty officer) a dozen years later ended their lives in the *Dakar*.

✡ ✡ ✡

Life aboard a submarine is demanding and stressful, especially during long voyages. Much can go wrong with such a complicated machine, and the crew's competence and training are offset by a marginal environment that degrades performance. I drew on my experience as a submariner to try to imagine how circumstances on board the *Dakar* could have contributed to her demise.

My days on the USS *Kamehameha* in the late 1970s differed dramatically in many ways from life on the *Dakar,* with much owing to its World War II heritage despite modifications and modernization. I sailed in an 8,000-ton behemoth; the *Dakar* was but 1,700 tons. Our normal complement was about 150 crew, and most had their own bunks; the *Dakar* sailed with 69, in very cramped quarters. Everyone could take showers on our boat, provided that the evaporators (which made freshwater from sea water) were working properly; we had plenty of power to run them. There were no showers on the *Dakar*; once a day everyone filled a basin with water and washed himself, a process that was mandatory to everyone on board. On my boat, most people observed the "submarine shower" method: quickly wet down, secure the water (a handy button on the shower head was provided so you didn't have to change the hot/cold mix), soap down, then quickly rinse. Anyone who let the water run was accused of taking a "Hollywood" shower, and didn't repeat the event. Still, some sailors are basically slobs, and they used the circumstances to allow themselves to accumulate a patina of filth and odor that probably rivaled the standard of a *Dakar* crewman.

In the confines of a submarine, even a big one like mine, it only takes a few examples to saturate the environment with that special smell. Add to this the omnipresence of diesel and lube oil fumes. Even nuclear submarines have a diesel engine for emergency power, and we ran it frequently for training and the occasional real emergency. In my day, smoking was allowed, so everyone smoked. Even if you didn't light up your own cigarettes, you breathed enough secondhand smoke to start to crave a nicotine hit from time to time. Cooking fumes, paint, electrical smells, burning paper from the sonar recorders . . . all of that added to the stench, the unmistakable "submarine smell." When I would return home from patrol, I would not wear my uniform in the house. My clothes, sea bag, and all gear were left on the porch, to be hung outside for at least a few days in "laundry purgatory."

Submarines are expensive assets, and their growing variety of post–World War II missions made them in short supply, in anybody's navy. So ships tend to be kept operating almost all the time, and that means a very demanding schedule for the submariner. Between operating at sea, repairs, maintenance, and training, there is time for little else (including family). This problem was addressed to a large degree on my submarine by having two complete crews, which would take turns operating and maintaining the ship. Our "off-crew" time could be devoted to training and R&R. But, of course, the *Dakar* crew did not have this luxury, and time in the shipyard is always the busiest.

Adding to the stress of long hours and demanding technical work are the special circumstances of submarine life. You have very little space, you work and live in very close quarters, and you don't see daylight for long periods of time. In a modern nuclear submarine, it is true that the only real limitation for submerged endurance is the amount of food you can carry. The nuclear reactor doesn't require air, so it can operate completely underwater indefinitely. Thus, life support and habitability are key to extended operations.

In a nuclear submarine the atmosphere is largely artificial. "Oxygen generators" make fresh oxygen from distilled sea water, using electrolysis. The carbon dioxide (CO_2) the crew exhales is removed by CO_2 "scrubbers" and pumped out to sea, and a host of other airborne contaminants are filtered, scrubbed, precipitated, or burned from the air to keep it breathable and somewhat clean. This is supplemented by periods of ventilation with outside air, but since this requires the ship to extend a snorkel mast above the surface, this time is kept to a minimum. Submarines are always stealthier and safer from the enemy when completely submerged.

On the *Dakar*, the time spent submerged differed from one mission to the next. The usual pattern was to stay dived from sunrise to sunset and snorkel (snort) in intervals during the night to recharge the batteries. However, periods of as much as thirty-six hours continuously submerged without snorkeling were not unknown.

More than any other factor, I think the submarine atmosphere had the biggest effect on comfort and performance of the crew. Although the systems to clean the air are remarkable and quite effective, the burden of emissions they must deal with is overwhelming, especially when they are not operating at peak performance. The most important thing to remove from the air is the CO_2 that is continuously being exhaled into the living spaces. Levels in normal air are only around 0.035 percent (350 parts per million); although this is rising from the preindustrial age level of 280 parts per million, and there is concern that elevated levels of this "greenhouse gas" will eventually contribute to global warming, these levels are perfectly safe for breathing. In fact, the recommended CO_2 limit for continuous safe breathing is 5,000 parts per million (0.5 percent). The CO_2 scrubbers in submarines are designed to maintain the CO_2 level below this limit. The scrubbers worked by taking in air and spraying it with an inorganic liquid called monoethanolamine (MEA) that absorbs CO_2 when cool, and gives it off when warmed. The "scrubbed" air, less most of its CO_2, is filtered and returned to the living spaces. The cool MEA is pumped through a heater, which causes it to give off its CO_2, which is in turn compressed and discharged overboard. The chemical is recooled, then recycled to start the process over. Unfortunately, MEA is corrosive and toxic even in small amounts, so it is itself a contaminant and must be handled carefully.

The more traditional way of dealing with CO_2 buildup, which was the primary method used on the *Dakar*, was by using a dry chemical (lithium hydroxide) that has a natural affinity for gaseous CO_2. This is also used on spacecraft, as highlighted in the movie about the Apollo 13 mission when the crew was faced with managing their life support with limited resources and damaged equipment. The most limiting factor was their ability to control CO_2 levels during the return from the moon. Unlike MEA, lithium hydroxide cannot be recycled on board, and once used, must be discarded.

The problem with both of these systems is they don't always work perfectly well. My nuclear submarine, the *Kamehameha*, carried two CO_2 scrubbers, and they both had to be working to keep the CO_2 levels at or near the 0.5 percent limit. The machines were very finicky, and when they were not working properly or were being repaired, the CO_2 level would go up quite a bit. As levels approached 1 percent (thirty times the normal atmospheric level), people would become irritable, develop headaches, fatigue, and, in more extreme cases, nausea. So it was a bad day on the ship if one of the scrubbers wasn't working.

And I believe that this was a more common state of existence on ships like the *Dakar* during periods of submerged operation. Long after it becomes impossible to light a match through lack of oxygen, a human can still work and think, but high levels of CO_2 can make life miserable and degrade performance.

Of course, oxygen has to eventually be added to replace what is consumed by normal breathing. That was done on a nuclear submarine by taking seawater from the infinite supply surrounding the ship, distilling it with an evaporator, and applying electricity to the pure freshwater to split it into hydrogen and oxygen. The hydrogen is pumped overboard, the oxygen is pumped into oxygen tanks, and then fed into the ship's living spaces at the rate needed to support breathing. So, if the oxygen generator failed and needed to be repaired, the stored oxygen in tanks would last a good long time. And even if the oxygen tanks become depleted, you could always come near the surface, raise the snorkel, and ventilate the ship, but that was something we always tried to avoid. The *Dakar* would have spent a fair amount of time snorkeling; if they needed additional oxygen, having no oxygen generators, they used more primitive "oxygen candles" which give off oxygen when burned.

A certain amount of explosive hydrogen and deadly carbon monoxide would escape into the living spaces or would be introduced into the air from the batteries or various other sources, and had to be burned away using a $CO-H_2$ burner. This device oxidizes (burns) the hydrogen, carbon monoxide, and other hydrocarbons into CO_2 and harmless water. The air was full of particulates, of course, from cooking, cigarettes, and any other source of dust; electrostatic filters helped control this (but could not effectively remove many odors). The usual rule on the *Dakar* was that smoking inside the submarine was forbidden. However, at specific times, with the permission of the captain, everyone was allowed to smoke one cigarette.

In our submarine, we made a great effort to keep contaminating chemicals out of the ship, but some things were unavoidable. Freon, for example, that was used in the air-conditioning units. We worried about that a lot. Greases, oils, or discharges from other equipment could also introduce contaminants, so we had a strict list of things that could not be brought on board including common everyday items such as pressurized shaving cream cans. The fuel in torpedoes was a particularly hazardous substance, so we had safety drills for how to deal with a ruptured torpedo.

Next to flooding, fire is the most dreaded event on a submarine. It doesn't take very long for compartments to fill with smoke or for oxygen to be consumed, even in a small fire. We carried a limited number of protective suits and self-contained breathing systems to fight fires if one occurred. Throughout the ship were air pipes that were hooked into the main air banks, which were otherwise used for blowing our main ballast tanks for surfacing, and for air-operated equipment on the ship. The pipes were fitted with plugs at regular intervals, and there were cabinets throughout the ship that contained breathing masks with hoses that would fit into the plugs. One could walk all around the ship, disconnecting and reconnecting the hose into different plugs as needed. So, if there was any kind of emergency on the ship that would contaminate the atmosphere, every crewman would first grab a mask and plug it in so he would have a source of breathing air. Then he would fight the fire or handle the emergency.

Part of our training was to learn how to quickly bring a ship to snorkel depth and start the diesel-powered generator, which we used as an emergency source of power. This would also allow us to ventilate the ship to remove smoke or any other contamination. Almost every day we would practice drills involving a reactor shutdown from some reason or another, and we'd quickly bring the ship near the surface, commence snorkeling and start the diesel running so we could bring power back into the ship without draining the batteries. One of the features of this exercise could lead to more trouble. If the officer of the deck was not very careful, and did not pay attention to the wind, we could suck diesel exhaust into the fresh air intake. Instead of ventilating the ship with fresh air, we'd fill it with diesel smoke. The captain would get very angry, as would the rest of the crew, and it was a good way to ruin everyone's day. As the *Dakar*, without the luxury of nuclear power, would spend many hours each day snorkeling, this circumstance was unavoidable from time to time.

✡ ✡ ✡

Submarines are all about secrecy. The Israeli Navy takes this to such a level that the identities of active submariners are protected, and their pictures are not published. In my day, most of the time the crew did not know where in the world we were operating—that was classified information. Even after a mission, the places the ship had been remained a secret. During a mission, the captain of the ship has his patrol orders, which, in the case of the *Dakar,* were to make a direct route to Haifa. The orders may be quite specific, but generally give a lot of discretion to the captain, allowing him the freedom of movement to accomplish his mission. This protocol became questioned as a result of the loss of the USS *Scorpion* in 1968 (the same year as the *Dakar*). The fleet commanders at submarine headquarters had no specific knowledge of the *Scorpion*'s position at the time of the sinking, and it was quite a feat to eventually locate the wreckage.

In my day, submarines on patrol were assigned a moving area of the ocean that they were to be in at all times, normally determined as part of the patrol order beforehand. This was not communicated to the ship by radio but handed in a sealed package to the captain prior to departure. So there was enough freedom of movement to remain stealthy and undetected, but if the worst happened and the ship sank, headquarters would have at least have some idea where the ship was supposed to be. In the particular case of the *Dakar's* voyage across the Mediterranean, she was given the general order to proceed directly from Gibraltar to Haifa, but there were no specifically assigned points along the way. By submarine tradition, the captain would have felt he had a large degree of autonomy in the details of accomplishing his mission.

One of the intriguing aspects of life on a submarine, and one that adds to the level of stress on the submariner, is the schedule. For our boat, it was convenient to operate on an eighteen-hour cycle because you had a sufficient crew for most of the watch stations to be covered by three people, and it was traditional in the U.S. submarine navy to stand six-hour watches. Three people working six-hour shifts each adds up to eighteen hours. There were exceptions where, due to lack of trained people, watches would be manned on a six-on and six-off routine (known as "port and starboard" watches), but that was avoided if possible.

During a watch, we were glued to a station or (in the case of supervisors) in the immediate presence of our watch team at all times, for the duration of the watch. The only acceptable break was for using the head (toilet) and, in that case, you needed to find someone not on watch to stand your position for the necessary few minutes. Each compartment included a complement of crewmen monitoring equipment, taking readings, and being ready for any emergency. Watch-standers monitored the reactor, engine systems, machinery spaces, sonars, electronics, navigation systems, weapons systems, buoyancy control, and ship control stations at all times; and, of course, the galley was in operation around the clock preparing, serving, or cleaning up from meals. As we were to remain always alert, this watch period did not generally include study time, equipment repairs, or entertainment in any form. So, in our time off watch, we weren't free. We had personal study, group training, administrative work, ship cleaning, and any other kind of work involved in running an organization. Then there was precious entertainment time, which mostly involved watching movies or reading, although some ship-wide activities would take place on special occasions.

So, it was a very, very busy routine, and left little time for sleep. There were times when you would stand your six-hour, midnight to 6 AM watch and go right into a morning cleanup lasting until noon. After lunch, if you were an officer or chief, you would conduct an inspection of the cleanup and make your report back to the executive officer (who was, by tradition, never happy with the results). That would take until late afternoon. At 6 PM, your next watch would begin and last until midnight. Generally, we would skip lunch to catch an hour's nap in the middle of that cycle, desperately needed since we commonly spent the prior evening watching a movie, instead of the more prudent choice of sleeping.

The interesting aspect of this ship's routine is that most crewmen live on an eighteen-hour day, with six (or usually fewer) hours sleep in eighteen instead of eight in twenty-four. Your body had to adapt to the shorter sleep cycle. It normally took most of us a week or even two to become comfortable with an eighteen-hour cycle. Meanwhile, the ship's official routine is still run on a twenty-four-hour day. In other words, there's still breakfast, lunch, dinner, and "midrats" (midnight rations), a full meal at the turnover of each watch. Training schedules were on a regular weekly basis, a Monday-through-Friday work routine, with Saturday for ship cleanup (known as "field day"), and a relaxed schedule on Sundays. There were still watches on Sundays, of course, but there was no training or drills or ship cleanup that day. All-hands drills, allowing us to practice our response to ship emergencies, were conducted regularly, some scheduled, some a surprise. So our personal routine was on an eighteen-hour sleep cycle, with many interruptions, but the ship's schedule kept up with a seven-day week and a twenty-four-hour day. Of course, when we returned home after maximum adaptation to this schedule over the course of months, we would have to readjust to the regular day-night cycle, which would take about as long as the original adjustment.

Then there was another twist. Once we submerged for our patrol, we would usually set our clocks to Greenwich time and leave them at that setting for the entire patrol. Because of that, as we cruised around, we didn't have to worry about switching time zones, and from that moment on, we could keep a twenty-four-hour, seven-day schedule without further adjustment. The world outside, however, was on its own schedule, with day and night according to the sun, depending on whatever part of the world we happened to be in. That mattered to the officer of the deck in case we needed to come near the surface and he had to use the periscope. It could be midnight by ship's routine, but he had to know whether it would be bright sunshine daylight or pitch-black night when he put his eyeball to that lens.

So the ship would be fully lit in all operating spaces all the time, with sleeping spaces kept dimly lit except for drills, real emergencies, and "field days." But the operations compartment where the officer of the deck (OOD) stood watch would be brightly lit if it was daytime outside, dimly lit in red light ("rig for red") if it was nighttime outside, or lights out ("rig for black") if we were actually at periscope depth at night. Then, the OOD would be using the periscope, and his eyes would have to be adapted to night vision. If at any time during his watch while it was dark outside he had to go where it was more brightly lit, the OOD would wear red goggles to keep his eyes night-adapted. So all these different routines interleaved, acknowledging the watch standing cycle, weekly/daily activities, and the "real world" day/night cycle, all going on at the same time.

In the *Dakar*, there were some differences in this, borrowing British tradition and adapting to their own military practices, but the ship's routine had to accommodate all of these factors, and the crewmen had to adapt. As described by Commander Yoram Bar-Yam:

> Normal procedure for the watch duration was 4 hours. I mention normal procedure because it was not cast in concrete. There were other routines, too, where the watch duration was only three hours but this was not the regular case.
>
> The number of watches per day all depended on the routine of operation. In training usually it was two watches in twenty-four hours. In snorting conditions the number of personnel required to run the boat was so that the whole crew was divided to two watches only, four hours on, four hours off. In a routine dive, like passage from one point to another underwater, we were split to three watches.
>
> No reading or eating was allowed during the watch. If a meal was served during the watch time, people were replaced by crew members from another watch to take the meal.
>
> If one takes in account the different stations, like diving stations, combat stations, or any kind of training and add to it the time spent to replace people from the watch for meals, you can see that at least half of the time between watches was consumed, and the time having a rest between watches was very little. And I did not yet take in account time needed to perform maintenance work, which was always between watches.
>
> Not enough space is available in a submarine. That is the reason why very few people had their own bunk. The captain and the cook were the only people with their own bunk. All the rest—every three people had two bunks, taking in account that at least one out of three was always on watch.
>
> This process is called "hot bunk" as the bunk never gets cold. (March 5, 2005)

Tight quarters, poor environment, crazy schedules, demanding tasks, constant vigilance . . . combined with homesickness and a yearning to be back in Israel again after two years. It was a lot to take, even for an elite crew.

✡ ✡ ✡

It is said about professions like submarining that they involve hours of crushing boredom punctuated by moments of sheer terror. There is some truth to this, and there is great danger in succumbing to either boredom or terror. The symptoms of either circumstance can be mitigated by good procedures, strict discipline, and effective training.

Many people's impression of submarine life is drawn from Hollywood. The movie (and book) *The Hunt for Red October* is a recent example. The film was, thankfully, quite accurate in its depiction of the jargon and procedures on a modern nuclear submarine. Of course, it was quite dramatized; the characters were larger than life, and you did not get a sense of the routine because it was episodic. The movie only featured the occasional very dramatic events, not even a few minutes of ship routine—that would be boring to the audience. Of course, there were other aspects of the movie that were dramatized or contrived, with a boatload of literary license in the idea that one could drive ships around underwater canyons—that just doesn't happen.

However, certain scenes were very accurate, including the idea of tracking and closely following an enemy submarine by lurking in its "baffles." This is the area directly behind a submarine, where the noises of its own propeller can mask the sounds of other ships. In this "shadow zone," the ship is essentially blind, acoustically. My ship was concerned about being followed, not following, so we did a lot of things to try to maintain our secrecy and stealth, including keeping track of our baffles. This involved procedures, discipline, and training.

The technique for checking for snooping submarines, or to see if any ship is unwittingly in your blind spot, is known as "clearing baffles." We would routinely, but randomly, make maneuvers to detect anyone that might be following. We had a list of half a dozen or so kinds of maneuvers involving turns to the left, to the right, circling, changing depth—different ways of moving the baffle area that would reveal a following ship. We kept a set of dice in the control room, and the OOD would throw the dice to determine which type of maneuver to do and what time of the hour to do it. This ensured the process was random, and that is how we avoided getting into any pattern.

When you have strict routines and a busy, repetitive schedule, it's very easy to get into a pattern, which can lead to boredom, predictability, and inattention. Part of running a six-hour watch is a time management exercise, because there are many things you have to accomplish in that time to keep the ship running properly. Some of those things are very time-sensitive or periodic, so it would be easy to fall into a routine of doing certain things exactly after one hour of watch or at a particular time of the day, and a very observant opponent will note those routines and adapt to them. There are stories of U.S. attack submarines that were tracking Soviet subs for days on end, following them around the ocean. They established the routines of each watch-stander on the opposing ship, so they knew when to expect a particular maneuver. At that time, they would back away, out of detection range, wait for the enemy baffle-clearing maneuver to be completed, and then creep up close again. We would try to avoid falling into that trap.

The crew of a submarine was highly educated and highly trained, and usually included a higher proportion of "prima donnas" than the average complement of sailors. Many enlisted crew members had two or three years of college behind them, and would be graduates but for some financial need (or other more creative problem). Before arriving on the ship, the submariner would undergo a four-month intensive submarine school program that included theory and practical training in submarine operations, watch-standing procedures, damage control, firefighting training, even submarine escape training. Sailors in the Nuclear Power Program would spend a year at school, including classroom instruction akin to a college degree in nuclear engineering and a period of practical training while operating an actual nuclear plant ashore. However, when a sailor arrived on the ship, he was considered to be completely unqualified to do anything. Every crew member, from the officers to the lowest-ranked enlisted man, was required to follow a program of apprenticeship, which would typically last at least one entire patrol.

Part of the training included School of the Boat lectures, but most of it was self-study, watch-standing under supervision, or one-on-one with a mentor. The trainee would learn the detailed layout of the ship, the location of every pipe and valve for every piping system (seawater, freshwater, pressurized air, hydraulic oil, fuel oil, and all others). Also, he would learn the location and function of every switch, breaker, generator, and motor in the electrical system. Piping and wiring diagrams were memorized, and the trainee expected to be quizzed regularly by his mentor or during qualification checkouts. Often, these "quizzes" were conducted under some kind of pressure, to try to simulate the demand of responding in an emergency. "Find MSW-22! Now!" the mentor might say, expecting the trainee to, without hesitation, describe in detail exactly where main sea water (MSW) valve number 22 is located, what systems it attaches to, and how to operate it. More realistically, in a drill, one would have to take the proper action to respond to fire or flooding by securing the right combination of valves and switches, hopefully without disabling something important on the ship. In this way, every crew member became "qualified" to respond to emergencies anywhere on the ship, regardless of his job specialty or watch-standing task.

And then you had to learn the operating principles of ship's equipment: propulsion, weapons, communications, environmental systems, auxiliary systems (seawater cooling, freshwater evaporators, air compressors, and so on). And then, of course, all the procedural activities—how to bring the ship to periscope depth; how to change the reactor operation from low-speed to high-speed configuration; how to commence snorkeling, for example. And most importantly, how to respond to emergencies—immediate actions to take for fire in the ship, flooding in a compartment, failure of a diving control system—any possible danger that could be imagined.

Crewmen falling behind in this process would be placed on the "dink" (delinquent) list, and liberty privileges revoked. Most crew members would take the majority of their first patrol to become qualified to stand a watch station without instruction. Finally, the crewman would sit before a qualification board for an intense oral and written exam, and it was only after clearing that hurdle that he was considered to be a "qualified submariner" and was awarded the coveted dolphin insignia. So, it was a long, demanding, and arduous training regimen, in many cases lasting over two years from enlistment or commissioning. When the dolphins are first ceremoniously pinned on by the captain, above the breast pocket of the uniform, it is customary for other qualified submariners to make sure they are "tacked on" by slapping the man on the chest, leading to serious bruises (more so if the man had been a particularly difficult trainee). Newly qualified submariners usually had to endure one more trial before full attention was turned to the next in line: a celebration upon return to port involving dunking the dolphin insignia in a pitcher filled with beer (at best), or some random concoction of liquor, and expecting the man to drink down the entire pitcher to rescue his badge. Owing to some serious incidents arising from this massive consumption of alcohol, the ritual is not sanctioned anymore, but no doubt it still survives.

☆ ☆ ☆

All submarine navies, like all military groups, thrive on tradition and ritual. Although to an outsider the practices seem mysterious, foolish, or even juvenile, they serve to bind a crew together, occupy the mind during idle hours, and sometimes even drive home important lessons. The traditions of the Israeli Navy, as described by Commander Bar-Yam, were not unlike those of the U.S. Navy, as sailors everywhere draw from an ancient heritage of seafaring, and share a common understanding of the risks, trials, and rewards of their craft.

> In order to help the crew to overcome boring periods, where very little activity happens, and in order to motivate the crew in a positive direction, a daily bulletin was prepared and published in the living quarters. This bulletin included news from the world, news from the navy, letters from crew members, some funny stories, etc. This was usually organized by one volunteer from the crew with a few more helping him.
>
> It was customary to arrange a party in the last evening at sea of every long trip (two weeks or more). In many cases the preparation

for this party took days of hard work. In the parties it was customary to have humorous competitions. One in particular that I remember was a competition to crown the ugliest person on board. Now that I describe it I know that the reader may think that there is some cruelty in it, but this was always received with good spirit and even the chosen person was laughing at it.

Crew members also prepared some competitions between the different compartments (torpedo compartment versus the aft compartment), or different disciplines (mechanics versus electricians).

Another tradition was the welcome ceremony of a new crew member. The very first day of his stay in the submarine was always terrible. It was full of traps that the crew prepared for him. The poor guy was sent numerous times from the torpedo compartment to the Engine room and back with all kind of funny tasks (like bringing from the engineer the material to clean the outer window of the periscopes while in diving position, etc.). I know that this first day was at times a little traumatic for the new guy, but everyone accepted it and when it was time that a subsequent new guy came, the same ceremony was performed. The previous new guy participated in it, enjoyed it and forgot all about his initial frustration. (March 5, 2005)

And my favorite of all:

Since the flotilla was very small, and not too much experience was available, it was emphasized to all of us in every opportunity how important was the Continuous Improvement Process (CIP). Many "lessons learned" sessions took place, many updates were made to the written procedures, and of course very many drills of all kinds of emergency situations were developed.

As part of the CIP, in the *Dakar*, Yaacov Ra'anan (the commanding officer) established a very unique ground rule. Whenever a silly mistake was made by anyone on board, he had to write a poem describing the error, possible consequences and the lessons learned from this case. It was also recommended to combine the lyrics with a melody (either a known one or a new one). This "Dumb Song" was then taught to everyone and was added to the culture of the boat.

Bar-Yam discovered a fragment of the poem that Ra'anan wrote giving the instructions on how (and when) to write a "Dumb Song." His rough translation (with an attempt to put it to rhyme):

Everyone feels now and again
He completely belongs to the Idiot Clan
Especially after committing some foolishness,
That seems to lie right on the verge of sad senselessness.
Officers of the *Dakar,* and I with them
Are sure to be counted among that Clan
And such kind of folly—it is quite clear
Will not be found scarce in the next couple of years.
So as you feel frustrated, once it's all done,
Instead of saying, "Damn it" and just moving on—
In perfect rhyme and poetic expression
Will each officer write his own declaration.

Ra'anan understood the critical need to recognize and correct mistakes, knew that even he was not immune, and demanded that his crew follow this philosophy. These lessons he taught while encouraging good morale and professional pride. These are rare qualities of a great leader.

✡ ✡ ✡

The primary mission of a submarine is to carry weapons, and to be ready to use them at all times. We found it to be quite curious that the *Dakar* was sent to Israel unarmed. Even during sea trials, it is normal to include at least a partial weapons load on the ship in case it would be called to duty in an emergency. Despite this, and although the *Dakar's* mission was complicated by its intelligence and special-forces capabilities, the protocols for use of weapons would have been well understood by Captain Ra'anan.

In the modern navy of city-busting submarine-launched nuclear weapons, the main job of a U.S. attack submarine is to locate, track, and, if necessary, destroy Soviet nuclear ballistic missile submarines to reduce the threat that they would be used against our country. However, with the Israeli Navy of 1968, submarines like the *Dakar* would have taken on a more traditional role of attacking surface ships when called upon, helping to protect surface ships from attack, and collecting intelligence. The *Dakar* was also outfitted with that large diving chamber to allow commandoes to be put ashore. In the shaky peacetime after the Six-Day War, the intelligence mission would have been most important.

Of course, there are very elaborate procedures and safeguards for both maintaining communications with our commanders and ensuring that control of weapons is assured, especially nuclear weapons (which can only be released by National Command Authority—essentially, the president and secretary of defense). There are several levels of authority that are granted, depending on whether you're at war or at peace and what kind of weapon you're wielding. On a tactical level, this is called "rules of engagement," which in peacetime, of course, is highly restricted to extreme defensive situations. On the *Dakar*, the captain had much more autonomy than a U.S. submarine captain, and he would have known that opposing Egyptian and Soviet submarine commanders enjoyed similar freedom. So even though he carried no weapons on *Dakar*, Ra'anan had to be keenly aware of the threats against him and how opposing forces might respond to his presence.

✡ ✡ ✡

All of this submarine experience gave me an advantage when the first committee meetings were held in Israel. For one, I had more credibility in the eyes of the committee members. Also, I could readily grasp the technical aspect of the problem, and had grounding in basic submarine operations.

In fact, a lot of the equipment, procedures, and traditions that were developed in World War II for submarine operations did not change very much in the ensuing decades. Great advances in ship design, equipment, and instruments were made during wartime, and tried-and-true methods have not been lightly altered. Even the "look and feel" of equipment in a vintage 1940s boat is familiar to a Cold War sailor. The upgraded *Dakar* of the late 1960s was of a similar generation to my nuclear sub of the 1970s (launched in 1965); things have certainly changed a lot more in the twenty-five years since I last sailed on the *Kamehameha*. The submarine fleet, especially prior to the 1990s, was very slow to adopt certain advanced technologies because of their survivability; computers and electronics can be quite delicate and could completely fail in time of emergency.

For these reasons, submarine equipment (and shipboard equipment in general) tends to be very rugged, usually a couple of generations behind commercial equivalents, but highly dependable and highly functional. So, I could look at a World War II boat and find very familiar-looking features and very familiar procedures. It was possible for me to identify with and understand the actions, motives, and capabilities of the *Dakar* crew.

Together with Tom, we could understand the problem and relate it to our expertise in underwater navigation and deep-ocean search. We were a good team, and the Israeli search committee quickly accepted us.

Chapter ז

Black Saturday

I t is difficult to imagine how dreadful it must have been for the families and friends of the crew in the days of growing realization that the *Dakar* was lost. It was clear that something terrible had happened, but they could only speculate about the mysterious and horrifying circumstances. After the high of anticipation, of elation, that their men would soon be home, it must have been nearly impossible to bear. Only the closeness of the families, the support of friends, and the empathy of the entire country made this at all manageable.

It is January 24, 1968. The submarine is racing for home at record-breaking underwater speeds, averaging eight knots according to the captain's position reports. At this time, the ship is located just southeast of the island of Crete. Later that night, at midnight, a routine Morse code radio check is received at Israeli Navy Headquarters. The next message is expected at 6 AM the following morning, with a position update.

The message did not arrive.

Speculation began at Navy Headquarters on the nature of her communications difficulties. During the next day, *Dakar* was repeatedly called, using her international call sign, 4XP-Z. But no further signals came from the submarine.

On Friday morning, January 26, the search began. All available Israeli ships and airplanes joined these efforts and began methodically to scour the eastern Mediterranean. Over the ensuing days, appeals for international assistance were answered by naval and air units from Great Britain, the United States, Greece, and Turkey. Even Lebanon took part in the search.

The word was out.

In no time, the terrible news flashed across Israel, heard by family and friends. Black Saturday was upon them. Sixteen-year-old Michael Marcovici was completely unprepared for that trip down the stairs and the news that was waiting for him. "I remember it was Saturday morning. I was playing the accordion, and the neighbor Behi called. He lived one floor below us, was the same age, and a good friend of mine. He said, 'Listen, come down, I want to speak with you.' I was not aware about anything because that morning I didn't hear the news. . . . I didn't know anything" (2002 interview).

Michael was looking forward to his brother's exciting return to great fanfare on Monday, and was blissfully unaware of the growing concern at Navy Headquarters. But this anxiety swept across the country as people learned of the terrible news on the radio and from family and friends. It was only a matter of hours before Michael and the rest of the families of the *Dakar* crew began a new and tragic phase of their lives.

> I went down and I entered, and I saw everybody was crying. I asked, what happened? And they told me *Dakar* is missing.
>
> I started to knock my head on the wall; then I calmed down. My father was, at that time, on the sea, so I was alone with my mother. I told them nobody would tell anything to my mother. I went up to the room, turned on the radio and heard the news.
>
> And then my mother came home, and when I heard that she was coming, I turned off the radio. She said, "I want to hear the news." I said, "There is nothing for you." She said, "I want to hear the news." And then I had to tell her.
>
> We gathered with some relatives and went immediately to the Navy Headquarters in Stella Maris. And then we went down to the port. We're hearing rumors all the time, all kinds of rumors. We had forty-eight hours until my father arrived on Monday. He was on a ship which came to port in Naples, and then he flew to Israel. He arrived at night, and in the morning, he volunteered to sail on one of the ships that went to search for the *Dakar*.

The ensuing days were filled with uncertainty, as Michael's emotions swung from despair to hope and back again, over and over. The vacuum of real information was quickly filled with rumor and speculation, which fed the uncertainty in everyone's mind. Since nothing could be determined, anything was possible. A series of bizarre coincidences served to nurture the rumors and sharpen their details, leaving people wondering and hoping even more. As Michael describes it:

> And for ten days I was with my mother all the time, between the Navy, and listening to the radio, all the time hoping. Rumors were almost every minute. All things happened in such a tempo. I remember the *Dakar* was declared as being missing on Saturday. On Monday, the French submarine, the *Minerve*, suddenly disappeared as well.

Then on Monday or Tuesday, suddenly, the Israeli Navy informed everybody that there is a third submarine called the *Dolphin*. Nobody knew about the *Dolphin*. So in three or four days, you had one Israeli submarine missing, one French submarine missing, and one Israeli submarine coming out of the blue sky, named the *Dolphin*, on the way to Israel. It looks very, very strange. Everybody knew, in Israel, that the *Dakar* was on the way; it was on the radio, it was in the papers . . . the new Israeli submarine. Nobody knew anything about the *Dolphin*.

So people started to think, "What is going on here?" And I remember that on Tuesday or Wednesday, suddenly, across the whole of Israel, there were rumors: "The *Dakar* is rising." People were standing on the roofs here, waiting to see the *Dakar*. But it was the *Dolphin* that arrived.

And we were squeezed between hopes and sorrow. We were really in chaos, and nobody could give us a clear picture of what was going on. So, to think immediately about disaster? No. As I told you, people were thinking maybe it's kind of a drill. You see, there is another submarine. People said, "Okay, we are a part of the Cold War between the Americans and the Russians. The Americans want to know what the Russian fleet is doing." At that time, the Russians were in Alexandria; there were a lot of Russian ships. So when you are doing the so-called search after the *Dakar*, you can identify every ship, every submarine. Then, when it will be finished, we will see that the submarine will arrive.

But it was not a drill; it was nothing. The submarine disappeared.

Soon, people began to understand that something permanently dreadful had happened, and there would not be a surprise happy ending to the story. The men of *Dakar* were gone. The Navy made it official; the rabbi made a declaration; the Knesset deliberated and proclaimed a national day of mourning. But still, there was uncertainty. Still, the rumors persisted. Family members banded together in sorrow, which in time hardened into a resolve. A resolve to find out what really happened to *Dakar* and her crew. Michael continues:

And after ten days, all the families were invited to the Navy base, and we were told that the search didn't succeed to find anything. The *Dakar* at that time officially was declared as a missing submarine, and all the crew was declared as being missing.

And from that moment, we have to speak about a new chapter in our lives before this event, and after this event because everything was constantly changing.

I remember that after this, my father could not anymore go to work on the ship. He started to organize the families, and I was with him at that time trying to help him in all the administration, so all the meetings were in our home. I was listening, and taking a part in what became the Committee of the Families of the *Dakar*.

First, you have good people with good intention. They were calling us. Advising us to take this direction, or that direction. Then you have all the spiritualists. They hear voices or whatever you want. And of course there are a lot of people who want to take advantage about things like this.

After my father died, two years after the *Dakar* event, I joined, officially, this committee. And I saw exactly, for the last thirty years, how almost every month people were coming with rumors . . . Russia, Egypt, whatever you want.

In fact you have to live two different lives. The daily life that has to go on, and the life with memories and a strong will to discover what happened.

And you have to try to do both things, and it is not so easy; not so easy.

Four-year-old Odie Ra'anan was back home in Haifa, staying with his grandfather while his mother and brothers detoured through Paris for a few days of excursion and shopping. Mother and brothers arrived on schedule. And then came Saturday, when word was out that communications with the *Dakar* had ceased and the families were galvanized in grief and worry. The adults tried not to share their growing panic with Odie, but the boy gradually came to understand what was happening.

"Maybe I can smell it," he said.

Odie's mother, Naomi, took her position as the captain's wife seriously, working tirelessly to comfort the family of the crew and ease their anxieties as much as possible. With three children of her own (Odie, the youngest), Naomi had more than her share of responsibility, but somehow was a fount of optimism and reassurance to others. Though as much in the dark as everyone else, she shuttled back and forth between Navy Headquarters and family homes with what news she could bring.

One day during the crisis, after visiting a *Dakar* shipmate's home and inspiring much needed laughter with a few minutes of nonsense and gossip, she stood to leave. Consulting a list with the names and addresses of *Dakar* crew members for her next stop, she paused at the door. In the words of Uri Oren, writing in his book, *The Commander's Wife* (1968), "And by the door, all of a sudden, as if she was reading what we all were thinking about, she says, 'Say, am I getting crazy? Sometimes, I almost believe it. At Headquarters they told me yesterday that they simply don't understand me.'" No one could understand Naomi's source of strength and compassion, in the face of her own looming tragedy. "How can I? so they say, so let me tell you, and perhaps this may sound a little bit crazy . . . for twelve years I've been married to Yankale [Yaacov], and three more years before we got married. Well, I think, fifteen wonderful years I had, wonderful for me and wonderful for Yankale, and then I tell myself: Naomi, who really ever gets that?"

The families were glued to each other for information and to share their agony even as the entire navy and air force went to sea to search for the missing ship. Optimists hoped the submarine's communications systems had broken down. Pessimists, rumor mongers, and attention-seekers spread speculations of conspiracies, secret missions, and all manner of gruesome fates. News agencies in Israel and around the globe printed what they knew . . . and what they didn't know. Those more intimately acquainted with the dangers of submarines, probably kept their thoughts and fears to themselves.

One man who could easily have been on the *Dakar* was Gideon Raz, the flotilla executive officer for over two years while the submarines were being outfitted in Portsmouth, responsible for crew safety. When the Six-Day War suddenly broke out, Raz sailed quickly home on the *Leviathan*, just six months before the *Dakar*. It was a logical choice, but had circumstances and timing been a little different, Raz might have stayed longer in Portsmouth, sailed with the *Dakar,* and shared her fate. His closeness to the crew, professional experience with the submarine, and brush with personal disaster made the loss more immediate to him. Raz recalled:

> I was the first executive officer in Portsmouth, the shipyard, when they were fitting both submarines. I was responsible for both ships at that stage, responsible for safety and for the crews. I was stationed there for two-and-a-half years.
>
> I was very close to the *Dakar* ship company. I was a close friend with the first officer [Deputy Commander Boomie Barkay]. We were just from the same officers' course, and we joined the submarine service together in 1960, and also I was very close to the captain, on a friendly basis. Families were close. So, of course, it came to me as a big shock, the loss of the people of the *Dakar.*
>
> It's a small group, a selected group, and because there are few, they feel very unique and they keep "very tight" together. We are having gatherings several times a year. We are now close to two thousand people from the first day of the submarines, 1957 until today. I, by the way, have a submarine sign number of 105. And so we are very friendly and proud people.

The *Leviathan* left Britain about six months before the *Dakar*. We left in a hurry because the Six-Day War started, and we had an order to come as soon as possible. Our passage was mainly on the surface, so we managed to do eleven or twelve knots. Normally, a submarine should do submerged voyages. We did not find any technical problems with the *Leviathan*. There were normal maintenance problems, but we managed to overcome them. We did our best, but it was a Six-Day War, and you couldn't beat it.

When we received a report that the *Dakar* was missing, I was submerged in the *Leviathan*. It was after midnight, and we received a cable from the headquarters that we should surface and should participate in the search for the *Dakar*. They gave us a certain area to look in. I was a deputy commander, second in command in the *Leviathan*. My commanding officer was Yomi Barkay, brother of Boomie Barkay who was the first lieutenant of the *Dakar*. So I had to inform him . . . and we both, as experienced submariners, understood something: that most probably the submarine is lost, and actually he lost his brother. When he got this much of the news, he knew that his brother was gone. (2002 interview)

Shipmate Doron Amir had escaped fate by being bumped from *Dakar*'s overcrowded crew. He joined Raz on the *Leviathan*, and must have wondered why he was chosen to be saved.

It was Friday morning, I remember. The flotilla captain at twelve o'clock called us to say there is no communication with the *Dakar*. The *Leviathan* should go out and join the search and rescue forces. So, on Friday afternoon, we left and went outside to look for the *Dakar* . . . we wanted to believe that they are there somewhere. Maybe they have a problem that they are grounded somewhere in the sea. So, continuously, we had a watch on the underwater telephone. The days and hours passed. We continued to call, "*Dakar*, this is *Leviathan*. How do you read me? Can you hear me?" (2002 interview)

Gideon Raz understood and felt the emotional distraction, but made sure his crew did not forget their business, their duties.

Everyone had friends in there. They were very close; they came from the same group. Everyone understood that he could be in the place of his friend. People knew families; very close families. Still, the concentration was on operating the submarine, because the submarine was a very dangerous machine, if you don't recognize how dangerous it is, and you have to do everything very methodically, very carefully. Of course you could see groups of people, when they were off watch, discussing what could happen, and bringing back stories and memories of their friends and their families. (2002 interview)

They were strong people, but it was a big blow and the recovery took some months.

✡ ✡ ✡

The people were strong. They were accustomed to struggle, tragedy, and loss. Many had recently fallen during the Six-Day War, and everyone knew it was not over yet. But this was unexpected; it was a shock. There was no way to prepare for the disappearance of your friend or loved one under completely routine and uneventful circumstances. It was a big, big blow, and it fell hardest on women like Chava Barkay, who recalled:

I was living in Haifa near the base, on the fourth floor. Every day I see the whole sea; if the submarine goes and comes, I can see it—I was prepared. The flat was rented for one year, so I prepare the flat, and I make shopping. I have plans until Monday, when he comes. On Friday, I was in the window looking, and I saw all the Israeli Navy are leaving the port, and going to sea.

So I was living, feeling the Navy all the time. I know on Friday, nobody goes out. They come back, on Friday. I was thinking, "What happened?" But it was still war, you know. I think, "Maybe they have some mission, you know." So I thought, "Ah, *Dakar* is around, she's not far. Maybe also the *Dakar* goes with them." And I try to be relaxed. I try not to worry.

But something inside me was telling me that something was wrong. And in the evening, a girlfriend of mine called me. She had also a friend from the Navy. She asked, "Do you know why everybody is together now, at my friend's house?" I said no. She said, "Let's go and find out." I said okay, because I want to ask them, as they all were from the headquarters.

They all were submariners. We went there and I saw everybody sitting around. When I came in, they were quiet. So I sat with them almost two hours, and my heart was like this [pounding]. Then I took one of them to the kitchen and I said, "Don't tell me secrets, but tell me what happened, that all the Navy ships are going to sea today? I watched them from my house. I see everything." And he says they didn't hear from them [*Dakar*] for a few hours, so they decided to go out to the sea. But it could just be the communication. He said they don't think that something happened. Maybe just the radio. He was sure they are all on the way back.

But it was not true.

He said, "Let me take you home," and I went home. And I was not happy, of course. I was worried all the time.

I went to sleep, and at four o'clock in the morning, I get a phone call from my sister, who was living in Montreal. From England, from Portsmouth, I sent her letters, and she knew that Boomie was on the *Dakar*. She asked me, "Can you tell me what submarine is Boomie on?" I said you know that he's on *Dakar*. But in the minute that she asked me, I knew something happened. Why? Because when we were in the Six-Day War, in Portsmouth we listened to the BBC, and we knew before the Israelis at home what was going on.

So I knew she heard it—something happened to the submarine.

But I didn't have courage to ask her what she knew. I didn't want to hear from her anything. And then her husband came on the phone and he said, "Please, send us a telegram—yes?—if they come." I said, "What is the rush?" And I still didn't want to ask them. I felt something.

Then I knew that I must listen to the BBC, and I knew that there was no news until five o'clock, but I still was listening to the radio for half an hour, maybe, forty minutes, going between the stations. We had a small radio, and the connection was not so good like today.

Five o'clock. Then I heard on the BBC that everybody is looking for the missing Israeli submarine *Dakar*. That was the word. I remember it like it was today. This was the minute that I felt so strong that my life is now without Boomie. I went to the bed and covered myself, and I said, "That's it, Chava, your life now without Boomie."

After this, I don't know how, I wait two hours, until seven o'clock, because my son [Guy] was asleep [at her brother's house]. I didn't want to wake him, and I was afraid because my parents were living in the same street, but I needed to go there. So I ran over there and saw that my son was sleeping, and I asked my brother to come to be with me. And my parents say, "What happened?" I say nothing, nothing, I just was not feeling very well, so I wanted Yankele to be with me. And I ran back because I was afraid to leave Guy more than five minutes alone.

Nobody came from the Navy to tell me, because nobody thought that they were not going to find her. Everybody had hope. And they started to tell me that maybe there is hope. I told you, the first minute, I feel like my life is without Boomie. But after few hours, or the next day, everybody came and said don't be worried. So I say maybe they're right. Maybe I just don't feel very well. But I knew it. I knew it. And then we have a story, in the family, that his [Boomie Barkay's] brother was the commander of the other submarine, so this is the big story. He went with the submarine to look for the *Dakar*. His best friend was the commander, Ra'anan, and his brother was on board. His mother, she came to my house, and we sit, maybe ten days. Everybody came and say maybe here, maybe there. But when he [Boomie Barkay's brother] first came back to the harbor, he came to visit me, and I saw in his face that he didn't believe that he can find *Dakar*. He didn't tell me and I didn't need the words.

It's a story; it's a romantic story; believe me. (2002 interview)

Chava did not seek company in her misery. She doesn't even remember her darkest thoughts. At first, she preferred to have her husband, Boomie, in her mind, in her heart, and leave his body in the sea. She was not impressed with the ceremonies, or memorials, or speculation about what really happened. All she cared about was that he was gone.

After this, I heard from friends of mine, that her husband told her that if something happened in the Mediterranean, there's no chance to be alive, yes? And yet he never told me . . . he said it's very safe. He tried not to worry me. And he was so happy there. From age twelve or thirteen, he was with boats, and then he went to the merchant navy for three weeks, and then to the Navy. All his life was with the sea.

So, I went with the hopes of the other people, I said, "Maybe they're right," but in my heart, I didn't believe that. But I couldn't believe that it would be more than thirty years, and then we would find her. It changed my life. I was still with him all the time. I mean, it was like he was with me. But he wasn't.

Tell you the truth, I was at home and I don't remember very much from the first three months. We sit Shiva of dead men [traditional seven days of mourning in Jewish homes], but if a rabbi come to you after one and a half months, and they cut the shirt, they say you sit now seven days because they are not coming back.

I was just going through each day. I don't know what was in the newspaper, nothing. So I didn't know what exactly happened with the other families. I just know when the Navy said, "Okay, you come today, all the family." So then we saw Moshe Dayan, the defense minister.

And he said that now, officially, the submarine is not coming, and they are dead, and da, da, da, da, da. And then I met everybody [the families]. I didn't know them all, only my friends that were in Portsmouth. Most of them were mothers and fathers who had lost a son. And they started the memorial day, every year.

But Chava could not leave it be. No one would allow that, and in time, as months wore on, she began to see that the only path to personal recovery was to know the fate of the *Dakar*, and of her Boomie.

✡ ✡ ✡

For some who weren't even family members, the recovery took much longer than mere months. For many, it took more than thirty years and still inspires prayer and commemoration at annual ceremonies. Shlomo Cohen, a youngster who lost no relatives when the *Dakar* went down, felt the fraternal commitment of the Navy to rush out to find the ship and their lost colleagues. It was literally a matter of family, in some cases, as many submariners were related by blood or marriage. In other cases it was a natural brotherhood among those elite who trained together for the unique challenge of submarine service. In all cases, it was a national commitment to bring back the dead from the battlefield—no matter what.

Young Shlomo felt the call of the submarine service, and the call of the *Dakar*. He joined the Navy, sailed on missile boats, and fought proudly in the 1973 Yom Kippur War. But he still was attracted to the elite, to the submarine service.

I wanted to be submariner. I was ASW [Antisubmarine Warfare] officer, and one day, the flotilla commander of submarines came and asked me to join the submarines, and to convert myself to be submariner. I wanted it very much but I had a veto. I got a veto from my wife. The only veto that I got all my life was: "You are not going to be submariner." I don't know why she decided this way but I respect her decision, because that's family.

I didn't join the submarines. (2002 interview)

Cohen, who rose to the rank of captain and the post of chief of naval personnel, was only twelve when the *Dakar* was lost, but he clearly remembers the impact on the city of Haifa and how over time, the *Dakar* families came to know pretty much everyone in the Navy as they pressured for continued and more extensive searches.

I live in Haifa, and as probably you know, most of the crew came from Haifa. Some of the sailors in the crew were classmates with my brother, with my sister, and one of them was a brother of one of my classmates. So it's hard, it's something that was close to us as a family. We feel that something touched us.

I remember, on Saturday, we were watching football, soccer. I was in the field and the atmosphere, even in the soccer field, was something different. People talked about the *Dakar*. People were trying to find out what happened, where is she? So even on the football field, during this Saturday, the only issue was the *Dakar*. Where is the *Dakar*? What happened to the *Dakar*?

And I remember a few days after it, there was some rumor that the *Dakar* is on her way to Haifa. I remember myself and with other people going to the Carmel Mountain and try to watch and see if there was something . . . hundreds—thousands—of people were over there, trying to see from the Carmel, if the *Dakar* is coming. My memory is from when I was twelve years old, at Haifa, when the *Dakar* was lost.

We are a very small service in the military. We are the Navy. We are about 6 or 7 percent of the military. Some are in Tel Aviv, but most of the Navy is in Haifa. Most of us also came from Haifa. So it's a small family, the Navy. You know all the officers in your age, about five to ten years, up and down, from your age, you know all of them. Each one in the Navy knew somebody from the *Dakar*.

We have a promise. As a sailor, as an officer in the Navy, I know that if something will happen to me, my friends will look for me. That's a value that we teach our cadets and sailors. That we never forget our friends in the Navy. It's something that probably comes also from the religious side. It says in the Bible, we have to bring our remains to be buried in the country, in Israel, in the land. We don't leave it as unknown. You have to try to make the effort to know what's happened with the remains of your friends or family.

A warship of 1,700 tons of steel and sixty-nine men doesn't just disappear, without a trace. They were missing, not gone. And they could be found. Must be found. Thus began the search for the *Dakar*.

Isaiah Chapter 10

Tom and I started our second day with the *Dakar* Search Committee with much more confidence, having overcome the anxiety of the first day and knowing a little more of what to expect. We settled into the process of becoming educated in the details of the submarine's disappearance. The night before we had a chance to look over an information booklet summarizing prior work on the *Dakar* loss, which began with a message from Admiral Raz:

> Dear Gentlemen,
>
> I the undersigned was nominated by the commander of the I.N. [Israeli Navy] to head a committee tasked to coordinate the efforts of the search for the missing I.N. submarine DAKAR.
>
> I hereby approach you on behalf of the I.N. requesting that you will cooperate with us in our efforts to locate the position of the missing DAKAR, solving the mystery which continues to haunt the I.N. and the Israeli people during the period of the last 29 years.
>
> Attempting to provide you with the necessary background information, we have prepared a summary of the data accumulated by the I.N., based upon research efforts conducted during the last 17 years.
>
> We hope that the attached summary document will assist you to develop your own method and recommendations as to the way to continue the search for the missing submarine.
>
> Sincerely yours,
> GIDEON RAZ
> Admiral (Ret.) I.N

Three things immediately jumped off the page to us: first, we were being given a great responsibility, and much was expected of us; second, this went way beyond any technical project we could have envisioned, as we were being asked to help solve a mystery that gripped an entire nation; third, we were encouraged to think independently and come to our own conclusions.

The booklet went on to summarize what was known and provide technical information and data, all of which was explained, discussed, and dissected over the ensuing days. The first page of my notes (which eventually tallied eighty pages plus handouts) established a shorthand for identifying facts: a letter "F" in a circle in the margin. Also, there was a notation for a piece of information or data which could be a fact, but was not known for sure: a question mark in a circle. My notes were scattered with question marks, and dotted with a few F's. But not very many F's.

The key facts of the case were quickly summarized after introductions. We did know that the submarine was lost, and almost certainly sunk (although even that was subject to debate, fueled by the rumored boastings of Egyptian submariners and wild speculations that the crew was rotting in a Cairo military prison). We knew that they carried no weapons, but were outfitted with an advanced ELINT (electronic intelligence) system, the Tavlit. They only had rough sailing orders, but were told to proceed from Gibraltar to Haifa with a particular time of arrival, and were not to venture within fifty miles of Egyptian territory without special orders. They had communicated at least three times per day, reporting position daily, and were ahead of schedule.

We knew many facts about the submarine and its refit upgrades. We knew about the weather, we knew the content of messages received, and we knew something about the disposition of military forces in the region. And we had one piece of wreckage: a single orange submarine rescue buoy, slightly damaged, clearly from the *Dakar*, found on the Gaza Strip over a year after the ship vanished.

Besides that, we had only mystery.

The details of these facts were interesting and took some time to go over thoroughly. The speculations were even more intriguing, and got the benefit of more time and attention. It was hard to keep the facts sorted out from theory, expectations, and occasional wild conjectures, as the Committee members had indulged in them so regularly and for so long. Even our first day's briefing on the history of submarines in Israel and the refitting of the *Dakar* collapsed to a long discussion of the propulsion mechanism and how certain failures of hydraulics could lead to a fatal casualty. Fortunately, Raz was not too patient with these digressions and got us back on track.

The eighteen official members of the Committee were an impressive group, and all had something to offer to the proceedings. Most were in the Navy, or retired, but a few were pure civilians. Assisting Admiral Raz was Captain Michael Kaisari, a submarine commander; Captain Yehuda Laniado represented Navy Intelligence; retired Captain Mike Koren covered submarine communications.

Our new friend who met us at the airport, Commander Baruch Peretzman, was from the Navy Hydrographic Branch and an expert in underwater surveying. Commander Dan Avidor of the Navy Engineering Branch could discuss all aspects of ship construction and technologies. Underwater systems, covering technologies explicit to submarines, were represented by Commander Shy Davidi. Commander Eitan Simchoni covered submarine operations and retired Commander Ami Yahalom covered submarine communications and radar.

The importance attached to the rescue buoy was such that an officer, retired Commander Ilan Duvdivan was assigned to focus on buoy research. Ilan was also a former *Dakar* project officer. The current project officer was our new friend Lieutenant Commander Yechiel Ga'ash, who had been involved with the project his entire career. The liaison to our U.S. team was Lieutenant Commander Barry Grinker, also a hydrographer, and graduate of the Naval Postgraduate School in Monterey, California. Retired Lieutenant Commander David Rutenberg rounded out the military presence on the committee.

A few scientists also contributed to the brain trust. Academic Officer Eldad Palachi was a meteorologist, Professor Eli Zipperman was an ocean currents expert, and Professor Zvi Ben-Avraham, a geophysicist, also head of the Dead Sea Research Center at Tel Aviv University. Doctor Asher Gitay was a marine biologist who had a special interest in the study of the buoy, and Doctor Abraham (Abe) Ariel was a geographer, as well as a master mariner. Abe is also an author of books and magazine articles, and we became good friends, maintaining a long-distance relationship over the years.

One thing we were sensitive to was the spelling and pronunciation of everyone's name. The former was almost impossible for us, and the latter was even more baffling. I have spelled everyone's name above as it was given to me in the official proceedings. However, hardly anyone seemed to be particular about how their name was spelled and some even changed it themselves at will. For example, Mike Kaisari was often Kasari, but sometimes Kesary or even Cesari. I just called him Captain K. I suppose the translation from Hebrew to English is phonetic, and there is no real standard for spelling. But it was refreshing that most of the Israelis did not stand on ceremony or put on airs, preferring to be judged on their merits and substance. At least, this was the impression I got from the majority of the Committee.

Our general overview was followed by an intelligence briefing. As one can imagine, the geopolitical situation in the Mediterranean in January 1968 was confusing, threatening, and difficult to assess in any detail. There were many Soviet intelligence trawlers, known by their NATO designation "AGI," present in the eastern Mediterranean. These vessels were always a Cold War thorn in the side of U.S. forces, as they were constantly present wherever the Western allies were deployed. Lurking in the bubble of a naval task force's radio and radar chatter, AGI's looked like fishing trawlers but bristled with antennae and electronics gear.

Two Egyptian submarines were known to be operating with antisubmarine forces just off the Israeli coast—to all appearances, a routine exercise. The USSR operated continuous aircraft and submarine patrols in the region, with as many as ten submarines deployed. It was almost certain that the *Dakar* was being tracked; in fact, a U.S. antisubmarine aircraft shot a photo of the *Dakar* at periscope depth just after departing Gibraltar. Traveling at high speed, with all masts raised, the ship left a huge wake that was highly visible. Despite this, there was no evidence that the USSR made any direct contact with the *Dakar* or produced any useful intelligence on its disappearance. Secret inquires to the U.S. intelligence community revealed that no underwater "event" was detected by any ships or underwater listening devices that could tie to the *Dakar*.

At the same time that the *Dakar* was missing, the French submarine *Minerve* was lost with all hands in waters two thousand meters deep off Toulon in the western Mediterranean. No connection could ever be established between the two disasters—it was apparently a gruesome coincidence. Nonetheless, this event fueled suspicion and speculation of the sinister circumstances of the time. Another complication in the intelligence picture at the time was the weather. Although skies were clear in the region through January 25, severe storms blanketed the eastern Mediterranean for many days after. This could have affected communications, and certainly hampered search efforts when they were launched on January 26.

✡ ✡ ✡

When you don't know very much about what happened, you tend, for better or worse, to think a lot about what was supposed to happen. Sometimes this helps to connect sparse information and profitably guides speculation; other times, it leads to useless dead ends. In our case, what was supposed to happen was contained in the Sailing Orders.

Sailing Orders really came in three parts: the Israeli Navy Headquarters (INHQ) Regulations, the specific written orders for the mission, and pre-mission briefings given by the squadron commander. The former included the general regulation that the ship was not to approach within fifty nautical miles of the Egyptian coast. This fact continued to be emphasized to us repeatedly and came up many times in our discussions. There were strong reasons to think that Captain Ra'anan violated this order.

The specific mission orders directed the ship to cruise mainly at snorkel depth. It was suggested to Tom and me that the rest of the time they would be completely submerged. The cruise was originally planned to take twenty-three days from Portsmouth; at over three thousand nautical miles that would require a speed of advance of five and a half knots. The date originally planned for arrival in Haifa was February 2. The route home was defined as "direct," but no courses or geographical positions were given as "waypoints." Also, the commander was permitted to conduct training along the way. Since the ship could cruise at eight knots while snorkeling, there was plenty of leeway in the schedule. That also provided much leeway for speculation: what did Captain Ra'anan do with the extra time?

Another major point of the Sailing Orders was the protocol for communications. The commander was to report to INHQ at least every eight hours, including a daily report of the ship's position at 6 AM. In fact, Ra'anan faithfully reported his position to INHQ daily at around 6 AM, and transmitted at least a radio check every six hours thereafter each day. All transmissions were made using Morse code. We were given a complete transcript of messages between the *Dakar* and INHQ, transcribed from Morse to Hebrew to English, a total of fifty messages after departure from Gibraltar. Most of the *Dakar*'s reports were simply a radio check, with no other information. The daily position reports included their fuel status and a few words summarizing events of the day, for example: "Unit exercises on route to Haifa." Messages back to the *Dakar* were much wordier and contained information on the disposition of Egyptian and Russian naval forces, as well as merchant traffic in the area.

Amidst the technical and formal military transmissions is an exchange that opens a window into the personality of Captain Ra'anan. During the first two days of transit from Gibraltar, INHQ apparently became anxious that the radio checks from the *Dakar* were coming a little late; even though the timing was not specified, only the number per day, the squadron began expecting a message on the hour at six-hour intervals. One can imagine impatient admirals asking about the *Dakar* when their noon radio check did not arrive until 12:20 PM, or even 12:50. So, on January 18 at 9:45 AM, INHQ sent the following message to the *Dakar*:

HQ TO DAKAR
> YOU MUST TRANSMIT COMMUNICATIONS FOR CHECK REPORT ACCORDING TO ORDERS. ANY DELAY CAUSES CONCERN.

Captain Ra'anan chose not to answer this upbraiding directly, but I dare say more effectively than a standard acknowledgment:

DAKAR TO HQ
DAKAR TO SQUADRON COMMANDER
> IN REPLY TO YOUR MESSAGE OF 180945—SEE ISAIAH

CHAPTER 10 PARAGRAPH A AND PSALMS CHAPTER 115 FIRST
PART OF PARAGRAPH 6.

According to the Bible, New International Version, Ra'anan said: "Woe to those
who make unjust laws, to those who issue oppressive decrees . . . they have ears,
but cannot hear." INHQ made no reply or further complaint about communications delays.

By January 21, the *Dakar* had already reached the southern tip of Sicily, and
was halfway home. Averaging eight knots, she was well ahead of schedule. Thus
began an exchange that was to fuel much speculation about Ra'anan's intentions
and actions after the *Dakar* lost communications. Just after noon that day, the
Dakar made an unusual request:

DAKAR TO HQ
DAKAR TO SQUADRON COMMANDER
   THE UNDERWATER TRIP FROM GIBRALTAR IS GOING
WELL AND FASTER THAN PLANNED. CAN AND WILLING TO
GET TO HAIFA ON SUNDAY 28 JANUARY AT 1000.

Ra'anan and his crew were certainly eager to return home. It was also noted
that an arrival as early as January 28 would have meant the *Dakar* continuing her breakneck pace, setting the speed record for a submerged transit of the
Mediterranean. Further, if she kept her speed as high as eight knots, she would
arrive even earlier.

INHQ was sympathetic to Ra'anan's request, but not completely flexible.
After mulling over the issue for a day, they replied:

HQ TO DAKAR AND OTHER UNITS
   TO YOURS OF 211200. APPROVE ARRIVAL AT HAIFA PORT
AT 291000. ACTIVITIES PLANNED FROM SUNDAY 4 FEB. EARLY-
MORNING REHEARSALS FOR OFFICERS' COURSE CEREMONY.
MONDAY 5 FEB. 1500—OFFICER'S GRADUATION CEREMONY
AND SUBMARINES RECEPTION. FULL TRAINING ACTIVITIES
FROM 11 FEB 68.

So, they could shave a few days off the trip. A full week of ceremonial activities
was planned, followed by a few days of rest. Then it was back to work for the
busy crew of the *Dakar*.

Ra'anan continued his eight-knot transit speed. By the morning of January
24, he was passing the island of Crete, within two days' cruise of the Israeli
coast. At this rate, he would arrive three days ahead of even the new schedule,

sooner than he himself had requested. Why was Ra'anan in such a hurry to reach Haifa?

One clue was contained in a message Ra'anan sent as he approached Crete on January 23, asking for details and times of operation of coastal radars he would expect to detect en route with his new Tavlit electronics intelligence gear. INHQ responded with information of Israeli radars at Haifa and Ashdod. Was Ra'anan planning to spend some time loitering near shore, training his crew in the operation of the new equipment, and testing its capabilities?

As the *Dakar* approached the eastern Mediterranean, INHQ provided as much information as possible regarding the disposition of forces opposing the Israeli Navy along the submarine's route. A summary of the messages sent on January 21 and 22 helps one appreciate the huge numerical inferiority of the Israeli naval forces, and how much they desperately needed the *Dakar* and her sister ships.

The Russian Navy had two auxiliary ships in Alexandria, Egypt. In Port Said there was a *Kashin*-class destroyer and a frigate. The waters between Egypt and Cyprus were patrolled by a minesweeper, with several auxiliary vessels. Just south of Cyprus were surveillance vessels (AGIs) and an unknown number of Russian submarines. A *Kotlin*-class destroyer was on the way to Port Said from the North.

The Egyptian Navy boasted four destroyers, sixteen missile boats, twenty-two torpedo boats, a dozen antisubmarine warfare (ASW) patrol boats, six mine-sweepers, a number of auxiliary craft, and ten submarines. Most of these were in port, but many were in readiness to go to sea within a few hours. Later, on January 23, INHQ reported that four vessels were at sea near Alexandria, and the next day a submarine deployed. The readiness at Port Said was raised, apparently due to fears of Israeli activities. Activities continued in waters near the Israeli border over the next days.

None of the message sent by *Dakar* revealed any hint of trouble, and there was no indication of impending disaster. There were no obvious clues to the cause of her demise. A routine maintenance report was sent on January 22, asking that the shipyard be prepared to assist in repairs upon arrival. Items included replacement of the aft auxiliary pump electronics, repair of the refrigeration compressor, and aligning of the periscope sextant, among other minor items.

A few messages of a more personal nature were sprinkled among the official communications. Headquarters informed *Dakar* that Ensign Yosef Lahav and Ensign Amnon Paz were to be promoted to lieutenant (junior grade) and included their congratulations. Also, INHQ reported that a Lieutenant Shorer, who had been on the boat in England, left a camera on board. The *Dakar* reported back at 12:07 on January 24:

DAKAR TO SQUADRON HQ
DAKAR TO HQ
LT SHORER CAMERA IN THE HANDS OF AMNON PAZ.

There is an added measure of fortune and tragedy in the mention of Eran Shorer, a Navy reporter who sailed from England with the *Dakar*. In Gibraltar, he left the boat, to be replaced by Yehezel Mizrachi. Mizrachi was granted leave to stay in England for a short while after the *Dakar* sailed because his wife was in labor with their second child. The *Dakar* left England with sixty-nine on board, and departed Gibraltar with the same number, but one lucky man disembarked while another equally unlucky joined the ship to keep the tally of men and misfortune in balance. Shorer went home to write of his experience in the book *Six Days in the "Dakar"* (Tel Aviv: Am Hasefer, 1969).

Other than two more terse radio checks at 6:15 PM on January 24 and 12:02 AM on January 25, that was the last message from the *Dakar*.

✡ ✡ ✡

It was difficult for the members of the Committee to stick to the facts, few as they were, and resist indulging in theories. So we spent some time discussing possible scenarios of the loss of the *Dakar*. Some scenarios might have a bearing on the location, so there was some profit in this. Our collective wisdom regarding submarine operations and the sketchy details of the *Dakar* transit led to four general possibilities.

The first possibility we considered was a hydraulic failure. Most major systems, including the control surfaces (known as diving planes or hydroplanes, and including the rudder) were operated using high-pressure hydraulic fluid, which pressed against pistons and moved the heavy planes against the drag of the water and their own weight. A major leak in this system, or failure of all of the hydraulic pumps, would make it impossible to control the ship's depth or heading. If the ship was traveling underwater at high speed at the time of this failure, and the diving planes became jammed in the dive position, the ship would nose dive toward the bottom. This is a casualty scenario that all submariners practice. The first action is to reverse engines, which helps reduce speed and mitigates the depth of the uncontrolled dive, hopefully before the ship reaches its crush-depth or hits the bottom, whichever comes first.

In the *Dakar*, this scenario was further complicated by its engine configuration. As with all diesel-powered submarines, the *Dakar* used a hybrid diesel-electric drive system, not unlike modern hybrid automobiles. The diesels were connected to generators that fed electric power through the battery to electric motors, which actually turned the propellers. But in order to achieve higher speeds while snorkeling, there was a more efficient direct-drive option that allowed the diesels to be mechanically linked to the propellers.

This direct connection was made through a hydraulically operated clutch. So, in order to reverse engines, hydraulics were required. Manual operation was possible, but that would take minutes, much too long when the ship is plunging toward the bottom of the sea in an uncontrolled dive. So, under direct-drive operation while snorkeling, a hydraulic failure, however unlikely, could be disastrous. Direct drive was not recommended for long periods, and it imposed an extra strain on the crew, requiring two officers to be on watch at all times. Yet it seems that Captain Ra'anan must have used this configuration much of the time, judging by his speed of advance.

The next scenario we discussed was a fire in the ship, a dreaded occurrence for any submarine. There are many sources of fire, but the one of most concern in a diesel submarine is the battery. Designed to power and move the ship for many hours while completely submerged, the ship's battery stores a huge amount of energy and can discharge it with violent effect under the wrong conditions. One of the biggest hazards to a submarine battery is contact with seawater, which is highly conductive. Also, age and mechanical stresses can cause a battery cell to short, generating lots of heat and deadly gasses. One of the products of battery discharge is hydrogen, which can be highly explosive if allowed to accumulate in a confined space like the battery compartment. A serious battery casualty can lead to fire, explosion, and loss of the ship.

Other sources of fire can present a major hazard unless combatted quickly. Since the *Dakar* was not carrying weapons, there was no concern of a torpedo casualty, but the ship still carried many small explosive devices, flammable liquids, and burnable materials.

An obvious possible cause, always a hazard at sea, was collision. A submarine at snorkel depth presents a very small visual or radar target; this is by design and key to its stealthy nature. The conning tower and hull itself lie just below the surface, easily within the draft of a large cargo ship. With only a periscope and one pair of eyes to look for surface traffic, it is conceivable that an unwitting merchant vessel could bear down on the submarine undetected, especially at night or in conditions of poor visibility. One could imagine such a collision damaging the submarine fatally, especially if the pressure hull was pierced at any point. One could go on to speculate that a collision between a large merchant ship and the conning tower or periscope of a submerged submarine might go unnoticed by the merchant crew, but sink the sub. One could even imagine that such a collision might damage the submarine, including the radio antennae, but fail to sink it immediately, allowing some time for the ship to cruise to shallower waters, unable to communicate, before succumbing to the persistent flooding and sinking short of land.

Several merchant ships were known to have crossed the *Dakar*'s path during its transit, and the eastern Mediterranean is a busy place. Collisions between ships have been a persistent feature of marine commerce, and many on the Committee favored this scenario.

The fourth and last major scenario we discussed was hostile action by enemy forces. There was absolutely no concrete evidence of this, but there were rumors. When you know nothing, anything is possible.

Curiously, the Committee did not seriously entertain the idea that the ship experienced a sudden and severe flooding casualty. This in spite of the fact that the *Dakar*'s hull was cut and modified, and there was concern about the design of this modification. The ship's operating depth was reduced from 360 to 300 feet, and the sister ship *Leviathan* underwent further structural modifications in response to ambiguous test results. Also, there were some reports of minor leaks in the forward part of the ship during sea trials. The possibility that flooding occurred without warning could not be dismissed.

✡ ✡ ✡

By the end of the second day of briefings, we turned to the topic of the infamous *Dakar* rescue buoy. Being the only piece of physical evidence of the disaster, this small orange cylinder received an inordinate amount of scrutiny, and was the prime subject of discussion. Seven of the first fifteen pages of my handwritten notes were devoted to facts, studies, and speculations about the buoy.

Our information booklet gave us a plain vanilla description of the event that led to three decades of fruitless search:

> INS DAKAR emergency marker buoy was found at E 34° 18.5' N 31° 24' (Han Yunis beach, Gaza Strip) on the 9th of January 1969 at about 1700 hours. The buoy was found in relatively good external condition. It was taken to the Israeli naval base at Ashdod where it was identified as the aft emergency marker buoy of INS DAKAR.

The finder was described as an Arab fisherman but his name is not mentioned. The details of the circumstances of the event are not clearly known, and many people felt compelled to criticize the initial handling of the evidence and lament that important information was lost. Was the buoy cleaned up before being turned over for study? How long did it lay on the beach before the fisherman found it? Did he turn it over immediately, or did he tamper with it in any way? We will never know the answers to these questions, and there is no real evidence to say that anyone is at fault for the handling of the item. In any case, investigators found plenty to work with upon careful and extensive scrutiny.

The rescue buoy on the *Dakar* was a relic of the original ship design, and was a concession to the unlikely scenario of a submarine sinking in shallow water, with crew alive but unable to escape. There were two buoys attached to the superstructure, secured in cages under wooden doors below the decking. The buoys were attached to two-hundred-meter-long wire cables, and could only be deployed manually from inside the ship. If the submarine found itself unable to surface, but otherwise intact, the crew could open the doors and reel out one or both buoys. Upon reaching the surface, they would begin automatically transmitting SOS in Morse code for forty-eight hours. Painted orange for visibility, the top of the eighteen-inch high, two-foot-diameter cylinder included a flashing light, "cat's eye" reflectors, and a six-foot antenna. Also, inscribed on the device was the following legend, in English and French:

S O S H.M. SUBMARINE DAKAR S O S
FINDER INFORM NAVY, COAST GUARD OR POLICE
DO NOT SECURE TO OR TOUCH

The "H.M." ("His Majesty") was presumably a relic of the ship's British heritage. Similar devices were installed on U.S. Navy submarines; however, a scenario for use was considered so remote, and the possibility that the buoy would deploy by accident (revealing the ship's position unintentionally) such a concern, that on my submarine the doors were welded to the deck, forever shut.

The buoy was rushed to the lab and studied carefully. Several initial observations were made. First of all, the buoy was largely intact and still buoyant. This was a key fact which told everyone that it could not have been submerged very deep, or it would have been crushed by sea pressure. The antenna was broken at the root; however, it was noted that the SOS transmitter had been activated. About two feet of cable was still attached to the bottom of the buoy, with the end frayed and, curiously, freshly broken. This was clear as there was shiny metal at the breaking point. The cable end could not have been broken for more than a month, or corrosion would have been evident. In fact, a more detailed analysis suggested that the cable had broken only three to six days before the buoy was found.

These initial observations led to the following key conclusions:

1. The buoy must have been attached to the rest of the cable and, hence, the *Dakar*, until a short time before discovery.
2. The buoy could not have been held deeper than its collapse depth, designed to be 350 meters (but tested to be 326 meters). Adding the maximum 200-meter length of cable to this, it was concluded that the *Dakar* must rest in water shallower than around 500 meters.

To refine this estimate, the buoy was subject to an extensive array of testing, conducted at the Navy laboratory, the Israeli Institute of Technology (Technion), the Israeli Oceanographic and Limnological Research Institute, Tel Aviv University, and the Geological Institute of Israel.

Our technical booklet included no fewer than sixteen eight-by-ten glossy photographs of the buoy, its cable, broken antenna, and its basket (the latter taken on the ship while in the shipyard in England). The initial studies noted that the short broken cable segment had a kink and a loop on the free end (not attached to the buoy), resembling an elongated question mark. This almost certainly corresponded to a curved guide pipe which directed the cable from the reel, through the basket, and to the buoy. It was an inescapable conclusion that this bend and kink in the cable was formed by the pipe; furthermore, the position of the break in the cable matched the spot where the cable entered the basket, so there would have been stress on that point. It was simple to thus conclude, with apparently overwhelming physical evidence, that the buoy had (for reasons unknown) been partially deployed, but that the cable jammed after a short length, and the buoy stayed straining against the cable trying to float free, for almost a year. Eventually, the jammed point on the cable failed, and the buoy floated free, to arrive in Gaza several days or weeks later. This was a pretty tight argument, and logically led to the conclusion that the buoy was attached to the *Dakar* by a very short tether for a very long time. This result placed an even shallower limit on the depth of the *Dakar*.

It also led to the disturbing conclusion that at least some of the crew of the *Dakar* were alive for some time after the ship sank.

✡ ✡ ✡

The analysis of the *Dakar* buoy had hardly begun. Next, the cable break was scrutinized for clues to the timing of the event. It was noted that there were actually two fractures on the cable. One was old, showing much corrosion, and probably dated to the unknown events of the time of the submarine's disappearance. The other fracture, which led to complete parting of the cable, was fresh. But how fresh? Professors Bodner and Yahalom at the Technion concluded that the wire had torn less than a month before it was found. To further quantify this, an extensive "Buoy Mooring Wire Experiment" was carried out at the Navy Architecture Branch. A buoy was tethered at a site about three miles offshore. Attached to the buoy were wires, of similar type to the *Dakar* cable, torn in a similar manner. Care was taken to electrically insulate the wires, and to try to replicate the assumed circumstances in all respects. After one day, one of the wires was retrieved and examined for comparison with the actual *Dakar* cable. Each day for the next thirty-eight days another wire was retrieved, and others were deployed. At the end of the trial, a collection of wires had been exposed to sea water for the entire range of times, from one day to thirty-eight days.

The result showed that the shiny gleam on the freshly broken wire, observed on the *Dakar* cable, would not last for more than a few days in seawater. It was concluded from this experiment that the wire had broken within six days of the buoy's discovery, and by further logic, that the buoy had been attached to *Dakar* within that time. But they weren't finished teasing information out of the cable. Similar wires were subjected to breaking tests to see what kind of force was needed to tear the cable as observed. Not much was learned from this, but it added to the growing body of buoy lore.

One of the key features of a buoy is that it is designed to float, and the *Dakar*'s buoy was no exception. In fact, when found it was still buoyant. The outer metal cylinder was actually only a housing for a collection of small closed aluminum cylinders which acted as floats. These surrounded a larger cylinder which housed the battery, clock, and transmitter. The cover plate of this cylinder was deemed to be the most vulnerable to leakage at high sea pressures. Pressure tests of the cylinder and all other components were conducted to establish the maximum depth the buoy could have reached; 326 meters was the result. Since the buoy had not leaked, it must have never exceeded this depth.

Some of the most involved tests, leading to the most intriguing results, were the biological studies of the buoy. Every piece of the device was scoured for marine organisms and many inferences were teased out of these findings. Mollusks, barnacles, polychaetes, and other more primitive organisms were identified, but as they were ubiquitous in the Mediterranean they gave no clue to location. Tiny hard-shelled creatures identified to us as "black spots" covered the buoy; these are found in lagoons, such as along the north coast of Egypt. This caused much head-scratching, and caught the interest of Professor Gitay, the biologist, who became convinced from this and other evidence that the *Dakar* was captured by the Egyptian Navy and towed to a lagoon in Egypt for hiding. His patience with any other theory grew thinner as the days progressed, and I can still hear him shouting, "But, the lagoon! The lagoon!" or "Impossible!" whenever we tried to discuss the clues in an objective manner. Gitay eventually resigned from the Committee in frustration.

The marked lack of marine plant growth on the buoy's surface was a clue. It strongly suggested that the buoy was submerged at a depth below the "photo zone," where photosynthetic organisms can live, for most of the time. This was reinforced by the lack of a waterline, indicating that the buoy was not floating on the surface, but was held underwater somehow. There was some concern that the evidence had been cleaned up before it was turned over for analysis, making these results ambiguous.

The mollusks were studied to determine their age and thus infer the temperature of the water in which they were living. Water temperature profiles all around the eastern Mediterranean were collected to compare with this. A byproduct of these and other physical oceanographic measurements taken during these studies was a great increase in our knowledge of the Mediterranean, and some surprising findings about ocean circulation patterns.

The most sophisticated tests conducted on the buoy were spectrographic analyses of samples of sand collected from the nooks and crannies of the device. The idea was to determine the chemical composition of the samples, and compare them with samples collected from sands around the Mediterranean coast. These tests were not conducted until 1981 (repeated again in 1994), so there was some concern that the samples had changed or were contaminated; also, there could have been plenty of contamination at the time the buoy was retrieved. Nonetheless, the work was done at great effort.

The closest matches were found with sands from the Aegean Sea south of Greece. No samples were taken in Portsmouth, England, nor from the location in Gaza where the buoy was found, to see if those known sources were overwhelming the data. Also, no samples were taken from Egyptian lagoons, which deepened Professor Gitay's suspicion that the Israeli Navy was part of a conspiracy to hide the *Dakar* in Egyptian territory, for unimaginably sinister reasons. He was vehement about the lack of peer review on these studies, and rejected them, not without cause.

One final bit of information was possibly attributed to the buoy, but only deepened the mystery. During the searches conducted by the Israeli Navy and other nations immediately after the *Dakar* disappeared, some intriguing radio signals were heard at various locations. The British radio communications center at Famagusta, Cyprus, reported possible beacon transmissions on Saturday, January 27 (Black Saturday). These signals were in Morse code, and appeared to be an SOS transmission, but were very weak and garbled. Similar, but weaker yet, signals were reported at Tel Aviv. On January 28, the destroyer *Jaffa*, operating near Cyprus, received a continuous weak transmission on the frequency of the buoy, but other vessels in the vicinity did not. Over the next two days, the *Jaffa* chased these weak and intermittent signals, and was joined by two missile boats that also reported Morse code signals. But whenever one of the ships would approach the source of the signal, it would disappear.

A board of inquiry concluded in March of 1968 that these signals were not from the *Dakar* buoy. It was even suggested that the original "false" reports may have spurred others to hear weak and garbled signals where there was only noise.

One of the curiosities of human nature is the compulsion for mischief, sometimes to deceive for a purpose, sometimes just for "fun." It is common in disasters at sea, while search parties are desperately seeking the lost vessel, that false radio transmissions will be sent. In the case of the *Dakar*, there was a message received late on January 26, over a day after the last verified transmission from the submarine. It was just a radio check, but it was on the correct frequency, and included the *Dakar* call sign.

Upon further questioning, the radio operator wasn't sure he actually heard the call sign, or just wrote it down by habit, but the transmission did purport to be from the *Dakar*. Nuances of the message were suspicious, and experienced operators can even identify an unfamiliar "hand" in Morse transmissions. It was concluded that this was one of a number of "foreign" transmissions that had interfered with normal communications over the previous few days. Somehow, a mischievous radio enthusiast managed to "hack" secret frequencies and procedures to mimic *Dakar* transmissions, in a harmless but distracting way. It would not be the first time that such spurious transmissions were associated with a loss at sea.

All of the facts, clues, and analysis conducted over the many years of study by several different committees supported by the most learned institutions Israel could muster led to a refinement of the initial conclusions:

1. The buoy must have been attached to the rest of the cable, and hence the *Dakar*, until a short time before discovery. Further, the shape of the cable indicates that the buoy was in its cage on the *Dakar* deck for about a year after the sinking of the ship.
2. The buoy could not have been held deeper than its collapse depth, 326 meters, or shallower than the bottom of the photo zone, about eighty meters. Thus, the *Dakar* must rest in water between these depths.
3. The buoy drifted for a period of no more than three to four weeks after the cable finally broke and it drifted away from the *Dakar*. Hence, the submarine must lie at a distance of 150 to 200 miles from Han Yunis, Gaza Strip, where the buoy was found.

These almost inescapable conclusions were strongly held, and misdirected the search for the *Dakar* for nearly three decades.

✡ ✡ ✡

By Wednesday, Tom and I were growing comfortable with our surroundings and even beginning to enjoy our evenings. Our heads were filled with new information, and we spent a lot of time after the official work day trying to sort things out and get ready for the next barrage of data. At some point, we were going to have to stop listening and start producing some answers.

We were also picking up a few handy Hebrew words, like "b'seder," which our hosts seemed to use all the time when they meant "ok," "all right," or "no problem." There's a version that translates "Hey, it's really no problem at all, no kidding," which actually means "We're in big trouble." In that case, I think a "balagan" is happening. We had also managed to recover pretty well from jet lag, and were anticipating the "day of rest" being Saturday instead of Sunday. My journal reads:

2/19 Wednesday, Tel Aviv: Today we learned all about previous survey efforts, along with other miscellaneous studies. The surveys have been very professional and seem conclusive in their elimination of certain areas. Our assistant Naval Attaché showed up long enough to show his face, mumble excuses about how busy they are, and ask for a copy of any reports we are planning to show the Admiral. No doubt they will be all over us when the Admiral shows up, wanting to take credit for how helpful they've been.

We were treated to dinner by El [Yechiel Ga'ash, the Project Officer and our guide] and Bar [Baruch Peretzman, the paratrooper who is the head of the Hydrographic Branch] at a place called "Dixie." To our mild disappointment, it was more American than anything else . . . they didn't even serve Israeli beer!

2/20 Thursday: Today is "Friday" (really Thursday, but that's Friday here, since Sunday is Monday). We had our first chance to work on the project on our own, and made a lot of progress. We even worked late (see, we're very busy and have little time for fun). After the semi-formal presentations of the first three days it was a little more relaxing, and also productive.

2/21 Friday: Our weekend started out to be a bust, as a raging storm blew in, bringing super high winds, sheets of rain, lightning, window-rattling thunder, and storm surges that inundated the beach. All very exciting (even to the locals), but not conducive to touring. We're taking advantage of the time to review what we've been learning and summarizing it for our eventual report. If things ease up tomorrow, we'll venture over to the museum or market. I tried to go running, and as soon as I got beyond the shelter of the building I was blown almost off my feet! I decided to wait for a break in the wind, but didn't get one all day. It's bound to be better tomorrow.

2/22 Saturday: The rain finally eased to a steady drizzle by evening, so Tom and I ventured out for a walk and possible dinner. We found a grill that served local draft beer (Maccabee) and specialized in shish-k-bobs. I got the mixed grill, which included pork, chicken liver, an unidentified (but delicious) sausage, and some other kind of meat (??). Included was a salad bar, but not your traditional Denny's variety. For one, there was no sneeze shield. Also, it was possible to confuse the decorations with the actual salad fixings. There were the ubiquitous chick peas & eggplant, peppers, olives, sauerkraut, various pickled things, tomatoes of various origins & treatments, onions, olives, and artichokes. I thought it was quite delicious!

2/23 Sunday: This morning (remember, it's "Monday" here, a work-day) broke bright and sunny. Figures. I have collected touring information for next weekend, so there's still hope that we'll get a chance to see some of the country.

✡ ✡ ✡

Yechiel Ga'ash was our constant companion and a source of confidence throughout the official proceedings, and spent many evenings and much weekend time with us. Baruch was usually with us as well, cheerful and friendly at all times. Yechiel became our closest friend in Israel, but also remained something of an enigma. He was usually quiet and easygoing, but sometimes forceful and stubborn. He was very friendly and likable, but clearly had many detractors. He was always joking, and even irreverent at times, but he was dead serious when it came to the *Dakar*. Yechiel had a delightful way of using American jargon in a slightly mismatched context, so that he sounded both foreign and familiar at the same time.

Yechiel was a member of the Israeli crew that conducted the first underwater search for the *Dakar* in the early 1980s, and was assigned as project officer in 1994. He threw himself into the task with a will, devoting his time and energies to the detriment of advancement and personal life. He realized immediately that one of his jobs must be to gain the confidence of the *Dakar* family members, who were suspicious of the Navy and disappointed with the unsuccessful efforts to date. In his words:

> We had a period of time that there was kind of a disconnection between the families and the Navy authorities, and later on we had to build their

confidence with the system that we are doing all of the efforts that we can do in order to achieve our goal, which is to find the *Dakar.*

So when you have a situation when somebody doesn't believe you, you have to convince him that you are doing your best. So it's not an easy situation . . . it took some time to rebuild the confidence between the two sides.

Yechiel was not the official liaison to the families, but took it upon himself to address a circumstance which he felt was important to his job. As there was some antagonism between family members and the Navy, this association sometimes put Yechiel on the wrong side, as far as the Navy was concerned. Tom and I gathered that Yechiel was not popular in some Navy circles, both for this and his single-minded determination to find the *Dakar.*

Yechiel's official job as project officer was to coordinate the search efforts. This was no small task, as it involved new and developing technology, evaluation of Committee findings, coordination with authorities in Greece, Egypt, and elsewhere, actual search operations, and assessment of the results. Somehow, he had to explain to his superiors and the families how days and weeks at sea accumulating into years of effort without success were actually measures of progress.

So, Yechiel's job was not conducive to advancement, and after a career's worth of service, he had not advanced beyond lieutenant commander. "There is nothing to do with promotion and the job that I made," he said. "I mean, ranks didn't bother me never ever." Still, he was dedicated and competent, and those who could look past politics and see the core of a man were counted among his supporters. These included Admiral Raz and Admiral Tal, who showed complete confidence in Yechiel and gave him every opportunity to succeed.

And he knew he would succeed: "I knew that we were going to find it. It's just a question of time. I mean, I believe in that thing every day, every time. To find the *Dakar* was, for me, just a question of time."

Chapter 9

The Commitment to Search

I t was the buoy.

The *Dakar* was lost at sea, with no clue to its disappearance, no idea where to begin to search, and no capability back in 1968 to search the deep water along its route. It might as well have been on the far side of Jupiter. Vice Admiral Yedidia Ya'ari, Israeli Navy commander in chief (successor to Rear Admiral Tal) said in a 2002 interview, "It is not like a destroyer who got hit by four missiles. She stays afloat, she burns, people are evacuating, and there are stories of heroism, distress, despair, pain, and tragedy. It's a ship that really dies on the surface, and only later after she is dead, she is sinking. This is not the case with a submarine. A submarine simply evaporates. One moment she is there; the other, she is gone—no traces, no clues, nothing."

It probably would have been left at that but for the appearance, out of nowhere, of the buoy, right on the shores of Israel. It was a stark reminder that the ship was out there, and the mystery unsolved. If the buoy could be found, why not the rest of the ship? The analysis indicated conclusively that the ship was in shallow water, somewhere. Could it be found?

The families thought so.

Wives, sons and daughters, parents, brothers and sisters, extended family members, and even close friends of the crew of the *Dakar* formed naturally and rapidly into a wider extended family for whom the *Dakar* was the glue. They consulted, commiserated, and relied on each other for the release of grief and nurturing of hope. They were bonded in bereavement, with sons or brothers vanished, children abruptly orphaned, and mothers with young sons and daughters suddenly on their own. Who else could understand?

But why search for the ship? How would that help? The motivations were many, and probably varied in importance with each member of the group. All certainly sought closure, a psychological need to craft a fitting end to a phase of life, so that one could look ahead and begin again. This was probably the primary motivation for most family members. Without knowing for certain the fate of their loved ones, there was no hook on which to hang their grief, and the imagination could always devise a new twist of their fate. This, for some, made it harder to handle, and a slower, more painful process. Included in this process was the honoring of fallen heroes, which helped unite the families with the rest of the small nation, all with the common need for closure.

There were religious reasons for finding the remains of the dead and bringing them home for proper burial on Israeli soil. Religious leaders made official declarations, technically settling the issue for orthodox observers, but the lack of physical evidence of death left many open questions.

Some were driven to find the submarine for more practical reasons. Many family members were themselves Navy men, some even submariners, and were keenly interested to know what happened before they would venture out in similar circumstances and risk a similar outcome. One could speculate as to the cause of the disaster and try to devise means to reduce future occurrences, but without a specific cause there is little justification for specific action. In the case of the loss of the U.S. submarine *Thresher*, detailed surveys of the wreck site and investigations of the cause led to many technical and procedural changes in American nuclear submarine design and operation. This motivation was common to the family members and the Israeli Navy, although means, methods, and the extent of this endeavor were subjects of great differences of opinion. Some came to believe that the Navy was reluctant to find a specific cause that would be detrimental to the careers of those who designed the modifications, refitted the ship, or authorized some ill-considered engineering change.

There was always the nagging doubt that maybe, after all, the *Dakar* crew was not dead. This was fueled by boastful Egyptian submarine captains who claimed to have captured the ship, and technical studies of the buoy that suggested the ship was ensconced in shallow water somewhere. Professor Gitay's favorite theory that the ship was in an Egyptian lagoon, based on soil samples found in the buoy, helped lend scientific credence to rash speculation. The darker fringes of this theory suggested that the Israeli Navy was even somehow complicit in the disappearance of the ship, in cahoots with the Egyptians to cover up a dire conspiracy.

In 1992, over twenty years after the *Dakar*'s loss, undersea explorer Dr. Robert Ballard played off this speculation in his fictional techno-thriller *Bright Shark*, which featured the submarine that "vanishes without a trace, burying its top secret cargo," engaged in a "mission so daring, so deadly and unthinkable that its exposure could forever alter the balance of world power."

Could the *Dakar* have been carrying top secret weapons, nuclear or otherwise? Was its disappearance staged, or real, but in either case arranged by its own government to cover up secrets or effect some political purpose? Were members of the crew still alive somewhere in Egypt, or living large in the Witness Protection Program somewhere in Montana?

Michael Shermer, publisher of the magazine *Skeptic*, explains how these conspiracy theories develop and proliferate. Shermer writes in *Scientific American* (May 2005): "Humans evolved brains that are pattern recognition machines, adept at detecting signals that enhance or threaten survival amid a very noisy world." He calls this capability "associative learning," and it explains how our ancestors could associate the seasons with the migration of game animals, or connect the position of the sun, change of season, and time to plant crops. Animals know some of these things by instinct, but human brains can reason out connections and make subtle inferences.

Humans can also communicate and pass on these learned associations to other humans. This awesome capability to reason out casual connections and pass on accumulated knowledge can be a great asset, but it also leads to false associations. Superstition, rumors, and conspiracy theories are all fueled by this associative learning ability. We do this naturally, whereas logical reasoning and scientific inquiry require more training and discipline to apply successfully.

Where facts are few, there is a great deal of room for speculation and false associations, and the *Dakar* disaster was a classic case.

In any group, there are leaders and followers. Within the family group, there were factions. Some simply wanted closure, and to honor their dead. Others were motivated by solving the mystery, for technical reasons or scientific curiosity. Still others believed that something bigger was afoot, and the Navy was dragging its feet, unwilling to find the ship and reveal its secrets.

One of the family members who tried to unite these disparate impulses and focus the energy of grief into positive action was Michael Marcovici. A natural leader, intelligent and well spoken, Michael was old enough to have felt the full force of the tragedy as a teenager when his brother vanished, but young enough to be able to energetically and doggedly pursue the answer over three decades. He served for a while as chairman of the *Dakar* Family Committee, which sought to represent the families in their commitment to find the ship and resolve the mystery.

Families, even family members who have been to sea and captained large craft, cannot venture into the depths of the great Mediterranean and find a lost submarine. Nor can they commission search parties or win unlimited access to the government or the military, or command even a small fleet of underwater search vehicles. They must rely completely on their Navy with help perhaps from the United Nations and the U.S. Navy and other sympathetic organizations. They share a common goal in this search, but that doesn't mean they will agree on strategies—or control funding or dictate the level of effort. Closure is the ultimate goal, but how to achieve it?

In a 2002 interview, Michael Marcovici stressed the psychological element of pulling the family members together to share their grief and deal with the tragedy as a group.

> I think that it's both things together. Definitely the feeling of being a part of a big family. It's not a relief, but when you see people who are sharing the same thing which you are sharing, the same pain, it's easy to communicate with them.
>
> The mandate that we received from the families was to try to do anything possible to convince the authorities, the government, the Navy, to go for the search and to find what happened with the submarine. This was our goal. This was our mandate, and for this we were chosen, and for this we were fighting almost thirty years.

But was it really a fight? Was the Navy reluctant to search? Marcovici recognized this as a very delicate question, but he still feels more could have been done at the outset.

> You have the official and you have the ongoing, and I can tell you that there is a big gap between the official and what was going on.
>
> Officially, in March '69, when they were declared officially missing in action, in the Knesset, the minister of defense, Dayan, said the government of Israel will do anything possible to find what happened to the *Dakar* and to bring them to be buried in Israel. This was a commitment from the Israeli government and I don't care if it is Likud or Labor, I don't care.
>
> But in '69, nothing could be done, because we didn't know anything. Then they discovered the buoy in Han Yunis. At that time, due to the fact that the buoy was found on the shore, [we thought that] the submarine is between 150 to 350 meters deep, and according to this, it should be alongside the Egyptian borders, but at that time it was still the war with Egypt. In 1977, until Sadat came to Israel, nothing was done, and nothing—if you want to be realistic—could be done.
>
> You see, we started to ask the questions, and then we started to discover a lot of things. The order is to go directly to Haifa, not to go to Egypt. Is it possible that Yaacov Ra'anan would do something like this? Of course not. But then what was the buoy doing in Han Yunis, and how is it possible? We go back to the rumors and to the speculations, that it was a kind of a Russian operation, Egyptian operation. Then we had all the rumors from Egypt. This general from the [Egyptian] Navy said, "I sank the *Dakar*," and, technically, everything is possible.

Regarding the decision to send the *Dakar* to Israel, just after the war with Egypt, unarmed, Michael says, "This is another story. How you can send submarine with no torpedoes? We went to the Navy and asked them. At the time, the chief of staff said, 'Listen, we wanted to save money, so we didn't send torpedoes from Israel to *Dakar*.' Doesn't make sense."

These facts and rumors and, over the years, lack of success fanned the flames. They gave Michael and the Family Committee motivation to be persistent, sometimes even a thorn in the side of the Navy and the government.

✡ ✡ ✡

Almost everyone we talked to who was associated with the Navy's efforts to find the *Dakar* avowed their own personal motivation for the search. They needed no thorns in their sides. However, from a practical perspective there needed to be a national will (including funding and technology development) to allow motivated people to work to achieve the goal.

It is true that some people in the Navy felt that, after so many years, the time and effort was a waste. Those whose prime concern was identifying technical shortcomings of the *Dakar* hull, equipment, or procedures were satisfied by the emergence of new, modern ships, and lessons learned from the mistakes of countless submariners since the *Totem* was designed and built in the 1940s. Money and talent spent searching for a thirty-year-old wreck could better serve Israel's defenses in other ways. There was a cool and irrefutable logic to this . . . but it was not a popular point of view.

Others in the Navy simply resented the second guessing, the accusations, and what they felt was harassment, being made to feel they were not doing their proper jobs or were complicit in a cover-up.

However, either through a genuine, Navy-wide sympathy with the cause, or a natural selection process of assigning the job of searching for the *Dakar* to those who wanted to find it, most people we worked with were serious about the job. One of them was Admiral Ya'ari, who, in a 2002 interview, had this to say about the desire, tradition, and national passion to bring every soldier back, that they should be buried in Israel, that everybody should be accounted for:

> The driving force behind this, if you like, obsession of ours, to find the *Dakar* and find out what happened, I think is more mental. It is rooted in our heritage as Jews. I don't think anyone else would have sustained that continuous effort for thirty-one years, trying every angle, every possible route and trying to cover every possible area within that Mediterranean that has some prospect of the *Dakar* being in it.

This type of commitment definitely goes beyond the military service or the Navy. It goes much deeper into the genetic code of us as a nation, as well as the genetic codes of the services in that respect. We still have teams right now that are searching at sea for missing pilots that were mosquito fighters from 1948. They are still active, still searching for clues, for evidence. This is probably something that is unique, but that's the way we are.

It is rooted in the Jewish tradition. That is a constant. We are going to search for our people everywhere for as long as it takes.

Admiral Ya'ari had his own special feeling for the role of the families and their relationship with the Navy.

It is, in a sense, an extended family, and the fact that every chief of the Navy since then, up to me, personally, knew the people in the *Dakar*, probably explains a great deal of where and how this thing evolved.

The families are looking to you for answers, and you need to supply them some answers, and that is your calling. So the Navy was busy for thirty-one years in keeping in touch. We would go every year for the memorial service. The entire submarine unit is there, all of the reserves, all of the retired crews, the families, everybody. We would gather every year in January in Mount Herzel, and spend an hour or so with the families.

And in the meantime they created a committee. The committee was the liaison with the Navy, and we were constantly updating them with the operations, and the different type of searches, in Egypt, in the Aegean Sea, around our coast, and so on and so forth.

I think, in a sense, we need the families not less than the families need us. We were actually looking for a constant reminder, and they were the constant reminder. We were looking for the influence of their pain to strengthen our commitment. It works this way. So this is, by any means, a family affair.

Admiral Raz was another who shared the passion to find the *Dakar*, but his role as coordinator of search efforts forced him to be practical and deliberate. His view of the family motivation was that they wanted to show that the crew was not at fault, and could not be blamed for the disaster. Whether anyone else could, or should, be blamed, was another matter entirely.

The families kept in touch with the Israeli Navy and with the prime ministers, all along the years. They never stopped pushing to continue looking for the *Dakar*. I believe that especially what concerned them was the fact that the Israeli Navy, for many years, had the view that the *Dakar* deviated from its original planning and sailed close to the Egyptian coastline.

The mere fact that people even thought that Lieutenant Commander Ra'anan took the liberty to deviate from his original orders, brought the families to bear a lot of pressure to find what really happened to the *Dakar*. They always managed to reach the prime ministers, and we always came out from the meetings with assurance that Israel Navy will keep on going, and will get the budget, and will have all the resources required to continue the searches.

I managed to appoint a committee of family members who were closely in touch with the Israeli Navy, and the other agencies, four or five people, mainly parents but also sometimes wives of the ship's company. Most of the time they were very adamant . . . pushing, pushing. I believe they, from their point of view, did a very good job.

When I was chosen to coordinate the search mission, I had my own position that we shouldn't be too much affected by the families' reactions, because we could not plan and do things methodically. That will never satisfy a parent or a wife. They wanted answers. They wanted answers now.

But at the same time, I managed to keep in touch, and in a very friendly way, with most of the people I knew from thirty years ago. Many, many years we are going together, and actually having the same feeling about what should be achieved.

✡ ✡ ✡

Tom and I were mostly oblivious to all of this history as we continued to learn about the events of 1968 and subsequent searches for the missing ship. Of course, we were aware of the families, and we knew from Raz's letter that they were counting on us, but Raz was careful not to let those motivations creep into the technical proceedings. He wanted a fresh perspective, and felt he could serve the families best by leaving them out of things, for now.

So, we learned about the searches conducted over the years, inspired by the rescue buoy and years of teasing scraps of information from the nooks of this little bit of orange-painted aluminum.

It was actually more than ten years from the appearance of the buoy until formal underwater searches were organized, under the auspices of the original *Dakar* Search Committee. Part of the reason for this was the time it took to study the artifact, develop theories of its appearance, and conduct experiments leading to specific search strategies. The first spectrographic tests of the sand in the buoy did not occur until 1981. Another reason for the delay was lack of available technology to search for something like a submarine hull on the sea floor over wide areas.

Some concepts are so obvious they are assumed. Sometimes as a result, the obvious can be overlooked, or given too little thought. There are two very obvious things that must happen if one is to find a lost item, regardless of whether it is a ship on the ocean bottom or a television remote control lost in the living room: one must be able to see the object, and one must look where it is. These two simple concepts are the key to any search, and of course, they are both necessary conditions. In the underwater realm, we must have an instrument which can "see," or detect, a ship hull or associated debris. One way to do this is by using a camera; in fact, the first underwater photographs were taken by Englishman William Thompson in 1856, and the first color underwater photographs appeared in the January 1927 issue of *National Geographic*. In order to light the subject, photographer Charles Martin used pans of magnesium powder explosives floating on pontoons that had to be triggered at just the right moment. This immediately suggests a limitation of underwater photography: there is little or no natural light available. In fact, seawater absorbs light (and other electromagnetic energy like radio waves, X-rays, and laser beams) so effectively that the ocean is completely dark below a few hundred feet, even in brightest daylight. The feeble light sources that we can deploy underwater serve to illuminate very small areas, and increasing intensity only serves to create debilitating backscatter into camera lenses, competing with reflections from the subject. At best, camera imaging is limited to distances of dozens of feet. Even specially tuned blue-green laser scanners are not effective beyond one hundred feet or so.

If one wanted to scour a square mile of ocean using a camera, over 300,000 photographs would have to be taken! A video camera, moving along at a brisk pace, would need the better part of a week to complete the task. The Mediterranean Sea is nearly a million square miles in area. Even if we are confined to coastal areas in the eastern part of the sea, thousands of square miles must be searched.

Of course, there are always exceptions. The RMS *Titanic* was actually found on the second search mission using an underwater video camera. Since the debris of the wreck was spread thinly over such a large area, the chances that a piece of debris might be seen even with a random search pattern was much more likely. Still, there are better ways to search underwater.

During the period between the world wars, the British commissioned a group called the Antisubmarine Detection Investigation Committee to develop techniques to use the hydrophone, an underwater listening device invented in 1906 to detect icebergs. The result was known by the British as ASDIC and by the American allies as "sonar" (sound navigation and ranging). The basic principle is simple: a sound is created underwater, usually by a piezoelectric crystal, having the property that putting an electric current through it makes it vibrate, and vice versa. Fortunately, sound can travel great distances underwater, and can echo off the bottom or objects in the water. The same crystal, called a transducer, detects these echoes, and the time between signal and echo is a measure of distance.

In 1963 Harold "Doc" Edgerton, a professor of engineering at MIT, performed a remarkable experiment with his newly designed sonar device called a "Sub-Bottom Profiler." The *Vineyard* lightship had disappeared during a hurricane in the fall of 1944, with the loss of all on board. Divers wanted to find it and determine why she mysteriously sank. Doc had ideas about how to widen the scope of the single-point coverage of sub-bottom profilers, and with the hopes of experimenting on a real search, he agreed to help. He mounted the transducer of the sub-bottom profiler so it could be aimed out to the side instead of straight down. In this configuration, the acoustic beam would propagate out at an angle perpendicular to the path of the vessel. When he got out to sea, Doc discovered that images of large targets were not very definitive; however, the uniquely mounted profiler did provide the location of one major anomaly in the sonar data. That anomaly turned out to be the *Vineyard* lightship.

Two years later, the company EG&G (now known as EdgeTech) was founded, and Doc's engineers refined the concept into one of oceanography's most remarkable undersea imaging systems. Although earlier work in long-range side-looking sonar had been done in England, this experiment provided the groundwork for the development of high-resolution acoustic imaging. The new instrument has revolutionized underwater remote sensing.

Doc Edgerton was a remarkable man, and is also known for his invention of the stroboscope for use in both ultra-high-speed and still (or stop-motion) photography. Besides applying this to many technical problems, Doc used his invention to photograph athletes in action, capture hummingbirds in flight, watch a bullet pierce an apple, and even help MGM Studios in Hollywood make movies. His photographs were exhibited at the New York Museum of Modern Art, his film work won an Academy Award, and his support of aerial photographic intelligence collection before the D-Day invasion of Normandy won him the Medal of Freedom. As recently as 1985, he was working with Jacques Cousteau to find Spanish underwater wrecks near Cuba, and his photography was featured on a Public Television documentary. The Edgerton-Benthos underwater camera was used to photograph the RMS *Titanic* in 1986. His productive and inspiring life ended in 1990 at age eighty-six.

With this new underwater imaging device, which came to be known as the side-scan sonar, great swaths of the sea floor could now be mapped, at least in terms of sound echoes. Fortunately, those echoes reflect differently from hard (sandy) and soft (silty) soil, and they bounce more strongly off raised ridges than flat bottom. Rocks echo stronger yet. So underwater topography and composition of the bottom could be inferred, to some degree. Also, sound echoes very nicely off hard metallic objects with sharp edges, such as ships and their wreckage. By timing the echoes and paying attention to the angles and geometries, one can even infer sizes and shapes from these underwater images. The results are subject to interpretation, but once an object is detected and its location is known, an underwater camera can be used to identify it without ambiguity.

Soon after Edgerton launched his invention, other companies such as Klein Associates followed suit with similar versions. By the time of the loss of the *Dakar*, the side-scan sonar existed as a search tool; however, it was still very new, somewhat experimental, and not readily available to Israel.

By 1981, however, the results of all of the buoy analysis were well accepted, the technology for underwater search was available, and the *Dakar* families were clamoring for action. Also, a new and dramatic development opened the door: Egypt and Israel signed the Camp David Accords in 1978, and a peace treaty in 1979. Since the most promising areas of search for the *Dakar* lay within Egyptian waters, this made way for a credible effort. Some cynics have contended that the opportunity to nose around in the waters off the military base at Alexandria was the real reason for interest in a *Dakar* search, but no matter . . . the searches began.

The Egyptian coast was chosen for initial surveys since it seemed most promising, and there was no guarantee how long the treaty would endure. Also, if *Dakar* had made the unlikely decision to enter Egyptian waters, the area off Alexandria harbor would have been the most interesting strategically, and the ship could have penetrated the outer limit of the area for a time between communications. Four expeditions were conducted in 1981 and 1982 using a side-scan sonar; more than one thousand contacts were detected and identified with a remotely operated vehicle (ROV). This tethered device, carrying cameras and lights, could be moved over a target using ducted-propeller thrusters, and operated remotely from the surface by a technician using a joystick. The search was very methodical; each swath was overlapped by half on the subsequent pass, so that in the end each spot on the sea floor was covered twice.

Nothing relating to the *Dakar* was found.

In 1986, the U.S. Navy offered assistance, and another expedition was launched to map the entrance to Alexandria harbor. This time, in addition to sonar, an airborne magnetometer was flown by the U.S. Navy. This device senses and measures the very weak magnetic field generated by the earth. Large ferromagnetic objects (such as the hulls of steel ships or undersea mountains of iron ore) will disturb this field, and if the anomaly is big enough it can be detected, even by low-flying aircraft. The U.S. Navy routinely operates such air-craft, called the P-3 Orion, for antisubmarine patrols. Again, the process was methodical, and the coverage thorough.

But, nothing relating to the *Dakar* was found.

Another magnetometer survey was done in 1989, farther to the east along the Egyptian coast. There were suspicious reports of fishermen snagging on some wreckage or outcropping at a depth of fifty-four fathoms (324 feet), a prime depth for the submarine. Later, in 1996, a local commercial company looked in the area, and claimed they found something, even publishing an image in the newspapers. They returned accompanied by the Israeli Navy and plenty of media representatives.

Still, nothing relating to the *Dakar* was found, and the sonar images were judged to be nothing more than shadows of rocks.

In spite of the failure to find the *Dakar* during these missions, the commit-ment to search was a great comfort to the families, as Chava Barkay gratefully notes in a 2002 interview:

> I wanted very much that the searching was every year, that they didn't stop until they found it. It was a very strong feeling for me. This is necessary to find it, to know what happened. Let it be the grave of them, yes, but I want to know where they are. And I was glad every time they sail, that we are keeping searching next season, next year, even if they say they're searching in another sea, in other places. I say OK, I can live. I can keep on my life.
>
> I just knew that someday, he'd be found. So don't stop looking for it, because I don't want to wait fifty or sixty years. I want it now.

As the months and years wore on, Israel always sought new approaches to the prob-lem and new technologies to apply. One center of this activity was the Weizmann Institute of Science, a multidisciplinary center devoted to research and teach-ing in the natural sciences. The Institute was founded in 1934 by Dr. Chaim Weizmann, scientist and statesman, and Israel's first president.

A visit to the Weizmann Institute was included in our itinerary, and we found the campus to be beautiful. One of the highlights was a Holocaust memo-rial which was a huge bronze Torah scroll broken in half, and inscribed on the outside with replicas of actual numbers which were tattooed on the arms of concentration camp inmates. These reminders of the recent past were power-ful and haunting.

Among the assets of the Institute was a Cray supercomputer, and it was being used to investigate water current modeling of the eastern Mediterranean which was relevant to our analysis. As part of this work, dozens of research buoys outfitted with tracking devices and recorders were released along the known and projected path of the *Dakar*. This was compared to simulated "buoys" that were projected according to computer models. Some interesting conclusions were derived from this. First of all, the ocean current circulation model was found to be significantly in error in some regions, and was updated. This explained an experience we had while searching in the eastern Mediterranean a few years earlier. We did not find our target until the analysis was updated with the actual current seen in the field, as opposed to the model data that had the current running in the opposite direction!

The actual buoys, to everyone's surprise, spent many weeks at sea before landing ashore, taking chaotic paths and sometimes even circling the island nation of Cyprus before reaching the Egyptian coast. This certainly conflicted with common wisdom and opened up the disturbing possibility that a buoy found at Han Yunis could have come from anywhere and taken any amount of time to get there.

Still, by ignoring the details of the buoys' paths and looking only at the start and end points, some general inferences could be made regarding trends, and these generalizations led the Israeli Navy to look beyond the frustrating and fruitless Egyptian searches and consider that the *Dakar* might lie farther afield. The logical place to look next was the Aegean Sea, in waters near Crete and Rhodes off the Greek coast. This was a conclusion of a second *Dakar* Search Committee, seated in 1987 to reconsider the loss of the submarine and all of the new research that had accumulated. The new Committee had the results of additional analysis of the buoy, including further biological and mineralogical analysis. This new analysis tended to suggest that the buoy had been in the Aegean, again in relatively shallow water. From an operational standpoint, this area was considered a possibility, since this was a common area for Israeli submarine commanders to use for training.

Four surveys were conducted between 1991 and 1994, again with a combination of side-scan sonar and magnetometer. Bolstered by new spectrographic analyses of the sand in the buoy in 1994, a fifth survey was conducted the following year using a modified multibeam bathymetry system. This device measured depth very accurately at many points over a wide swath, and had been shown to be capable of detecting shipwrecks. The surveys covered virtually all of the coastal areas between eastern Crete and Rhodes to a depth of 350 meters. It also included offshore areas of seamounts with depths of less than 350 meters.

And yet again, nothing relating to the *Dakar* was found.

✡ ✡ ✡

So, we return to the two obvious and necessary conditions to a successful search. The best imaging technology and the most professional team of operators will not be successful if they do not search where it is. After thirty years of fruitless searching, and hundreds of square miles of coverage, the *Dakar* team had learned something very valuable: they had a good idea of where the ship wasn't. However, their efforts still left countless square miles of Mediterranean coastline to scour. Also, no search is perfect. The probability of detection is never 100 percent, as even something as large as a submarine hull can be missed due to navigation errors, sonar signal dropouts, or rough terrain. The latter was encountered frequently in the Aegean, offering many rock outcroppings, cliff sides, and crevasses to hide a hull. Clearly, something had to be done to narrow the search, and make the best use of the capabilities the U.S. Navy was offering.

Having learned all we could about the ship and its history, it was time for Tom and me to begin coming to some conclusions. As we began our second week of work, I summarized our situation in my journal:

But then our Committee degenerated into speculation. Everybody has their pet theories, supported by logical suppositions based on weak evidence and flawed analyses. The professor of biology (who has a pet theory that the signal buoy found washed ashore must have spent some months in an Egyptian lagoon) will accept any evidence in his favor, but says everything else is "Impossible!" Most everyone else is open-minded for the most part, but Tom and I are trying our best to make them see that Assumption B does not always proceed from Fact A.

Tom and I spent a lot of time sorting out the information and trying to distinguish verifiable facts from assumptions, and trying to judge the quality of the information. Some things were quite certain, such as the communications with the *Dakar,* the positions they reported, and details of the ship's capabilities. And there was the stark fact of the buoy and the secrets it held. There were clearly two major areas of speculation: where did the buoy come from, and what was the frame of mind of Captain Ra'anan? Conclusions about these two issues had been the prime motive in all of the search efforts to date. Could we validate or refute these conclusions? Was there a new and better approach? How could we, in a few short weeks, come up with something new when the weight of Israel's technology had been applied to this problem for decades?

Fortunately, we didn't waste any time worrying about the odds, and pressed on.

The Three Threads

By Monday of our second week working with the *Dakar* Search Committee in Israel, we had learned all the useful information we could absorb. Tom and I had asked a lot of questions as we became more familiar with the facts and issues. I was intrigued by the mysterious transmissions heard in the vicinity of Cyprus right after the loss. Even though the board of inquiry judged them not to be from the *Dakar* buoy, I still had suspicions. I was unwilling to discount the information completely. We studied the transcripts of various radio operators in Famagusta and asked again about the details of the reports from ships.

Most of our questions could be answered by the people gathered, or the answers were contained somewhere in the volumes of papers in front of us, or clearly could not be answered. However, Raz was unwilling to allow the fourth possibility: that there was an answer, but we did not have it. In one case, regarding the radio transmissions, we had a question about the communications protocol of the day. It was a minor point, but Raz insisted that we send for a senior radioman who would know the answer from experience. We set the question aside. Several hours later, a smartly uniformed chief radioman appeared with a knock, was invited in, and asked for our question. We posed it, got a straight answer, and he left to return to whatever duties we had interrupted. We felt sheepish about the time and expense invested in this simple question, but that was fine with Raz. And we could never complain that any corners were snipped during the inquiry.

As the hours wore along, we sank deeper into trivialities, always alert for a point that had been overlooked. We learned about all of the oil stains encountered by the search parties just after the disappearance. We asked to once again go over the "foreign" transmissions that purported to be from the *Dakar* but probably weren't. We considered the weather. We looked at winds and currents. We talked about the buoy, and how it could have gotten to Han Yunis.

Tom, as I have said, had a lot of experience with submarine wrecks. He explained that as a submarine sinks, its pressure hull (if intact) will resist the force of the sea until it fails in a dramatic implosion. Until that point, the cylindrical hull will actually shrink by a surprising amount. I knew this from my own submarine experience: as we dove, the compression of the hull would cause the ship to get heavier (less buoyant), since the slightly smaller hull volume would displace less water. We had to pump a ton of water from our ballast tanks for every one hundred feet of depth, just to keep even.

Under these conditions, structures attached to the hull, such as decking, external tanks, fairings, and other equipment, would undergo stress at the attachment points. It is a factor in the design of the ship to make sure this stress is manageable. However, when the ship is sinking, descending far deeper than planned, the hull shrinks considerably beyond any measure of design. As the stress on the external structures builds, joints can fail and equipment can come loose or even pop off the hull. Then the hull implodes and all is reduced to twisted wreckage. This is the experience with wrecks like the *Thresher,* the *Scorpion,* and others Tom had seen.

Conversely, the wreck of the Japanese submarine I-52 was not imploded. That ship was sunk by a torpedo, which made a huge hole and allowed the hull to fill with water as the ship sank. So there was never any pressure buildup, and the hull never compressed or imploded. In this case, we couldn't be sure that compression and implosion occurred with the *Dakar,* but it was a good guess. Tom's rare experience with the nuances of submarine wrecks turned out to be the key to the mystery, but it took a lot of collective thought and a methodical approach to apply that knowledge and arrive at the right result. That conclusion was yet to come; validation and certainty was in the distant future.

Though our days and most evenings were focused on the work of the Committee, our hosts found time to entertain us and show us some of their country. My journal continues:

2/24 Monday: We met Baruch's family: wife Dina, who used to work for Prime Minister Rabin, his two daughters, ages 22 and 10, and his mother. His mother was very interesting, having a fascinating story which I'm sure is all too common here. She spent four years in Nazi Germany during the war in ghettos and concentration camps, including the infamous Dachau. She lost her mother and one brother, and was liberated by the Russians, all by age 20. She was headed back to Lithuania to find her family, when she by chance ran into an old family friend who knew where they were going and advised her to flee Russia. She found her father and the rest of her family back in Germany, then she spent three years trying to escape to the West, finally making it to

Israel in 1948, just in time for the War of Liberation. We heard all this in an hour or so of very intense storytelling.

2/25 Tuesday: More real progress at work. As a result, I think Professor Gitay is quitting. It's too much for him that we are objectively considering alternatives to his Lagoon Theory.

2/26 Wednesday: We are a little anxious about the Jerusalem trip, since there have been protests over the Israeli decision to build in a new neighborhood, and a Palestinian was killed by Israeli police. I think the danger is low (compared to, say, a drive down the New Jersey Turnpike), but Tom is a little concerned. We'll check with our hosts tomorrow.

2/27 Thursday: It's settled. Since we will go to Jerusalem with the government tour next week, we will do the bus trip to the Dead Sea and Masada tomorrow, and then Yechiel will take us to Nazareth and Galilee on Saturday. We also will go to the Naval base at Haifa (which includes Mt. Carmel and is supposed to be like San Francisco) on Sunday (which is like Monday), so we will get all our tours in a row.

By then we understood the situation, and were devising a plan. As a group, we suffered from a serious lack of consensus, but I saw that as an asset . . . after all, a consensus on a wrong answer is still wrong. Using a commonsense approach, I proposed that we methodically consider each person's idea and try to identify each step in each scenario. It seemed to me that every theory had something to offer, but that none of them could stand alone.

I also was able to sell the group on the idea that we should consider improbable events; in fact, I argued that something improbable was likely to have happened! This is hard to accept, since engineers, designers, and operators are trained to identify sources of failure and account for them, so that they become less likely. For example, the strength of a part is designed to withstand any likely stress. Of course, if you have two unlikely things, the chances of them both occurring is even more remote, and this principle is considered in the design and operation of safe systems.

In the case of a sunken submarine, or any disaster for that matter, we have to turn this thinking upside down. If nothing unlikely happened, proper design and operation would have averted disaster. The fact that something unusual did happen is why there was a disaster in the first place! So, we have to assume that some improbable combination of events probably happened. The understanding of this concept by the group opened everyone's mind to consider any reasonable chain of events, even unlikely ones.

We started the process with a known point in space and time: the report of the *Dakar's* last position. Although one could imagine that Captain Ra'anan, for bizarre and unfathomable reasons, falsified this report, we had to start somewhere and we could all agree on this. We then considered all of the possibilities that could ensue. Did the *Dakar* continue on its path? Did she change course or speed? Did Captain Ra'anan decide to head to Egypt or to the Aegean, or somewhere else? We tried to think of all of the things that reasonably could have happened, however improbable, and regardless of how that fit with our own theories.

Once we agreed on all of the possibilities, and grouped them into categories that represented essentially equivalent outcomes, we took each in turn and considered further. The rule was: given that this event has happened, however unlikely, what could reasonably happen next? We repeated the process for each outcome, generating new sets of outcomes. Before things got out of hand, I asked for some large flip-chart paper, and started mapping out the growing branches of this "decision tree" so everyone could see it.

As an objective exercise, it worked; pretty soon, everyone was enthusiastically "playing the game." As the tree expanded, I added sheets to the drawing, Scotch-taping them around the wall as space on the table was quickly consumed. Only one person disagreed with this approach, and that was Professor Gitay, as noted, who could not consider any idea that contradicted his own. He soon quit the Committee rather than be a party to the proceedings any longer. All the others were relieved to have some way to make progress, so we had a fairly enthusiastic participation.

✡ ✡ ✡

Of course, there was much continued discussion about the *Dakar* buoy, as any branch of the decision tree had to somehow account for its appearance at Han Yunis, and its uncrushed condition. The freshly broken cable and lack of biological growth on the buoy's surface were also key facts that had to be part of any solution. All previous studies came to the strong conclusion that the buoy was attached to the sub until shortly before it was found, and it was held underwater so it didn't get enough light to foster sea growth but wasn't so deep that it was crushed. That was the key set of circumstances that led many to believe the ship was in shallow water somewhere.

But the last position reported by the *Dakar*, and its planned route over the ensuing hours, was in very deep water. Was there some way the ship could have sunk in deep water, yet still produce the buoy as discovered? I was thinking about this, and listening to Tom's description of submarine sinkings, and mulling over the environmental studies we saw at the Weizmann Institute, when a scenario came to mind that just might fit.

The buoy was not crushed, but it clearly showed some damage, consistent with being forcibly ejected from its basket in the submarine's deck. The kink in the buoy wire corresponded to the top of a curved pipe (called a "horn"), which could have occurred when the shock of ejection stretched the wire in the horn. The antenna was probably broken by a pin that held everything in place, again as the buoy was ejected from its basket. The garbled Morse code signals heard near Cyprus could have been from the buoy, transmitting weakly with a broken antenna. All of this sounded as though the buoy was pushed out of its basket at or just before the time the ship imploded in deep water.

But what about the lack of sea growth and the freshly broken wire? Was there another explanation?

We decided to consider what might actually happen to the structure if the ship imploded, or if the deck was twisted due to hull compression to the point that equipment became dislodged. In the case of the buoy, the assembly consisted of nearly two hundred meters of heavy steel wire wound on a large steel reel, passing through a horn (guide pipe), and attached to the buoy. All of this was contained in a basket, or cage. If the buoy was forcibly ejected, the wire and reel could easily come along. It turned out that the weight of this extra gear was almost exactly the same as the extra flotation in the buoy, so that the buoy, wire, horn, and reel together would tend to be at the edge of sinking or floating. This condition is called "neutral buoyancy"; any extra weight or reduction in buoyancy would cause everything to sink.

But buoyancy does not remain constant in the ocean; many factors affect this, and the most important one tends to be water temperature. The tale of my first nearly disastrous dive as ship's diving officer taught me a lesson: floating objects will tend to sink if the water gets warmer. Of course, the surface of the Mediterranean is quite warm, especially in the summer, but it cools off considerably as one goes deeper. Temperatures on the surface vary from an average of 28 degrees Centigrade (82 Fahrenheit) in the summer to 17 Centigrade (63 Fahrenheit) in the winter; however, the temperature drops to a constant of around 14 Centigrade (57 Fahrenheit) a few hundred meters deep, year-round. There are also thermal variations as a result of day–night changes, mixing due to currents and winds, salinity changes, and other factors, but this drop in temperature from the surface is the main feature. This means that something that tends to sink at the surface, especially in the summer, would gain buoyancy as it dropped to colder waters below; if it was nearly neutral to begin with, it just might hover at some modest depth, and stay there indefinitely.

Could this be what happened to the buoy? Calculations based on its size told us that the buoyancy could change by as much as three kilograms from surface to the deeper level in the summer, a pretty significant gain. So, this led to the following scenario: the *Dakar* sank somewhere in deep water. Just before

The INS *Dakar,* underway from Gosport, England. (Courtesy Yoram Bar-Yam)

Captain Yaacov Ra'anan, commanding officer of the INS *Dakar*. (Courtesy Oded Ra'anan)

Abraham ("Boomie") Barkay, first officer on the INS *Dakar*, with his young wife, Chava. (Courtesy Chava Barkay)

Isaac Marcovici, twenty-year-old seaman mechanic on the INS *Dakar*. (Courtesy Michael Marcovici)

Crewmen boarding the *Dakar* in Gosport for their final voyage. (Courtesy Oded Ra'anan)

First Officer Barkay salutes as the *Dakar* gets underway. This is one of the last photos of the crewmen of the *Dakar*. (Courtesy Chava Barkay)

The emergency rescue buoy of the *Dakar*, found on the beach at Han Yunnis in Gaza over a year after the ship vanished. (Courtesy Nauticos)

U.S. Department of Defense representative Richard Boyd (left), with Israeli *Dakar* project manager, Yechiel Ga'ash. Yechiel searched for the *Dakar* for nearly two decades. (Courtesy Nauticos)

Nauticos vice president and *Dakar* operations manager, Tom Dettweiler. (Courtesy Nauticos)

Admiral Gideon Raz, retired deputy commander of the Israeli Navy and first officer of *Dakar*'s sister ship, the INS *Leviathan*. (Courtesy Gideon Raz)

Donna and John Coombs, shipmates on the *Dakar* search expedition, enjoying a tour of the island of Cyprus after the successful mission. (Courtesy John and Donna Coombs)

The EDT ship *Argonaut,* which along with the EDT *Flying Enterprise* conducted successful search operations in 1999. The following year, another EDT ship, the *EAS,* was used for salvage of the *Dakar* bridge. (Courtesy Nauticos)

Deploying the Williamson & Associates AMS-60 deep-towed side-scan sonar. (Courtesy Nauticos)

John Coombs and shipmate working at sea. (Courtesy Nauticos)

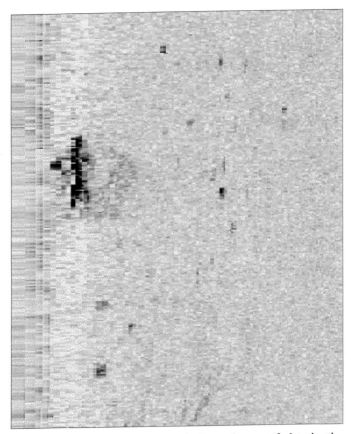

The side-scan sonar target B-310, which was later verified to be the *Dakar*. In the crude image of just a few pixels, one can see the main hull, the sail (conning tower) laying to one side, the tail cone laying to the other side, and a circular "down blast crater," created when tons of metal and an entrained stream of water hit the bottom with great force. Surrounding the wreck is a "debris field" of various sized objects, including the bridge fin (later recovered). (Courtesy Nauticos)

The bridge gyrocompass of the *Dakar* rests on the silty bottom, still indicating the course the ship was following when it sunk. (Courtesy Nauticos)

The bridge fin of the *Dakar,* resting on the bottom before recovery. This was the first piece of wreckage seen by the search team. Note the cone-shaped ladder enclosure, a feature unique to the *Dakar.* This four-ton piece was later salvaged and today serves as a memorial to the sixty-nine lost sailors. (Courtesy Nauticos)

The *Dakar*'s anchor, still housed in the undamaged bow of the ship. (Courtesy Nauticos)

A section of the *Dakar*'s two-inch-thick steel pressure hull, originally smooth, but twisted and extruded like taffy by the force of implosion. (Courtesy Nauticos)

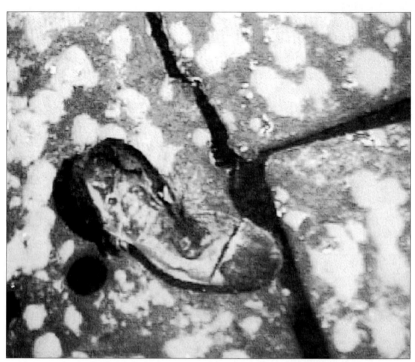

A crew member's shoe lies on the deck of the ship. Though organic matter is normally consumed by the sea rather quickly, materials such as tanned leather, metals, ceramics, and even some kinds of paper can last for decades or even thousands of years in the cold, quiet, deep ocean. (Courtesy Nauticos)

The bridge fin of the *Dakar* is gently placed on the dock in Haifa, recovered after over thirty years on the bottom of the Mediterranean Sea. (Courtesy Nauticos)

The bridge fin as it now appears in Haifa, as a memorial to the men of the *Dakar.* (Courtesy Shelley Wachsmann)

This plaque was placed on the bow of the ship, honoring the men of the INS *Dakar*: "Never Forgotten." (Courtesy Nauticos)

sinking, or as it imploded, at some depth shallower than 326 meters, the buoy was ejected from its basket, damaged, and trailing wreckage by its wire, including the horn and reel. At that depth, it had enough buoyancy to float; since it was wintertime, it probably made it to or near the cool surface. Weak transmissions from its broken, partly submerged antenna, were heard in the vicinity of Cyprus where currents took it during the first days after the sinking.

During the daytime, as the surface warmed, the buoy probably sank to colder waters; this is consistent with the fact that the garbled signals were only heard at night. After a few days, the transmitter battery was exhausted and the SOS signals ceased. As the spring came, and then summer, the surface became warmer yet, and the buoy lost buoyancy and hovered, somewhere just below the photo zone, but above its crush depth. In this condition, the buoy wandered around the Mediterranean at the whim of the currents, detectable by no one.

A year after sinking, as the currents by chance carried the buoy toward land near Gaza, the wreckage trailing below the buoy touched ground off-shore. Maybe it got tangled in some other bit of wreckage on the bottom, or just started dragging, like an anchor. Now the wreckage is lodged in the surf zone near shore, and at some point, the weakened, kinked wire, damaged a year before when the buoy was thrust out of its basket, failed. The buoy quickly washed ashore, and within days was found by the famous fisherman with a freshly broken wire and no sea growth, and eventually came to us.

Everyone was interested in how the buoy might have gotten to the beach in Gaza, so we went back to the test buoys that were dropped all around the Mediterranean and tracked. Sometimes you have to look at things differently from the way they are presented to you. Everybody focused on the complicated and random-looking paths the buoys took from one place to another, but I chose to ignore that and simply looked at where they started and where they went ashore. What I found was that buoys dropped along the *Dakar*'s intended route, but not far from where it was last heard, almost all eventually found their way to the Gaza shore, after an average time of eighty-three days. One of them took over four hundred days. Buoys that were dropped a little to the south or farther from Israel went down to the Egyptian coast west of Suez after about sixty days on average. Those dropped closer to the Israeli coast ended up going north in some cases around the island of Cyprus before going ashore at Syria, in an average of ninety-five days. This was all consistent with the outcome of the *Dakar* buoy landing in Gaza, having started off along the submarine's original route, and taking many months to get there.

So it was plausible, and opened the door for consideration of the deep water possibility.

Based on all of this discussion, Captain Kaisari proposed that we consider three distinct "threads," or scenarios regarding the buoy, and include them in our decision tree work. These were:

1. The buoy was attached to the deck of the ship for some time after the sinking. This implied that the ship lay in water depth less than the collapse depth of the buoy (about 325 meters). This was the conclusion of the previous committees.
2. The buoy was attached to the cable, but deployed to some length (up to 180 meters) for some time after the sinking. This implied that the ship lay in water depth less than the collapse depth of the buoy plus the length of the buoy cable (about 500 meters).
3. The buoy was released from the ship at or near the time of the sinking, possibly with the cable and some wreckage attached. This implied that the ship could be at any depth.

Finally, after nearly two weeks for us, and three decades for some of the Committee members, we had a new approach to take. We eagerly set about the business of filling out the decision tree branches, hoping the process would lead us to new and better answers.

✡ ✡ ✡

One nagging question that was a hotbed of speculation and charged with emotion repeatedly occupied our deliberations: was Captain Ra'anan a fool to speed for home? Or, more charitably, what was his purpose in being so far ahead of schedule?

The most popular theories held that he rushed home from Gibraltar because he wanted to break a speed record for a submerged crossing of the Mediterranean Sea. Ra'anan's position reports showed he made very fast time, averaging about eight knots. He asked for permission to arrive five days early, on January 28. Headquarters in Haifa told him to delay twenty-four hours, until January 29, and the Navy would move up the arrival ceremony from the original date of February 2. Even after that, his position reports showed he was driving the *Dakar* at record-breaking speed. On the morning of January 24, she was just southeast of Crete; at such a pace, she would be in Israeli waters by January 26, even earlier than he had requested.

Some felt Captain Ra'anan was taking unorthodox risks in racing for Haifa at speeds beyond those recommended in England, and that the Navy was not happy with the pressure this placed on ship and crew. If he was simply trying to break a record, this was a dubious reason for such a risk. Whatever the opinions, he was as much as three days ahead of the accelerated schedule by his position reports, and must have had some purpose in mind.

What would he do with the extra three days? The most popular theories held that he picked one of three choices: diverting to the Aegean Sea to conduct tracking exercises on commercial shipping, a common training practice for Israeli submarines; running south to the coast of Egypt to test the new Tavlit electronics equipment; or running to the Israeli coast to conduct training drills in home waters. All of these ideas were consistent with the interpreted evidence of the buoy, that the ship sank in shallow waters. But were these good enough reasons to ignore or rationalize his Sailing Orders to make a direct route to Haifa?

Other, more inventive theories, held that the ship was captured and taken to another location. Or that Ra'anan's position reports were falsified and he was really somewhere else all along, for unknown reasons. Or even that there was a government conspiracy afoot, possibly a scheme by ultraconservatives to create an excuse to go back to war with Egypt. Psychics, mystics, and fringe elements weighed in with ideas tied to alien encounters or a Mediterranean Bermuda Triangle. Naval officials were not the only ones with these questions. There was also Ra'anan's family, including his sons who would grow up under the cloud of their father's death at the helm of the great *Dakar* that went down with sixty-nine countrymen on board.

The Committee spent a lot of time discussing the psychology of Ra'anan and his crew. The conclusion of every prior committee was that the ship had sunk in shallow water somewhere, and thus was way off its intended and ordered course. Therefore, the ship was either captured and taken somewhere else and sunk, or the captain decided to go somewhere else. It was hard to explain how such a hand-picked, highly trusted, dedicated man would disobey essentially direct orders with Israel's second new submarine. Prior committees developed psychological profiles and tried to explain how the captain could have made such a choice. After all, he was very independent-minded and a strong personality, known for questioning his superiors; these very traits made him an attractive choice for leadership in the Israeli Defense Force, which valued initiative and independent thinking. On the one hand, it was hard to find the leeway in his orders that he could have honestly rationalized using his extra time to conduct training far from his directed path. Could the pressure of his situation have been so great that he went off without having to rationalize it?

Fortunately, our accepted approach helped us avoid fruitless speculation and helped us to methodically assess the pros and cons of each reasonable theory. We took each in turn, and tried to imagine every reason for or against such a scenario. Why would the captain decide to visit the Greek Islands southeast of the Aegean Sea for exercises? On the supporting side, there were several arguments. It was a common training area for the flotilla. There was, at the time, a large volume of shipping traffic in the area because the Suez Canal was closed, resulting in much less traffic around Israel. He had spare time, and had recently been informed that he could not arrive as early as he asked. And, finally, there are reported, but uncharted, submerged reefs that could have been the source of a collision leading to sinking in shallow water.

On the other hand, Ra'anan would be risking a late arrival in Haifa, although with three days to spare, it was a small risk. He was on his track to that point and reported no deviation up to the last communication; it would have been an abrupt change in course for him to head due north at that point. Plus, he was not on an operational mission, but on a delivery mission, with a specified track in the Sailing Orders. It could be argued that it was within his purview to choose that option without violating any orders; nor was he specifically required to report this activity. It was common to be given a planned route in the Sailing Orders, but to make reasonable deviations as the circumstances dictated. Still, this was quite a significant deviation, and he would have been stretching the boundaries of his initiative beyond reasonable limits in the minds of many of his superiors. Clearly, we could go back and forth on this point without generating any new information or coming to any conclusions that could not be easily refuted.

Or, why would Ra'anan decide to visit the Egyptian coast for exercises and intelligence collections? On the supporting side, he had an upgraded ELINT (electronics intelligence) system on board, with the project lead engineer accompanying. He had spare time, and had recently been informed that he could not arrive as early as he asked. It was not a large deviation from his track, certainly not as drastic as going to the Aegean. There was an attraction to the area from an intelligence standpoint. Acquisition of ELINT intelligence would have been a dramatic accomplishment. There was no air search around the area that might have revealed wreckage. Caveats, though, were that Egyptian radars were low, and could not be heard outside the fifty-mile limit specified in the sailing orders, so he would have had to interpret his orders very generously, or intentionally disobey them, to gather any useful information. Other questions against this scenario parallel the Aegean scenario: how could he rationalize such a choice and fail to report this extraordinary deviation from plan? In this case, one could further speculate that he didn't want to alert Egypt to his intentions by making radio broadcasts, but that would clearly violate his orders.

Why possibly head to Cyprus for exercises? There were reasons similar to the Aegean scenario to support this, and it would require only a modest deviation from the direct course, easy to justify. He could possibly receive radar signals from Nicosia on his ELINT, with a small deviation from direct course. And he could have gone around to the north of Cyprus, gathering Syrian intelligence on the way south to Haifa. This, however, was well out of the scope of his orders, and he had no operational or training reasons to go there, except for hearing the Nicosia radar.

Or why continue along his track and arrive in the vicinity of Haifa early? This would not contradict his orders at all, and he could spend time near the Israeli coast evaluating the ELINT system. He asked for information about radars in the vicinity, so this seemed plausible. There was, however, little shipping in the area useful for training exercises. And there was no shallow water along that direct route that would offer a location for the sinking consistent with the interpreted buoy evidence.

By the time we exhausted all reasonable possibilities, and felt that we had identified all of the likely outcomes, we had quite a large and complicated decision tree, with many branches. In the evenings, with the help of Tom and Dick Boyd (who joined us in the middle of the second week), I tried to reduce all of the discussion and debate into a few succinct statements that captured the essence of each point. The "three threads" identified by Mike Kaisari focused on the buoy, and as they all related to the question of the depth of the *Dakar* this became known as the "vertical problem." The remaining issues related to the location, regardless of depth, and became known as the "horizontal problem." Of course, the two had to intersect in a consistent manner. The horizontal problem was the basis of the decision tree, and it consisted of a collection of statements and alternatives that we crafted as a result of our investigations:

1. The last known position was at 1/24 0600 at 34° 16′ N, 26° 26′ E. He could have had a visual and/or radar observation of the island of Gavdo 1/23 1600. We have no reason to doubt this position within normal navigation accuracy.
2. The last report was at 1/25 0001 (eighteen hours later). The most likely speed and direction was along the track at about 8 knots. Possible alternatives:
    a. He could have changed speed to as low as 5 knots, or as high as 8.5 knots, while remaining submerged under normal operations.
    b. He could have changed course at this point to the northwest (Aegean), the southeast (Egypt), or due east (Cyprus). These all led to further alternatives.
    c. He could have had an error in steering, causing some deviation from base course.
3. He could have lost communications between 1/25 0001 and 0600 because he missed his report. Possible alternatives:
    a. He could have sunk during that time, through collision, accident, or enemy action. The most likely speed and direction was along the track at about 8 knots.

    a1. He could have changed speed to as low as 5 knots, or as high as 8.5 knots, while remaining submerged under normal operations.

    a2. He could have changed course at this point to the northwest (Aegean), the southeast (Egypt), or due east (Cyprus).

    a3. He could have had an error in steering, causing some deviation from base course.

  b. He chose not to communicate for tactical reasons (e.g., being in the vicinity of enemy vessels/airplanes). Note that this is a higher probability if he chose a southern route and was near to Egyptian waters, traveling at a speed between 5 and 8.5 knots.

  c. He had a problem that disabled communications, but he did not sink. Examples include: antenna failure (note that the antenna is a single point of failure), or, collision with the sail, but not an immediate sinking.

    It is unlikely that he drifted very far without sinking, since if on the surface he would have had other alternatives to communicate. It seems very unlikely that he would have remained alive, adrift, and submerged for more than an hour or two after an accident.

4. The ship could have communicated at 1/25 1220. The communication seemed normal, but was incomplete. There is some probability that this was a genuine communication. Possible implications:

  a. The ship was proceeding along the track submerged at a speed between 5 and 8.5 knots. This assumes he (for some reason) felt he communicated successfully at 1/25 0600, or he felt his missed communication did not require him to surface (in spite of the briefing from the flotilla commander).

  b. The ship had surfaced after failing to communicate sometime after the last planned transmission, and proceeded at maximum surfaced speed (11.5 knots).

  c. The ship was heading to some other area or had a steering error, as mentioned before, proceeding at 5 to 11 knots, depending on circumstances (considered to be a low probability).

5. Since there were no genuine ensuing communications (eliminating the very suspect 1/26 1755 message), the sinking most likely occurred within six to eight hours of the last genuine communication. Alternatives:

    a. The ship was proceeding along the track submerged at a speed between 5 and 8.5 knots for up to eight hours.

    b. The ship was proceeding along the track surfaced at a speed up to 11.5 knots for up to eight hours. There is very little reason for this, since he had communicated successfully up to that point.

    c. If he failed to communicate after eight hours, but was still operating, he would proceed along track, probably on the surface, at maximum speed (up to 11.5 knots).

    d. The ship was heading to some other area or had a steering error, as mentioned before, proceeding at 5 to 11 knots, depending on circumstances.

6. At the time of the casualty leading to the sinking, the ship could have:

    a. Sunk almost immediately.

    b. Proceeded toward Haifa at best speed until sinking.

    c. Proceeded toward nearest landfall at best speed until sinking.

    d. Drifted with the current for several hours. Considered to be unlikely.

I also collected the array of sketches on flip-chart paper, taped to the walls all around the conference room, and converted them into clean drawings, indicating each path, or branch of the decision tree, and each node, or place, where the tree branched. These nodes represented decision points where alternatives caused the scenario to diverge. In the end, we had one starting point: the last known position of the *Dakar,* and thirty-seven reasonable outcomes, all ending in the sinking of the vessel. There were nearly sixty branches in the tree, representing steps in each scenario leading to outcomes. The picture on the next page only shows the beginning of this tree, and only includes three of the outcomes, so the complexity of our problem should be evident.

By Thursday of the second week, we were making much progress, but it was time to start bringing the process to some conclusion. The tone was set very well by Gideon Raz. I considered him to be a terrific leader because he recognized that success could only be achieved by allowing others to do their job, and he took the role of facilitating that rather than trying to be the source of that success himself.

The entire proceedings of the Committee were conducted in English. However, from time to time, the Committee members struggled to express themselves and had to have some side discussions in Hebrew. They would always apologize and ask our permission if they could clarify their issue with each other by speaking in Hebrew for a few moments. And then one of them

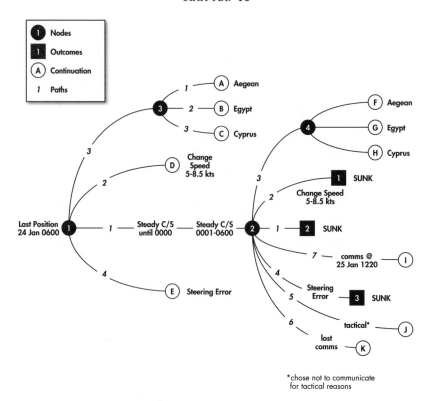

Figure 1. A small portion of the decision tree used to help assess the probabilities of different outcomes for the loss of *Dakar*. Three outcomes are shown here; the entire tree included thirty-seven possible outcomes.

would relate the gist of that discussion. When these occasions arose, they were very careful not to have any side discussions that appeared, in any way, to be hiding anything. So there was a lot of trust.

Tom and I generally shared ideas after the meetings. He is quieter than I am, and would rather not speak up without a lot of consideration, preferring to keep his counsel. I was more willing to put ideas on the table and create an atmosphere for discussion, so I fell into that role more readily. Tom and I always worked successfully together because he is far more experienced and effective at operating in the field, but has a healthy grounding in analysis, whereas my strength has always been in the analytical end, but I also have experience in the field. It is a good combination because one person cannot be good at everything, and it helps to have an appreciation for another's talents.

Our visit to the Weizmann Institute the day before had offered a little digression from sitting in the conference room, which was very helpful to us. What started as a way to organize our discussion became a means to a solution:

to use the decision tree to help us make a prediction and select an area to search. The way to do that was to examine each node or decision point in the decision tree and consider the likelihood of each of those steps taking place. If you do that, then you can determine the likelihood of each outcome.

I spent some time describing each of the decision points in narrative form, including all of the relevant information we had collected, and then I created a questionnaire in which all of the key decision points were identified. I circulated these papers, and asked the group to rate, on a scale of 1 to 5, the likelihood of each event on the decision tree. The rule was to assume that all of the events up to any given point had occurred, and then to judge the likelihood of each ensuing alternative. We took a huge leap to assume that those judgments by reasonably objective experts represented statistical probabilities. We could not justify this formally to a statistician, but we felt that it would reflect the collective wisdom of the body of experts in a systematic and objective manner.

To reduce everything to some conclusions, I took everybody's rankings, averaged them, and combined them through the decision tree to yield the likelihood of each of the thirty-seven outcomes. This would represent the probability that each branch of the tree actually occurred. But we could do a further consolidation by grouping the outcomes that predicted similar locations for the ship, and could be combined in the same search area.

At the end of Thursday, I had all of the results and presented them to the group. By then, we were all so supportive of the process that I was confident we would collectively accept any outcome the numbers justified. Our conclusions:

1. There was no strong evidence for the *Dakar* being in shallow water based on the buoy; in fact, our buoy findings slightly favored a deep-water scenario. This was important, since previous committees had arrived at strong conclusions to the contrary.
2. It was 70 percent likely that the ship sank somewhere along the direct route to Haifa in deep water.

I can still see the look of satisfaction and relief on the faces of the Committee members. To have reached such a strong consensus in spite of the original differences of opinion and historical precedent was a major breakthrough.

Still, we had to work out where exactly to search. Tom was the one who put together the search plan in the end, based on the most likely courses and speeds favored by the decision tree. In the end, we cast aside the sophisticated software and navigation analysis techniques that were so effective in the Japanese I-52 submarine discovery, in favor of simple computations based on a few bits of information. But the process came to a conclusion based on the same experience, analytical approach, and leadership common to all of Nauticos' discoveries.

With the week's work reaching a satisfying conclusion, we set out to see some of the country with a clear conscience. On the one hand, we were just tourists. However, the opportunity to see historical places relating to events spanning many thousands of years helped us gain a little perspective on the quest for the *Dakar*. For people used to thinking in terms of millennia, a mere three decades is a blink of an eye.

2/28 Friday: What a day! We took a bus tour to the Dead Sea and the fortress at Masada today. The route went through Jerusalem, which was a tour in itself. Once we left Tel Aviv, we found the road lined with orange groves, source of the famous Jaffa oranges we have been enjoying. Next, we passed the Ben-Gurion Airport, which used to be called the Lod Airport after the nearby ancient town. We also saw lots of vineyards along the way.

Next we came to Latrun, which was famous in the War of Independence as the key fortress blocking access to Jerusalem. After several unsuccessful attacks, the 100,000 Jews in the city were finally relieved through a bypass road through the mountains, using mules and manual labor. Latrun is also the site of an old Trappist monastery, and the legendary town of one of the thieves crucified with Jesus.

We noted our entry into the West Bank, and the Judean Mountains. Carcasses of trucks and armored vehicles left over from the War were preserved along the road as a memorial to the battles fought there (presumably the actual trucks which didn't get through). They were all freshly painted with primer red, so they looked neat and tidy, and more effective as a result. We also saw a kibbutz, and some beautiful neighborhoods along the hillsides.

Leaving Jerusalem, we passed the Mount of Olives and saw the towers of the Old City from a distance. Besides its role in Christianity, we were told that both the Islamic and Judean faiths believe that the Messiah will descend from that mountain. It also separates the city from the desert, and from its 850-meter height we began our descent to the Dead Sea, 400 meters below sea level.

On the road to Jericho, we saw the Bedouins, with their camels and desert camps. The desert had a tinge of green on the northern slopes, a brief condition in winter when there's a bit of rain. We passed the Inn of the Good Samaritan, ostensibly built on the site of the biblical event. There was also a stone marking our descent past sea level, with quite a ways to go. Off in the distance was a small church which, according to Islamic belief, is the burial place of Moses (the Old Testament disagrees).

Jericho, to the North as we passed, is considered to be the first organized city in the world. From that spot, we saw Jesus' mountain of temptation, the mountains of Moab in Jordan, and our first view of the Dead Sea.

As we passed along the east bank of the Sea, we saw several oases, green with palm trees and shrubs in stark contrast with the dry, red desert. We stopped to look at the caves which held the Dead Sea Scrolls for 2,000 years, which I thought was awesome. We learned that Cleopatra claimed areas around the Sea, valued for its healthy mineral treatments and (even better) the balsam trees which are a source of embalming fluid. The sandstone cliffs are breathtaking, even from below.

Finally, we reached Masada. This was a fortress built by King Herod to help defend Judea from Egypt and the Arabs in Mesopotamia. It also served as a possible refuge, and included an opulent palace (complete with Roman baths and mosaics) on the 450-meter high plateau. Later, around 50 AD, it was taken by Jewish zealots, who were resisting Roman rule. In 73 AD they were attacked after a long siege and chose to kill themselves rather than surrender to the Romans. Since suicide is a mortal sin, they killed their families until there were ten left, at which time they drew lots to select one to kill the rest. He was obliged to commit the sin of suicide. They have found what they think are the actual lots!

Rediscovered in 1938, the site is under extensive archaeological study, and is accessible to tourists by a (very long) footpath or a cable car. Besides the moving stories of events that took place there, the engineering and construction is remarkable. The ingenuity of the Roman baths and the way they were supplied with water was fascinating. There were dams in the surrounding canyons, and complicated networks of cisterns, pipes, and channels to collect the mere three inches of rain which the desert averages in a year. Herod's palace was a three-story affair hanging over the cliff, and it appeared to have been opulent. There are remains of beautiful tile mosaics in some of the buildings.

Leaving Masada, we headed to Ein Gedi, a spa on the Dead Sea. We bathed in the warm sulfur springs, covered ourselves with "special" black mud, and floated in the Sea. The water had a cool surface layer, probably an inch or so of fresh water from the recent rains, covering the warm, briny water below. The brine was so salty it was almost thick, and you could see the wavy fluid as you swished it with your hand. Anything that floated or touched the surface developed salt pillars, almost like sculptures. The place makes the Great Salt Lake seem bland.

3/1 Saturday: Today Yechiel picked us up at the hotel and we started another amazing tour. We drove up the coast to Haifa, where *Dakar* was to sail, and continued on to Nazareth. The town is fairly large today, and has an old section which is probably laid out much as it was during the time of Jesus. Although the buildings are all more recent, they are made mostly of the same limestone seen everywhere. One relic of the old era is the Church of the Annunciation. As was described to us, a small church was built on the site, which fell into decay over time. Recently, a new (and very elaborate) building, walls, and gardens were built, containing the remains of the original church. The new edifice, besides being huge, is very ornate and decorated with modern mosaics and artwork from various countries. I really enjoyed seeing the old stones of the modest original church, and imagining the things that Jesus and his family may have done on that very spot. I also enjoyed walking the narrow streets, feeling the history. The new church, however, was something of a distraction. It was showy, overly elaborate, and, to me, missed the point. It reinforced my feeling that Jesus was more interested in being followed than worshipped.

Next we drove to Tiberias, and the Sea of Galilee, known in Israel as Lake Kinneret. We had a great lunch sitting right at the water's edge, eating fish (mullet) and bread (pita) that was probably similar to meals of 2,000 years ago. We also had "black beer," which is sort of like root beer. You could see to the far shore, and the Golan Heights on the other side. The strategic advantage of the Heights is obvious, and one can imagine how uncomfortable it would feel to have Syrian guns looking down over the near shore and city. Now, of course, everything you can see is Israel, except for parts of the snow-covered mountains way to the Northeast.

After lunch, we headed north around the Sea to Tabgha, one of the traditionally attributed locations of the rock upon which Jesus laid the loaves and fishes to feed the multitude. A primitive church was built around 350 AD, using the actual Rock as an altar. It was decorated with tile mosaics, and rebuilt in the Byzantine style around 450 AD. Destroyed during the Persian invasion in the early 600s, it was hidden for over 1,300 years. In 1932, archeologists unearthed its remains, including the Stone altar, and built a monastery around it. The Benedictine Monks care for it. You can see the Rock and look at the original tiles. The new monastery is unassuming and quite the opposite of the church in Nazareth. I think it served the purpose of providing a place for people to come and worship or meditate, or just look, while not detracting from the object of the site.

We reversed course back to Tiberias, and continued along the Sea to its southern end. There, we entered the Jordan Valley and saw the place where the Jordan leaves the Sea of Galilee. There is a facility there for baptizing, and it was crowded with dunkees. The road south along the Jordan was lined with olive trees, and there was a kibbutz to the East in what used to be Jordanian territory. Evidence of the wars was still around, including a destroyed power plant on the Jordanian side of the river.

As we entered the green hills of Samaria, we came to a real treat. In Bet-Shean there are extensive ruins of Roman amphitheaters and other structures, covering many acres. They are being slowly reconstructed into a park. Later, on the way back to the coast, we passed through the valley famous for the battle between David and Goliath. I imagined the armies arrayed in the fields there and the history that was made in that place.

Jerusalem

Buoyed and inspired by our country tours, we began our third week in Israel with two final tasks. We had to propose a search area based on our prior week's analysis, which was mainly Tom's job. And we had to prepare a briefing for the admirals who were coming to hear what we thought, which was my job, with Dick Boyd's help.

The search area was a complicated matter. First of all, although we had a strong consensus arising from our efforts over the prior two weeks, this did not tell us exactly where to search, and it left the door open for alternatives. We were going against the conventional wisdom; in fact, our result was contrary to the original mission of our visit: to recommend where the *NR-1* submarine should search. We had to present the good news that we thought we knew where the *Dakar* was to be found, but the bad news that it was much too deep for the *NR-1* to search.

After considering this dilemma, we decided that the best plan was to work up a search in the primary area in deep water, and present the justifications for that. But, also, we had to admit that our results were uncertain, and there was a smaller probability that the *Dakar* did sink in a shallow area, accessible to the *NR-1*. Since the *NR-1* was operating in the area on another mission, and there was extra time in its schedule, it would make sense to investigate these lower-probability areas while we had the chance. So, we also worked up search areas specifically for the *NR-1* as part of the presentation. This focused on some areas around Cyprus that had never been searched but were within *NR-1*'s reach. Our analysis rated that as an 11 percent probability—small, but a chance. We also noted one interesting area along the extended track of the *Dakar* that was relatively shallow: the Eratosthenes Seamount. This dramatic rise in the sea floor, south of Cyprus, had a small area within the depth capability of the search submarine, so it was a prospect, however unlikely. Inspired by all of the biblical references surrounding us, we referred to this spot as "Mount Ararat."

We summarized our findings in a written report that detailed all of our investigations and analysis:

> Through a structured analytical approach, this committee concluded that the highest probability is that the INS *Dakar* will be found lying in deep water along its intended track, which is a new outcome as compared to the previous two committees' findings. Much of the buoy evidence which strongly steered those earlier outcomes has now been drawn into question, and alternate scenarios which support the deep water site without contradicting buoy evidence have been presented. Although the *NR-1* cannot search the high probability areas, the identified areas within its range cannot be ruled out until they have been covered. They represent a significant contribution to the search effort until deep water search assets can be brought into play.
>
> There is very little direct, hard evidence supporting this investigation, and the INS *Dakar* may yet hold some surprises for us in the final chapter.

On Monday, Admiral Krol arrived, and we had our first official dinner. The gathering included the U.S. Naval Attaché with his wife, two of his assistants, the admiral, two *NR-1* submariners, and a liaison officer. Although it is true that the U.S. Navy folks did not spend any time with us until the admiral arrived, I came to enjoy their company and appreciated the wonderful hospitality they showed us, especially during our visit to Jerusalem. From that point forward, our schedule was filled with trips, meetings, presentations, dinners, and little spare time. So we wrapped up our preparations for the formal presentation on Thursday the best we could, and looked forward to the next two days.

On Tuesday, we were scheduled to visit the naval base at Haifa. Yechiel made sure we were not attached to the admiral's party so that we could have some flexibility. We had a chance to see the survey ships that the Israeli Navy had been using for hydrographic work and the *Dakar* searches, then took a drive around Haifa before joining the entourage at the Haifa Naval Museum. Of greatest interest to us was the actual *Dakar* buoy on display as a memorial, surrounded by photographs of the lost sailors. We had seen many pictures of the buoy, but seeing it for real helped make our endeavor a little more tangible. Tom and I were both moved by the photos. This was the first time we had seen the images of the lost men, and at that moment the project became much more than a very challenging job. The pictures are on display on the Web site of the Israeli Submariners Association (http://www.dolphin.org.il/), and I have looked at them many times since. I am always reminded of that day.

On the way back to Tel Aviv, we stopped at the huge port city of Caesarea, which was built by King Herod. The two-thousand-year-old city has been largely ravaged by time, and much of the stone rubble is under water. However, some structures are being refurbished including a four-thousand-seat theater. There is also the largely intact remains of a huge Crusader castle, built with the stones of the Roman structures over its old foundations. The evening events included dinner at a seafood restaurant on the harbor in Jaffa, the oldest port in Israel (and maybe the world).

But the best was yet to come. Wednesday was our scheduled tour of Jerusalem, which we eagerly anticipated. Our glimpse of the golden limestone city during our earlier trip to Masada was tantalizing. To add to the excitement, we were seriously cautioned about travel procedures and the dangers we should be aware of while visiting there. By presidential directive, U.S. citizens in official capacities could not be accompanied by official Israeli personnel into East Jerusalem (known as the Old City) or the West Bank. It seems that the Israelis were more of a target of terrorism than Americans. Also, our five-page travel orders mostly addressed policies and cautions regarding travel in these areas. As if danger from traditional terrorists was not adequate, our orders noted: "Ultra-orthodox Jewish neighborhoods should be avoided on Saturdays (Shabbat). Assaults on secular visitors, either in cars or 'immodestly dressed,' have been known to occur."

To reduce our exposure, our group traveled together in a special Chevy Suburban van, which was rumored to be bulletproof. We did not have occasion to verify this. Because of the VIP status of Admiral Krol, we had opportunities to see sites that were not open to many visitors, and certainly not the general public.

My account of our visit is based on descriptions by Commander Richard Holzknecht, the U.S. Naval Attaché. Rich had been in Israel for a couple of years, and as part of his official duties he frequently took people to the city, so he was an excellent tour guide. He had made a serious study of the history, religion, and culture of the city; also, he tried his best to distinguish fact from legend (or, in some cases, outright fiction) that some tour guides are known to pass on. My Christian training probably lent a heavy slant to my recollections, although I am fascinated that most everyone in the world can trace their religious roots to common places, people, and legends associated with this city. We were referring to a book called *The Holy Land* by Jerome Murphy-O'Connor (Oxford University Press, 1980), an authoritative text on the subject (not just a travel guide), I am told. My journal of the visit reads:

We followed the same route to the city that I described the other day. We learned that Latrun, besides being a strategic location during the

War of Independence, has always been a spot to control access to Jerusalem. During the final attack on the city by the Romans in 70 AD, Latrun was the staging point.

On the way, Rich made some calls to one of his many pals in the city, the chief of police on the Temple Mount. Apparently, when the Sixth Fleet was in town, Rich arranged for the chief to visit one of the aircraft carriers and observe flight operations. So he gives Rich special treatment on tours. Surprises were to follow.

Our first stop was the Mount of Olives. This place has great significance to the three major religions. It is revered as the place of the Ascension of Jesus by Christians. Jews, Muslims, and Christians all expect the Messiah to return to this place. From the heights, one has a fabulous view of the Old City Eastern Wall. In the valley that separates the Wall from the Mount of Olives, lies Gethsemane and many old tombs. The slopes are a major burial ground, for those lucky enough to be resting there when the Messiah returns someday. One used to be able to buy a spot there (for more than a few shekels), but I'm reasonably sure they're sold out. The Jewish aboveground tombs are littered with small stones, as it is the custom for visitors to place a stone on the lid when paying respects. There are many private homes on the mountainside, some of which include historical archaeological sites on the property.

The Eastern Wall as we see it today was rebuilt in the 1500s, and only a few stones can be seen from the Herodian era. The rubble from the earlier walls has piled up around the base, so that current ground level is much higher than earlier. As a consequence, we are only seeing the top half of the walls today, and excavations have revealed lower gates hidden in the slope. The Golden Gate is visible, but walled up by Muslims to help defend the holy places just inside from Crusader assaults. A Muslim cemetery also lies against the wall at that point, a way of thumbing their noses at the Crusaders.

The most prominent feature is, of course, the Dome of the Rock, which shines brightly golden in the sunshine (the roof was recently refurbished). The rock inside is the highest point on Temple Mount, and is revered as the place where Muhammad began his Night Journey and where Abraham offered the sacrifice of Isaac. To Muslims, it is the third most holy place in the world (besides Mecca and Medina. . . . I'm not sure how they score it). It was also the site of the First Temple (built by Solomon and destroyed by the Babylonians), and the Second Temple (built by Herod and destroyed by the Romans). But more on all that later.

We descended the Mount of Olives by a path to Gethsemane, first seeing the Church of Pater Nostre. In this church are over a hundred tiled plaques, about four feet tall, with the Lord's Prayer, each in a different language. Next we saw the traditional tombs of Malachai and Haggai, folks you may remember from the early Old Testament days. Since the tombs were on private property and nobody was home, we couldn't go in. But we saw the cave entrances from a gate just outside.

We passed along a number of Jewish cemeteries, and could walk among the tombs if we wished. Some were quite old, but others were very new-looking. All had various numbers of stones on the lids. We saw a crypt where, in Jewish tradition, corpses were placed after burial and allowed to decay to bones, at which time the bones were placed in the tomb with other deceased family members. This was called being "gathered with the fathers."

Next along was the Church of Dominus Flevit, or the Church of Tears, commemorating the spot where Jesus wept for Jerusalem, and, earlier, where he taught the disciples to pray. Also nearby is the Church of Mary Magdalene, a Russian Orthodox church.

Finally, we reached the Garden of Gethsemane. This has always been a significant place to me, and I really felt the power of it. I think this is mainly because it is a simple place, probably closer to its condition at the time of Jesus than many of the holy places in the area. "Gethsemane" is derived from the Aramaic *gath shemani*, which means "[olive] oil press." Thus, Gethsemane was an olive orchard and, in its day, it covered much of the lower slopes. Now there is a small fenced-in grove near the modern Church of Nations (the third basilica built on the site). The olive trees in the grove are incredibly gnarled, and are thought to be more than 1,500 years old. Since the trees were all cut down by the Romans, they are not the original trees growing during Jesus' time, but they may have sprung from the existing roots.

Nearby was a grotto that was probably visited by Jesus, and is claimed to be the site of the betrayal. We also visited Mary's tomb deep in caves, which had hundreds of ornate Arabian oil lamps hanging from the ceiling.

Our driver, Gadi, brought the Suburban down so we didn't have to walk back up. There is a continuation of the trail across the valley and up to the Eastern Wall, and I certainly would have walked it if it was up to me. We drove to the Lion's Gate, which is also known as Stephen's Gate since it was the site of the stoning of Stephen. It may be the start of the Via Dolorosa, the path that Jesus walked on the way to his Crucifixion, but we aren't sure about this. This is also the entrance to the Muslim Quarter of the Old City. We entered on foot and immediately came upon the Pools of Bethesda.

The pools were constructed in the third century BC, and were part of the water system of the city. Great cisterns supplied water to the Temple, which was needed for religious rites as well as more practical purposes. A lot of excavations have revealed some of the extent of these constructions. On the site is a small Crusader cathedral, which had great acoustics inside and had attracted an informal choir who entertained us for a few minutes. Having just learned about echo chambers and cathedrals, it was particularly interesting. This site is mentioned in the Bible as the place where Jesus healed the paralytic who was trying to get to the Pools but was unable.

Leaving through the same gate, we went to an overlook with a view back to the Mount of Olives. The traditional tombs of many Old Testament prophets were visible, including Zacharia, Absalom, Bene Hezir, and Jehosaphat.

On to the Zion Gate, entrance to the Jewish Quarter. It is the place of Peter's denial, and thought to be near the house of Caiaphas, the high priest, who judged Jesus. Just outside of the gate is a cemetery where Oskar Schindler was buried, famous for the rescue of many Jews from the Holocaust in World War II. The most significant site near the Gate is the tomb of King David (and other Judean kings), which one can visit. In a small room above the tomb is possibly the Passover room where the Last Supper was held. It is reasoned that Jesus would have held the event at the place of his fathers, and the room certainly fits the image. We took a brief walk into the Armenian Quarter and David's Citadel, and then on to Jaffa Gate.

Here we reentered the Jewish Quarter and the entrance to the Temple Mount. There we met the chief of police, Eli Assaf. He is in charge of security on the Mount, a challenging job, to say the least. He seemed to be a gentle, but firm man, described as an effective peacemaker. On Wednesday, when we visited, things were rather quiet, but on the Holy Day as many as 300,000 people crowd onto the Mount, and he routinely brings in a force of three thousand army troops for crowd control. Eli arranged for an escort for our tour of the area.

As we climbed the steps, passing the Western [Wailing] Wall, we saw scads of uniformed personnel, and young men and women not in uniform but carrying their weapons. Apparently, part of basic training is to visit all important locations in the country, so you have an appreciation of what you are defending, and you are required to carry your weapon even when on an off-duty tour. In spite of all that, I didn't sense any real danger, as life goes on there. As we later walked along the temples, and through the streets, I tried to imagine the pitched, house-to-house battles that took place in 1948, not to mention the repeated episodes of destruction over the centuries.

Finally, we reached the Temple Mount. We first visited El-Aksa Mosque, the huge Muslim temple on the south side of the Mount. Shoes off before entering, and no pictures inside! We were guided by a very nice Muslim fellow who explained the significance of all the sites for us. The mosque is the size of a football field or more, completely covered inside with Arabian rugs, some simple, some very beautiful. Only men are allowed to pray at the mosque, although women can visit (they can pray at the Dome of the Rock). The temple was once much bigger (!), and was damaged by earthquakes on a couple of occasions. Beautiful new columns of Carrera marble have been installed, I believe donated by King Hussein of Jordan. One of the columns near the entrance bore the mark of a bullet from recent clashes.

Our next stop was a real treat. They have recently opened Solomon's Stables, a huge area of tunnels and caverns under the floor of the mosque and adjacent terraces, very open and spacious, extending all the way to the corner of the Eastern and Southern walls. This area is not open to the public, and is jam-packed during the holy day. When the Crusaders were there, they used the area to stable horses, and some of the supporting columns have holes drilled in them for horse tethers. No pictures, unfortunately.

Back up, shoes back on. We were allowed to walk through some garden areas which the police have closed for the time being because it's too easy for troublemakers to lurk there. We didn't see any, and tried our best not to appear to be lurking. This took us to the inside of the Golden Gate (which we saw from the Mount of Olives), closed by Saladin to keep out Crusaders, as I mentioned before.

Finally, on to the Dome of the Rock. This temple was built between 688 and 691 by Abd-al-Halikon over the top of the famous rock. It is very ornate and covered inside with very beautiful Turkish carpets, also donated by King Hussein. There is a cave into the Rock, but our Muslim guide didn't let us tarry to look in. The Rock itself is the exposed centerpiece of the temple.

Before leaving the Mount, we were invited into the police headquarters for coffee and a chat with Eli. We were then allowed to climb to the roof of the headquarters, which probably has the best view in all of Jerusalem.

Back down the way we came, and to the Western Wall. Jews worship this as the location of the wall of the Second Temple, and the Orthodox will not visit the Muslim-occupied Temple Mount because it is considered to be defiled and must be purified. So the Wall must do for now. There is a men's side (next to tunnels which go deeper along the Wall, and a smaller women's side. We had to don cardboard skull caps (as we did in David's Tomb), but we got to keep our shoes on. People write prayers on papers and push them into the cracks between the stones. The entire base, and a long way up, are the Herodian stones of the Second Temple wall.

Next to the open-air section are tunnels, built to carry water by the Hasmonians (or Maccabees), the Jewish kings before Herod. Inside the tunnels are mainly Orthodox Jews, dressed in black with broad-rimmed hats, beards, and ear locks, reading, praying, and bowing toward the Wall. They bow by bending stiffly at the waist very vigorously several times in succession. The bobbing motion seems most unusual, for those of us not used to it.

There is an ongoing dispute between the Jews and Muslims over excavations in the tunnels. The Muslims are afraid they will tunnel under the Mount. Even when the other side of the tunnel was opened, allowing two-way passage through the existing tunnel, there were big brouhahas.

Leaving that area, we walked to the Cardo, a wide avenue during Roman times, leading all the way across the city to the Damascus Gate. There are the remains of twin colonnades, along which were shops and markets. Some of the excavations reveal three-thousand-year-old Hasmonian walls. Today, they have built part of it into a modern shopping area, arranged as the old one must have been.

The last major stop within the city was the Church of the Holy Sepulchre. This huge building contains one of the possible sites of Calvary (Golgotha) and the tomb, and it is controlled by an uneasy arms-length agreement by seven different churches. They are always at odds with one another over the nature of the control. One faction is a group of Ethiopian priests who trace lineage back to Solomon and the Queen of Sheba. They live in very modest quarters—single rooms, with stone floors, very small, on the roof of the Church.

Anyway, if this really was Calvary, it is the end of the Via Dolorosa. The site was discovered by Helen, the mother of Emperor Constantine, who was commissioned to locate certain holy places in the region. She built the church in 325 AD, but the modern structure dates to the eighteenth century. The evidence for this as the site of the tomb of Christ is based on strong oral tradition and some physical evidence, although no tomb fitting the description has been found. It is also questionable that the site was located outside the walls at the time, as described in the Bible. The rock indicated to be Calvary has a prominent fissure in it, as described. Some frescoes were discovered in a deep cistern dating to the fourth century, which showed evidence of the site.

There is a cave in the rock where the tomb of Christ is thought to have been, and small groups could go inside and look. You couldn't wear a hat and you could keep your shoes on, but I was admonished twice for having my hands in my pockets in a holy place. I just couldn't keep track of all the rules!

On the way out, we were allowed twenty minutes to wander amongst the bazaars and do some shopping. I had already spent all my money, so I wasn't tempted. One curiosity was the "Holy Rock Cafe," using the same motif as the other cafe of similar name. Dick bought a T-shirt for his "irreverent" daughter. Lots of kids were trying to sell us stuff everywhere.

We left by the Damascus Gate, one of the busier and more interesting gates. An old one was found under the rubble beneath the "new" one. From there, it was a short walk to the Garden Tomb, the other possible place of the Crucifixion and burial. This place was discovered in the 1800s, after being used as a trash pit by the Ottomans for centuries. It is owned and maintained in a relatively primitive form by the British who bought it some years back for £100. There is much physical evidence in favor of this site, but it is not conclusive. For one, it is at the intersection of the roads to Damascus and Jericho, a very busy thoroughfare (even today), and a common place for crucifixions. (The Romans used to crucify by the dozens or hundreds, and they made the process very public.) Mount Moria is there, under the North Wall, as mentioned in the Bible. It was also a quarry site, used for stonings and, presumably, other punishments, so it may have been Golgotha/Calvary. Next to the quarry, a vineyard and wine press was discovered, as was a tomb which fits the description in the Bible perfectly. The tomb would have been owned by Joseph the vintner. There is even a channel for a large stone. We could enter the tomb (which was found empty, by the way). The British philosophy is to leave it in a tidy, but natural state, rather than building a temple around it. They say, "God doesn't want us to worship places," and they do not want to detract from the worship of God. After so many elaborate cathedrals, temples, and mosques, it was refreshing. The gardens were also beautiful.

The tour finally ended, and we wearily loaded onto the bus for the drive back. It was a very moving, inspiring, and educational experience, and the real highlight of the trip to Israel. It helped to understand how one's actions and passions can be influenced when surrounded by so much history.

Another official dinner that night, this one more informal at the home of Dan Smith, the assistant naval attaché. Also, we got to meet Admiral Raz's wife, Aviva, and we saw Baruch's wife, Dina, again.

✡ ✡ ✡

The following day, Thursday, was reserved for our presentation to the admirals. The gathering of around twenty included most of the members of the committee the *NR-1* officers, Admiral Alex Tal, head of the Israeli Submarine Flotilla, Admiral Chorev, department chief of the Israeli Navy, and Admiral Krol.

That morning, we had just completed final preparations. The presentation was created on Tom's laptop computer, which we placed out of the way on a shelf by the window. We were just catching our breath and anticipating the arrival of the admirals, when a gust of wind rushed in and blew the computer right off the shelf! It fell on the floor and never worked again! We looked at each other in horror . . . but then we realized we had already printed out transparencies and were planning to present them on an overhead projector anyway. The computer had all of our three weeks of work on it, but we had backed up everything so we didn't lose a byte of information, and Tom wanted a new computer anyway, so everyone was happy in the end.

Thanks to Dick Boyd, we crafted a clear and concise briefing that stated the problem, summarized all of the studies to date, described our analytical process, and presented strong conclusions. Knowing that style often counts as much as substance in that type of forum, we were careful to keep to the point and precisely on schedule. The presentation was very well received, and we answered all questions to the satisfaction of the gathering. There was a very solid consensus among the group by that time, which made me very proud, because if you had witnessed the situation before we arrived in Israel, you would have seen a dramatic turnaround.

In the end, we agreed that the *NR-1* should go ahead and search the areas of lower probability that we indicated from our analysis were possible (though not likely) resting places for the submarine. Although not likely to reveal the *Dakar*, this would eliminate some of the possibilities, and could be done immediately while we were considering how to search in deep waters.

After lunch, we held a planning session with the *NR-1* crew, and, after a long day, headed back to the Carlton Hotel for the last time. We were given some beautiful gifts by our Israeli hosts on the way out, including a coin in a stand made of olive wood.

3/6 Thursday: We left for the airport at 10:30 PM, and checked in with no problem. Everything was going smoothly, until the pilot told us he was having problems with the flaps and needed to taxi the two miles back to the terminal. We sat in the plane at the gate for over three and a half hours getting repaired! Finally, at 4:20 AM, we took off, and we were on our way! By then, I'm sure we didn't care if they fixed the flaps or not.

The flight lasted the predicted twelve hours and fifteen minutes, so we arrived at Kennedy 9:30 AM, EST after spending nearly sixteen hours in that damned plane. We missed our connecting flight to National Airport, adding to the delay. At 12:30 PM we finally arrived at National Airport, where our faithful wives Lynn and Hélène were patiently waiting. It's great to be home!

Two Long Years

We left Israel on a very high note. At the conclusion of our briefing, Admiral Krol offered our continued assistance to Admiral Chorev as needed, at any time. Dick Boyd, being practical and knowing he had other critical needs for our services back home, objected to "full-time" support and said we would work it out with Captain Meshita at the embassy. Still, it was clear that we would have an ongoing role in this endeavor, and we were eager to see it through.

Our last official duty before leaving was to conduct a planning session with the *NR-1* team. The research vessel was to be in the area that summer, and would have several weeks to spend in support of our mission. After completing operations with the Woods Hole team, led by Dr. Ballard, the ship would disembark the group in Naples, Italy, in early July, and board an Israeli officer to support and monitor the *Dakar* search activities. The first step would be to cover suitable search areas in the Aegean Sea, examine the Eratosthenes Seamount, if practical, and, in about three weeks, make port in Haifa. After a few days in port, the vessel would search areas of interest around Crete, then, if time permitted, look further around Alexandria, Egypt. There was much ground to cover that was deeper than previous searches (limited by the conclusions of the buoy studies), yet still within the depth limits of the *NR-1*. We were cautioned about publicity. Nothing would be released until operations were completed.

On the way back to our hotel to prepare for departure, Yechiel encouraged us to submit an alternative proposal to the Israeli Navy for a deep-water search, as we were not optimistic about the *NR-1*'s chances of success, and Israel had no deep-water capability. In fact, Nauticos was among the few companies in the world that could conduct such an operation. Yechiel promised to take our proposal straight to Admiral Tal.

But first, Israel would wait for the results of the *NR-1* search. This was a little frustrating to us, because in the Mediterranean it is not possible to do this kind of work year-round due to weather and sea conditions. May is about the earliest that one can effectively operate, and reliable weather persists only through August. It becomes very windy in the autumn, with high seas, and then winter storms arrive. Although regular commerce shipping is still possible, and military vessels can operate to a degree, towing a sonar at two knots at the end of thousands of meters of cable is practically impossible and downright dangerous. Even if you tried, your data would be worthless as the bobbing ship would impart a lot of motion to the sonar through the heaving cable, distorting any images beyond use. So, May through August is the only practical time for search operations; this is known as the "weather window." This means that every new approach or major mission costs a whole year, and so the rest of 1997 would be devoted to the NR-1 mission.

The NR-1 is a one-of-a-kind vessel. First of all, it doesn't really have a name, nor is it officially a U.S. Navy warship without the designation "USS." The commander of the NR-1 is called the "officer in charge" and, although this is a prestigious posting, it does not carry the official recognition of warship command. Conceived in the mid-1960s, at a time when nuclear submarine designs were maturing and the Cold War was becoming a prime motive, this ship was designed to conduct research and collect intelligence with an endurance far exceeding that of any conventional research submersible. Admiral Hyman G. Rickover, who headed the Naval Reactors Branch of the U.S. Navy, gave the ship the designation "NR [Naval Reactors] 1," imagining that this would be the first of a series. To date, no others have been built.

NR-1 was launched and placed in service in 1969, and for decades its activities and capabilities remained highly classified; even its existence was denied by the Navy. As the Cold War fizzled in the late 1980s, it became harder to justify the cost of the ship for military research only, and it became policy to make the NR-1 available to qualified agencies of the U.S. government or accredited research organizations for use in nonmilitary deep-ocean research. Some aspects of the ship remain classified or sensitive, but a glossy brochure produced by the Navy for public release tells us many interesting facts.

The NR-1 resembles a miniature nuclear submarine but, at around 400 tons, she is tiny compared to the typical U.S. nuclear attack submarine of the 1960s, that is, 5,000 tons for the venerable Sturgeon class. She is dwarfed by the 19,000-ton Ohio-class ballistic missile submarine of the 1990s. Even compared to the Dakar (1,700 tons) she is small. The pressure hull is only 96 feet long and 12.5 feet in diameter, two-thirds of which is filled with a compact nuclear reactor and associated equipment. This leaves just a few hundred square feet of crew space, most of which is crammed with electronics, research equipment, food lockers, and storage for consumables. This space is shared by as many as seven crew and researchers, who can theoretically spend more than forty days on a mission.

Unlike the *Dakar*, the *NR-1*'s endurance is not determined by fuel or battery power. With a miniature nuclear power plant at its heart, the ship and its equipment can operate submerged indefinitely. The people, however, cannot, and eventually food, oxygen, and lithium hydroxide (for removing carbon dioxide) will run out, and the ship must come home. The fact that it takes a special person to tolerate the cramped quarters and limited activities for so long a time, far more demanding than any other modern submarine, is assumed.

The Navy doesn't talk about the nuclear reactor; all unclassified drawings of the ship show a large blank cylinder comprising two-thirds of the pressure hull with a nondescript label such as "machinery spaces." It is a good guess, however, that the reactor can operate for many years without refueling.

Although small and cramped, the *NR-1* has many features absent on a typical nuclear submarine. For one, it can dive considerably deeper, advertised (in the brochure) to go 2,375 feet. This is impressive, and allows the ship to explore most of the reaches of continental shelves around the world. However, it is no good for "real" deep-ocean work. The Mediterranean Sea averages around 5,000 feet, and the deep-ocean abyssal plains lie at 15,000 to 20,000 feet. The deepest spot in the ocean, Challenger Deep in the Marianas Trench of the western Pacific, is just over 35,800 feet. This location was visited only once by humans, when U.S. Navy Lieutenant Don Walsh and Swiss scientist Jacques Piccard descended in the bathysphere *Trieste* in 1960. One interesting perspective on this: if you were able to lop off Mount Everest, the highest point of land on earth, and place it at the depth of the Marianas Trench, there would still be a mile of water over the peak!

But for continental shelf depths, the *NR-1* brings to bear other interesting features, including thrusters (allowing precise maneuvering), view ports, mechanical arms known as manipulators, cameras, lights, and various sonars. The ship even has a pair of tires allowing it to roll along the ocean floor! Special oceanographic equipment can be added, and there is no lack of power to keep instruments in operation for the duration of a mission. Because the submarine was designed for research, rather than speed or range, it is towed on the surface from place to place by a Navy support ship. Crewmen manning the submarine for these excursions certainly have an uncomfortable ride, even in modest seas.

So, in the summer of 1997, the *NR-1* set out on yet another shallow-water search for the *Dakar*. With Commander Charles Richard as officer in charge and Yechiel embarked, the research vessel spent weeks carefully mapping the sea floor. By the end of August, hundreds of square miles were added to the tally of area searched, and Admiral Boorda's promise to Israel to help search for the *Dakar* had been fulfilled.

But, yet again, nothing relating to *Dakar* was found.

Although this endeavor did not yield ultimate success, it was far from a failure. Three major accomplishments can be credited to the *NR-1*'s role in this tale. First, the crew completed the mission to cover the low-probability ground we identified, so this was eliminated from the search. We now knew other places where the *Dakar* was not, and the likelihood she was in our primary area increased.

Second, we gained another valuable member of our team. Young Lieutenant John Coombs was the operations officer on the mission, and he impressed us greatly as a smart and capable engineer with field experience—just the kind of person we were looking for to add to our growing staff at Nauticos. Although we never recruited Navy personnel, we were certainly open to those who were nearing the end of their military obligations and were looking for civilian employment. As it turned out, John was just at that stage. We kept in touch, had a subsequent chance to meet when the *NR-1* visited Annapolis, and, in December of 1997, John joined the team. This was just the beginning of John's personal contribution to the *Dakar* search, which was to offer rewards that were entirely unanticipated.

The third achievement of the *NR-1* mission was unrelated to the *Dakar*. The bottom of the Mediterranean continental margins is littered with the wrecks of ships and aircraft, downed by weather, war, or other dangers of the sea. Over time, most of these craft have been buried, dredged to unrecognizable bits, or dissolved by natural processes. Still, there are uncounted numbers of surviving shipwrecks in these waters, and any mapping of the sea floor is bound to reveal many. All have a history, usually hidden from any record, but some are much more interesting than others. Such was the case with one particular site that was discovered by the *NR-1* crew: two Iron Age cargo ships lying largely undisturbed at a depth of about 1,300 feet off the Israeli coast near Ashkelon. A remarkable discovery, the crew of the *NR-1* recognized the significance of this find but they were faced with a dilemma. With no success in finding the *Dakar*, and plans for further searches in the works, it was decided not to publicize the *NR-1* mission. Rather than immediately release news of this discovery, the crew passed the information on to Dr. Ballard, who had been working with them earlier in the summer. Two years later, in the spring of 1999, Ballard organized a return to the Ashkelon site and announced the discovery of the eighth-century BC shipwrecks.

Of course, we were a little disappointed that Nauticos was not given the news first, but as it turned out we were distracted with other events and probably would not have been able to launch another mission to the site as Ballard did. He was in a better position to explore the find, and undersea archaeology was probably better served. In any case, Nauticos would have its own opportunity for unexpected discovery in time to come.

✿ ✿ ✿

As 1997 came to a close, preparations were underway for the first deep-water search for the *Dakar*. Tom Dettweiler and the Nauticos team presented our findings back in Washington at the Israeli embassy and to our U.S. Navy bosses. Further thought and discussion, along with the negative results from the *NR-1* work over the summer, reinforced our conviction that the submarine was in deep water and our proposed search area offered the best chance of discovery. This area was an elongated rectangle sixty nautical miles long and eight wide, derived from the decision tree outcomes (see Chapter 10 for this tree) and taking into account the most likely times of sinking, speeds of advance, and course errors along the way.

The U.S. Navy kept its promise to continue to support the search for the *Dakar*, and Israel was grateful for the help. The obvious next step was to deploy the Navy's deep-ocean search system, called DSILOS (Deep Side Looking Sonar), which was operated by the Deep Submergence Unit (DSU) of Submarine Development Squadron Five. To share in a major cost of the effort, the Israeli Navy was to provide the vessel. In February 1998, Admiral Krol, Tom Dettweiler, and Dick Boyd again visited Israel for detailed discussions of search areas by the deep ocean sonar. Captain Ben Wackendorf, the development squadron commander, also joined the team.

Submarine Development Squadron Five was established in 1967 as the U.S. Navy operational center for submarine rescue, ocean engineering, and undersea research. Besides directly serving military needs, Squadron Five conducts cooperative programs with civilian scientific and academic institutions. The DSU was established in 1989 and is home to the Navy's manned and unmanned deep-diving submersibles. Originally chartered as a submarine rescue unit following the loss of the USS *Thresher*, the DSU operates the Deep Submarine Rescue Vehicles DSRV-1 *Mystic* and DSRV-2 *Avalon* (seen in *The Hunt for Red October* and other movies). The DSU has a mandate to be able and prepared to locate a disabled submarine, help keep surviving crew members alive, and rescue them. It also operates a variety of unmanned search and recovery vehicles, including DSILOS. Over $100 million worth of military and civilian hardware have been found and rescued over the years by the DSU.

Before the February meeting, Tom and Dick spent several days at the U.S. Navy Oceanographic Office in Mississippi reviewing bathymetric data collected in the mid-1990s. They were hoping that surveys had already been conducted in the areas that interested us. Even though those systems were for geological mapping and were not really of good enough resolution to detect a submarine, Tom and Dick were looking for anomalous data that might indicate a potential shipwreck. One bathymetric anomaly was found north of the primary

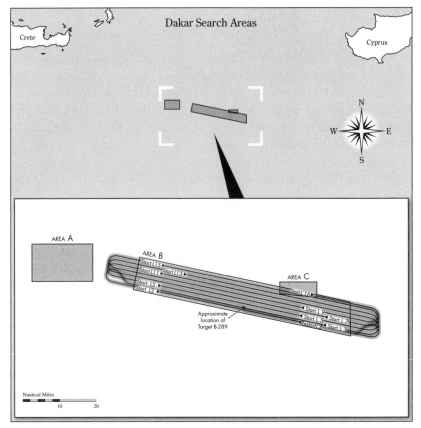

Figure 2. Search areas for the *Dakar* 1999 expedition, showing the sequence of sonar lanes and the approximate location of the discovery.

search area, and one to the west. The joint U.S. Navy–Israeli Navy team agreed to include coverage of these areas in the requirements for the DSILOS search. The western bathymetric anomaly became known as "Area A," the area recommended by Nauticos was "Area B," and the northern anomaly "Area C."

In the summer of 1998, the DSILOS system was mobilized on an Israeli research ship and prepared for search operations. According to unofficial reports, Israel also paid for the cost of shipping equipment, which further reduced the U.S. Navy commitment. The operation was fraught with equipment difficulties from the beginning, costing much valuable time. The sonar did not perform well, leaving to question whether complete coverage was achieved. Problems with vehicle navigation led to uncertainty in target locations. It is expensive to keep a ship and people at sea, and as time and expenses mounted with little progress, it became clear that "free" help could be very costly. Finally, a failure of the winch system that lowers the equipment to the ocean floor effectively put an end to operations. Heading for home, the U.S. Navy system could claim coverage of almost all of the small Area C and about 30 percent of Area B, the Nauticos region, primarily in the northeast quadrant. But the system failed to detect contacts with the characteristics consistent with those of the *Dakar* and, what is more important, failed to convince Israel that it could complete the job. In any case, the U.S. Navy was reluctant to invest more resources in this good-will mission. So, the Israeli Navy decided in late 1998 to issue a competitive request for proposal (RFP) for commercial help in searching the deep sea area.

✡ ✡ ✡

Meanwhile, Tom and I and the Nauticos team had been working to secure the job for ourselves. Although we supported the DSILOS effort by helping to define tasking and review of data, we were not directly involved (or tainted with) the unsatisfying result. We were sorely disappointed, however, when the government of Israel decided to open the job up for competition, as that meant we had to prove ourselves over again, this time to new people.

Dick Boyd had told us in May 1998 that although we had the best wishes of Admiral Krol and that he supported our efforts, he could do nothing to directly help as the decision should rest with the Israelis. The U.S. Navy did not want to get involved in vetting subcontractors; they had done enough already. We also spoke with Yechiel and Admiral Raz, whose hearts were with us, but they did not have the power to direct contracts our way. We were going to have to win the job the old-fashioned way: on merit.

Still, we made plans. This is another part of being lucky and taking advantage of it, as I mentioned earlier. It occurred to us that the *Dakar* was a great story, and a successful find would be a great opportunity for publicity and for a documentary. There was nothing secret about the work we were doing. Also, it would be a great historical event in Israeli history and should be recorded. So we made plans to film our work and began to discuss the prospect with documentary broadcasters.

This was an uphill battle from the beginning. Although he personally supported the idea (and thought there was an even chance it would be allowed), Admiral Raz warned us that many in the Israeli Navy were against having any photographers on board any search ship as a naval security matter. Undaunted, we took preliminary steps and thought about the prospect of adding documentary film production to our business.

Our leader in this endeavor was Gary Bane. In charge of our West Coast operations, and former director of ocean systems at Rockwell International, Gary was invaluable to Nauticos, finding new customers and taking care of current ones, as well as managing programs and strategic planning. Besides that, his location in Santa Barbara, near Hollywood, and his vast social and professional network made him well-suited to the task. We were also working on another ocean exploration project—seeking the Japanese fleet sunk at the Battle of Midway in 1942, which was a television documentary prospect—so we had more than the *Dakar* to consider. Our first steps were trying to predict the costs and rewards of such an undertaking, and find some help from someone already in the business. Gary started looking around and, in a short time, found David Brown and Passage Productions of Santa Barbara. David was a graduate of the Brooks Institute of Photography in Santa Barbara and veteran of underwater filming expeditions with Jacques Cousteau. We were impressed with his credentials, friendly personality, and eagerness to work with us.

With the help of Gary, David, and others, we visited the Discovery Channel, National Geographic, WGBH (Boston Public Television), many documentary production companies, and other people in the business. One of the more interesting personalities we had a chance to visit with was Jean Michel Cousteau, son of the late, great Jacques. Everyone thought the project was interesting, but since it had no clear "American" angle, no U.S. documentary broadcaster was willing to get serious about it. We hadn't found anything yet, of course, and there was no guarantee that we would even get a chance to try. It seemed that if we wanted to film this project, we were going to have to do it ourselves.

But first we had to win the opportunity to go to sea and search. We kept in touch with Israel through Admiral Raz and Yechiel, submitted proposals and variations on proposals without a clear idea of Israel's requirements, and saw a parade of new faces enter the scene who did not know Nauticos and had no real appreciation for our work. We had to be supportive of the U.S. Navy's work, even as it failed, without being tainted by the results or annoying our customer. But we did have ardent supporters both in Israel and the United States. One new friend was newly appointed Israeli Naval Attaché Yochay Ben-Josef, whom we met in the fall of 1998. He immediately grasped the significance of our work and the quality of our team.

Then we had some bad luck: Dr. Ballard was going to be operating in the area again and had some time available to help with the *Dakar* search. With equipment already mobilized for other operations, he might be able to do the job more cheaply and, of course, he had the notoriety of the *Titanic* and other discoveries to add to his allure. Israel might even be able to justify going right to Ballard, skipping a competitive bid process. By October 1998, Israel had decided that, available or not, they would politely decline further U.S. Navy deep-water search support in favor of either Ballard or going through the process of a competitive bid.

But, in December 1998, our luck changed, and we immediately took advantage. Admiral Raz contacted us, seeking a consultant to help the Israeli Navy

write a good RFP for the *Dakar* search. There are many details and considerations when specifying the requirements and bid process, and the better the
RFP, the better chance we had of winning. It was a great opportunity to offer
an expert who could help this process and make it less arbitrary. We replied in
short order with a name: Ken Lee. Ken was a former U.S. Navy submarine commander, veteran of Navy special undersea programs, and manager of Undersea
Vehicle Programs at Perry Technologies in West Palm Beach, Florida. He was
experienced, smart, and absolutely honest. He also had a lot of overseas travel
experience, and we knew he would work well with the Israeli people. In time,
Ken was hired for the job and helped write the RFP. We never discussed it until
long after the project was over, but we were confident that Ken would do everything he could to make sure the process was fair and the best bidder won.

Another lucky thing that happened to us in December was that Dick Boyd
announced his retirement from government service after over thirty years with
the Office of Naval Intelligence. After spending a few enjoyable days waking up
late and reading the newspaper for several hours, contemplating retired life, he
got a call from Tom. Nauticos immediately offered Dick a position as consultant on the *Dakar* project. In mid-January 1999, we received the RFP, issued by
Israel's ministry of defense procurement office in New York City, to conduct
the deep-sea search for the INS *Dakar*. We had three weeks to respond. The
race was on.

✡ ✡ ✡

Who was in this race to win the job to search for the *Dakar*? The basic requirements for deep-sea search in the vicinity of ten thousand feet immediately
reduced the contestants to just a handful. Eliminating the U.S. Navy reduced the
field further, and there were few European countries with enough capabilities
to conduct such a mission. Of course, the Russian oceanographic fleet, such as
we had hired to help us find the I-52, could do the job. Also, the French Institute
for Ocean Research and Exploration (IFREMER) could field deep-ocean assets,
including the submersible *Nautile,* which were put on display during the 1998
Discovery Channel live broadcast from the site of the *Titanic*. (Nauticos worked
for Discovery as ocean operations manager for that project, which included the
live broadcast, submersible and robotic vehicle operations, and even recovery
of a twenty-ton piece of the *Titanic* hull.) There were some developing commercial capabilities in the United Kingdom, including Ultra Electronics. Outside
of the United States and Europe, only Japan operated any deep-ocean systems,
and these were not typically used in mapping or search projects.

These few non-U.S. prospects were eliminated from direct competition
owing to vagaries of the sources of funds. Israel wanted to pay for the effort

using U.S. foreign aid funds, but there were restrictions to the use of this money, including requirements to follow U.S. government contracting practices and assurance that most of the contracts were with U.S. businesses. In the U.S., outside of Navy and defense programs, there were only a few organizations that could field such a capability. The top name in the business was Oceaneering International, a Houston-based publicly traded firm working mainly in offshore oil, that operated the Ocean Technologies Division of Oceaneering (OTECH) in Maryland. OTECH supported the U.S. Navy underwater salvage program, and also commercial projects. They were heavily involved in the Discovery Channel *Titanic* program, and had supported other deep-ocean projects seen on documentary television. Operating both deep-sea search sonars and underwater robotic systems, Oceaneering was a very serious bidder.

Then there was Robert Ballard and the Woods Hole Oceanographic Institution (WHOI) in Massachusetts. Ballard had the *Titanic* discovery to his name, and could field deep-ocean search equipment. He also had a personal interest in the *Dakar*, having written a fictional account of the episode, and having a connection through the *NR-1*. The Israelis could even imagine turning the job over to him under "sole source" justification; that is, he was the only source of technology available. On the other hand, WHOI rarely, if ever, took on commercial jobs, and it was recognized in Israel that there were other options. Still, Ballard and Woods Hole represented a capable resource and serious competitor.

A small business but significant competitor was Mike Williamson. Mike had founded Williamson and Associates in the early 1980s, having spent time as a Navy salvage diver and geophysicist for the Inco Deep Ocean Mining Project, the first large-scale recovery of manganese nodules from the deep ocean. Mike was a world expert in the use of side-scan sonar for geophysical surveys of the deep ocean, and his company made a living supporting ocean pipeline and cable route surveys, mapping projects for various purposes, and the occasional shipwreck search. Mike was a key player in the discovery of the SS *Central America*, and he had the equipment and talent to find the *Dakar*. He had even participated in one of the earlier *Dakar* shallow-water searches, so he had a history with the project.

Curiously absent from the list was Tommy Thompson, the engineer-explorer who masterminded the discovery of the SS *Central America*. Chronicled in Gary Kinder's book *Ship of Gold in the Deep Blue Sea* (1998), Thompson and his Columbus–America Discovery Group set out in the 1980s to "establish a working presence on the deep ocean floor and open it to science, archaeology, history, medicine, and recovery." Working independently from mainstream but still classified, military undersea developments, Thompson succeeded in 1989 with the discovery of the *Central America*, a Gold Rush–era steamer that sank in a storm off the

U.S. east coast. Lying at a depth of eight thousand feet, the ship contained a literal treasure of gold, and a figurative treasure of preserved artifacts and history of life in 1857.

Thompson designed and developed working deep-sea salvage systems and patiently recovered gold coins, bars, nuggets, and dust, as well as other artifacts, thought to be worth hundreds of millions of dollars. He had scored a stunning achievement, and should have been financially and technologically poised to launch commercial ocean exploration as a successful business. But the good news turned sour as dozens of insurance companies claimed ownership of the treasure to offset their long-standing losses. The ensuing legal battles have persisted ever since. Seemingly resolved at last in 1998, with 92 percent of the ownership awarded to the Columbus–America Discovery Group, negotiations collapsed in the face of accusations of secret deals, failure to live up to judicial rulings, and a myriad of appeals. As time continues to pass, the list of accusations grows. The complete inventory of the gold is still secret, and the process of converting treasure into money remains fraught with obstacles, not the least of which seems to be greed. Nauticos tried to interest Columbus–Discovery in participating in projects in the mid-1990s, but were unable to get beyond some polite phone calls. It seems that the distractions of gold and greed had removed this promising player from the table.

Another possible challenger was the Science Applications International Corporation (SAIC). A multibillion dollar employee-owned company, SAIC had the resources and interest to attempt the mission. In fact, Norm Estabrook, head of the Marine Operations Division in San Diego (and former director of ocean engineering for the Naval Ocean Systems Center), contacted Tom Dettweiler when he got wind of the project in 1998. At that time, the U.S. Navy was still supporting the effort directly, and we were under strict orders not to publicize anything about the work. So Tom was very uncomfortable when Norm called him, wondering if he and Nauticos would like to team with SAIC in preparing an unsolicited proposal for the Israeli government to look for the *Dakar*.

Norm remembers the phone call: "Tom was very nervous, he didn't act right. I thought that was very strange. He said he'd talk to Dave about it, but it was clear he was not comfortable about this idea. I was still puzzled by the U.S. Navy involvement, as no one had told me who that entailed. So, later, I called Tom again, and in the midst of our conversation, when he was again acting strange, I had another phone ring, a classified phone, and there was a fellow on the line who was an old friend of mine, Dick Boyd. He was from an intelligence organization within the Navy, and so I had two phones going in my hands. I went back to Tom and I said Boyd was on the phone and he said, 'Oh, thank God, you talk to him!' And immediately it started to become apparent why he was so nervous."

Dick asked Norm to back off for the time being, but promised to offer them a chance if the current efforts failed. Later, he invited Norm to come to Washington and review the work we had done. Norm said, "They'd done a really good job, so at that point, it was clear that it was in good hands, and we had no need to go forward, and I would just wait and see what happened." I believe SAIC was on the bidder's list for the Israeli RFP when it came out the following year, but I don't believe they ever submitted a proposal.

Nauticos had the talent, experience, knowledge, and ambition to find the *Dakar*. What we lacked was deep-ocean equipment. In spite of our efforts and successes, we had yet to obtain capital funding needed to develop such unique equipment. We had to rely on teammates and the pickings were very slim. How were we going to justify our case against the likes of OTECH, Ballard, and SAIC? Where were we going to get equipment? How were we going to handle the financing of the project, since Israel didn't want to pay until the end, and was even expecting a letter of credit from us! We were also at that time preparing to launch operations in the Pacific with the U.S. Naval Oceanographic Office to search for the Japanese Fleet at Midway. How were we going to field two teams simultaneously? These were all questions that needed good answers in the next three weeks.

✡ ✡ ✡

The first step was building the team. We needed three major and distinct elements to fulfill the project needs: a ship capable of operating for extended periods offshore and handling twenty tons or more of equipment; a search sonar system capable of detecting the *Dakar* at as much as ten thousand feet deep; and a robotic vehicle system with lights and cameras to allow us to photograph and identify whatever we found.

The last of the three was the easiest. We had established a teaming arrangement with a new company, Phoenix Marine, founded by Mike Kutzleb. Mike's father, Bob, was also involved in the discovery of the SS *Central America*, and Mike went on to his own career in ocean technology. He established Phoenix to develop a deep ocean robotic vehicle system, and to eventually compete with companies like OTECH for military and commercial work. Nauticos leased space to the fledgling Phoenix, helped with their technology development, and included them on our *Titanic* work with Discovery Channel. In turn, Phoenix invested in the development of the Remora, a small but effective robot that could descend to twenty thousand feet, be placed on a dime, point its cameras in any direction, light up the scene, and even manipulate objects using robotic arms. Mike was eager for the job, and we were happy to have his support.

The ship was a problem, but not because there were no ships. The problem was the requirements of the RFP, which insisted on all services being from U.S. companies. We did not own or operate a ship ourselves; that's an entirely different business, and even if we did own one, it would probably be in the wrong ocean whenever we needed it. So, we typically lease a "ship of opportunity" with the right characteristics for the job, near to the place we need it. The nearest U.S.-owned research ship that met our needs was on the east coast of the United States, thousands of miles from the search site. We would have to pay by the day for the ship to be relocated, including fuel, crew, food, insurance, and other costs. Our best choice, the R/V (research vessel) *Atlantic Explorer,* was owned by Marex Oceanographic Services and based in New Orleans. The ship was capable and an attractive choice, but we calculated a round-trip time of fifty-four days to transit from its home port to the search site and return. Adding up all the costs, at over $500 per hour, we would be spending almost three-quarters of a million dollars before we even started! Common sense would have to prevail somehow, but the requirements of the RFP were quite specific.

The search sonar was even more of a problem. Our best choice was Mike Williamson, but he was keen to bid the job himself. Without the restrictions on non-U.S. companies, we would have turned to Ultra Electronics or to the Russians. We finally solved the dilemma in an unconventional way. We worked a deal with Williamson so that he could bid the job himself, but also was listed as a member of our team. It was a win-win for Mike, unless one of the other competitors prevailed.

Besides those major problems, the RFP was a nightmare of requirements, clearly crafted by people who had little appreciation for the job we faced. This is typical of government procurement. The process is so complicated, and so regulated, that it takes specialists to manage it who usually know nothing about what is actually being procured. In the spirit of preventing any conflict of interest, or at least the appearance of it, people with a genuine interest and expertise in the matter are usually insulated from the endeavor. So, in spite of honest intent and the professionalism of the Israeli procurement people in New York City, we were left scratching our heads over some of the demands of the job.

Fortunately, we could see the influence of folks like Ken Lee and Yechiel in the technical requirements, although the procurement people seemed to delight in making these as stringent as could be imagined. There were many special requirements for the habitability of the customer, including "one shower and one lavatory, at least, for exclusive use of the I.N. crew." This was not trivial, as we were expected to accommodate as many as five Israeli Navy personnel, above and beyond the technical team required for operations and the ship's own crew. The required "air conditioning suitable for the Middle East climate" and "Kosher food for the I.N. crew" were interesting, but distracting details to be accommodated. Fortunately, the cook on the *Explorer* was Jewish and claimed to have been raised in a kosher household, but clearly we were going to have to do some research in fields unrelated to ocean exploration to be sure we met all the requirements of the RFP.

Some other requirements were scary. One that got our attention was, "Should the mission be delayed due to any malfunction or personnel availability, the cost shall be born by the participant." We were looking at costs of over $700 per hour during operations for ship, search equipment, and personnel. That elicited a collective "gulp" from our management team. How would we answer that one?

We also had an idea of what the market was willing to bear, and we knew a fully compliant proposal would have a price tag way out of range. The cost to do everything as demanded would approach $3 million, which, coincidentally, was just about equal to our entire company annual revenues at that time. We needed a strategy that would win this job without such a low bid that we would end up a big success but broken financially. And we hoped that the evaluators would be sophisticated enough to recognize a low bid from an organization that could not perform. Also, we had to worry if one of the big companies, like SAIC, would bid the job low (because they could afford to), just to get the publicity and opportunity.

With some collective thought on these matters, we decided that we could not do anything about unsophisticated bidders and evaluators, and we could not prevent a company from purposefully "low-balling" the job for whatever reason. We decided the best thing to do was to write a fully compliant bid, which we knew would be much too costly, but also offer some options for Israel to consider that would lower the price, but still get us the job.

So, our proposal included the *Atlantic Explorer*, but also two other options: using the Russian vessel, the *Yuzmorgeologiya*, which served us well in our 1995 discovery of the I-52, or engaging Darios Melas and his company EDT Towage and Salvage. Darios was born in Alexandria, Egypt, to Greek parents. Educated in Egypt and Europe, he eventually joined EDT shortly after it was founded by his uncle, Eas Tchacos, in 1980. Jointly owned and managed by Eas and Darios, the company had a fleet composed of seven vessels and two barges. Based in Limassol, Cyprus, their vessel *Flying Enterprise* was well positioned and capable, but not U.S.-owned. At $2.3 million, the price tag for this option was considerably more attractive.

The next two weeks were frantic with planning, negotiations, and writing. Having established the basic strategy of the proposal, we still had lots of tactics to work out, including how we were going to answer requirements about delay costs, how to handle subcontracts, and a long list of other important considerations. The process was led by Jim Moran, our project manager, with the help of

Julie Nelson, our in-house counsel. Jim worked tirelessly to get answers, and Julie worked through all of the legal and contractual issues we faced. Carla Bowling, our business manager and a ten-year veteran of Nauticos, worked on insurance and financial issues, and helped pull it all together. And, of course, there were the technical folks led by Tom, who would actually go to sea and deliver whatever we promised. It was frustrating to have to react so quickly after waiting for the chance for so long, but there was no future in complaining.

I felt very good about our team. Jim came to us with experience in building training simulators for major aircraft, and had managed programs of much greater complexity. He could wrangle a spreadsheet and make sure that the numbers turned into reality. Carla had been with Nauticos almost since the beginning, and I had complete confidence in her ability to deal with the complexities of maritime insurance, as well as money matters and personnel. Julie, who eventually became Nauticos' general manager, had an eclectic background. Starting her career as a Navy enlistee, she studied business and Russian language in college, joined government service as an intelligence research analyst for the Department of the Navy, then attended law school, culminating with a degree in admiralty and maritime law from Tulane University. Julie knew the vagaries of the law of the sea, as well as government contracts, business, and international relations. On top of all of these qualifications, Julie was able to work with diverse personalities ranging from engineers to artists to lawyers, and seemed to be able to get the most from all. She was great to be around, always positive, and truly enjoyed the challenges of her work.

Somehow, we managed to get price quotes from Phoenix, Williamson, and three different ships, answer every question in the RFP, and come up with a price that we could live with. As late as February 3, five days before submission, we were not sure if Mike Williamson would be on our team. But we all sighed with relief when the 150-page document went out the door to the Israeli procurement office in New York City on February 8, 1999. We were able to certify that our proposal included 100 percent U.S. suppliers, our costs were approved by U.S. government audit, we were fully compliant with all requirements, and even had provided a letter of credit as demanded. We had to scramble for that last item, and owe thanks to one of our business advisors, Bruce Crawford, who leveraged a personal banking relationship to prove, oddly enough, that *we* had the cash to do the job!

We knew our proposal would be much too costly, but we included an array of options and cost-cutting measures, if the Israelis were willing to be flexible with requirements. We also included a couple of offers that were not part of the requirements. First, we volunteered that our proposed fee, the profit for the job, would be paid *only* if *Dakar* was found. It was a risk, as there were many factors beyond our control in this matter even if we were right about the location. But it certainly showed our commitment to success. Second, we offered to provide, at our expense, an experienced documentary cameraman to help record the historic events. Of course, in return we wanted permission to produce the documentary.

✡ ✡ ✡

We didn't have to wait long for a reply. Ten days after our submission we heard from Kalman Lior, the assistant to the director of naval procurement. Our proposal passed initial hurdles, and Israel was moving quickly to the next step: a visit by a technical team for an in-person presentation, facilities tour, and questions. They would arrive on March 5, just over two weeks away.

We were pleased and excited that the procurement office was taking things seriously, and moving fast. It seemed that everyone in our office was engaged in the event. Besides hoping to make a solid technical showing, we wanted to be considerate of our guests. So we arranged for a kosher buffet lunch, prepared by an orthodox delicatessen in Baltimore. As it turned out, most of the members of the Israeli delegation did not routinely observe those traditions, and they politely chuckled at our efforts, but they seemed to genuinely appreciate the thoughtfulness.

I told our team that we had worked very hard to get to that point; the day would be fun and a chance to show off our capabilities and talents. It *was* fun, and I was very proud of the group. The day went well—and no computers were destroyed this time! We were finally rewarded for two years of work when Kalman Lior called on March 9 to inform us that our proposal had been selected as the "best value" to Israel, and to invite us to New York the following morning for contract negotiations! Tom, Julie, and Jim immediately volunteered to drop everything, get on a train, and head north.

As we suspected, the process that ensued was to develop a specific plan that would really work, considering the funds that were available. As we had already put forth some options for consideration, we had a head start, but it still took three days of long hours and hard work by the team. I chose not to go to New York, because I believe it is always best for the final decision-maker to stay out of the meeting. Anyway, I am not a good negotiator, as I tend to see everybody's side of an issue, so I set parameters and let the negotiators do their job. One of the key aspects of all of this was how and how soon we would be paid. We were committing close to $2 million of services, most of it going to subcontractors, and we had to be sure our little company could handle it. Julie made sure we had some breathing room, both in our negotiations with Israel and with our subcontractors.

Eventually, we reached a satisfactory agreement. A lot of what was specified in the RFP was costly but not critical to the search, as I mentioned above, so there was much room for economizing. Softening the restriction on U.S. content of services was crucial, as that would allow us to hire EDT to provide the ship. In the end, Darios actually provided us two ships at reasonable cost, one for the search system and one for the robotic vehicle, so our efficiency of operation was dramatically improved. This allowed us to split our team into two groups, one focused on search coverage with a sonar, and the other identifying contacts with cameras on the robotic vehicle at the same time. It also turned out to be the start of a great relationship with Darios and EDT.

So on March 12, 1999, Julie called from New York City to tell me we had a deal for a fixed-price $1.6 million contract. It was all too exhausting for me to remember clearly, but I'm sure we celebrated! We were taking a lot of risks, but they were calculated and acceptable. All of our subcontractors, EDT, Williamson, and Phoenix, came to our aid to make the deal work. Operations were to begin in the latter part of April; we had barely a month to make all preparations to go to sea. It had been two long years, almost to the day, since Tom and I returned from Israel in 1997, but we were finally about to embark on the deep sea search for the *Dakar*.

Of course, for the people of Israel, just over thirty-one years had come and gone since their ship and sailors disappeared. They were ready for some good news, and counting on Nauticos to deliver.

Just an Old Ship

"**I** believe that what really brought success is the meeting, face to face, with an experienced team of the U.S. Navy and the civilian company Nauticos. . . . I believe we found the best people, very devoted people, which together with the technologies they brought, was the foundation for success." Admiral Raz's kind words were spoken in hindsight. In April of 1999, this devoted team had yet to fulfill these expectations, and in fact was struggling mightily to get the expedition launched at all. Six weeks after getting the go-ahead from Israel, ships, equipment, supplies, and people from around the world had to come together in Limassol, Cyprus, and begin the mobilization. The daily costs began to add up immediately. The process is a contest between speed (so more time can be spent at sea searching) and thoroughness (as any forgotten supplies or malfunctioning equipment will have to be dealt with at sea for the duration of the mission). Underway was scheduled for May 3, leaving just four days to prepare.

I arrived in Limassol on May 28, just as things were getting started. Cyprus is an island nestled in the northeast corner of the Mediterranean Sea, about forty miles south of Turkey and sixty miles west of Syria, only a little farther northwest of Lebanon. The island is about one hundred miles long and fifty miles wide, and is marked by a mountain (Troodos) about six thousand feet high on the western side. The capital is Nicosia, located in the northeast part of the island to the northeast of Troodos. The city is traditionally Greek, but partly occupied by Turkey as it sits astride the boundary indicating the limit of the Turkish invasion of 1975.

Just to the south, on the coast, is the main international airport at Larnaca. On the east coast is the town of Famagusta, occupied by Turkey, but still used as a British naval base. This was the source of the mysterious and garbled SOS messages that may have come from the *Dakar* buoy shortly after the ship disappeared in 1968. Today, a modern expressway connects Nicosia with Larnaca and the towns to the west along the coast. About a forty-five-minute drive along the road is Limassol, where we were staying. There is a major seaport there, an ideal place to launch any operation in the eastern Mediterranean.

Less than an hour's drive along the south coast is Paphos, an ancient seaport and ancient capital of the kingdom of Cyprus. Back east, directly north of Nicosia, is Kyrenia, an ancient north coast seaport. The zone of Turkish occupation includes about one-third of the land area, and its boundary runs roughly east–west from Morfou Bay on the north coast through Nicosia and to Famagusta on the east coast. The zone of occupation includes the towns of Morfu, Kyrenia, Famagusta, and portions of Nicosia. The northern third of the island is dominated by Turkish settlers and Turkish Cypriots. The rest of the land, including most of the centers of commerce, is inhabited by Greek Cypriots, who strongly identify with Greek country and culture.

The island has been mined for copper and asbestos in the past, but these activities are shut down. Much of the island was once heavily wooded, and the trees provided material for a major shipbuilding industry, supplying the ancient pharaohs of Egypt with massive navies. However, the trees are sparse now and seem to be confined to the mountains. Other products of the island are almonds and other nuts, olives, seafood, crafts such as lace and pottery, and of course, tourism. The island is a favorite retirement spot for British citizens, and a vacation destination for Europeans and Middle Easterners. Due to friendly banking laws, Cyprus is the "Switzerland of the Mediterranean" for wealthy Russians. The excellent harbors and proximity to many popular Mediterranean destinations have fostered cruise ship business, with short and inexpensive voyages to Greece, Israel, and Egypt available.

Cyprus has been an important hub of commerce and politics since antiquity. Evidence is found of villages dating back to 2,000 BC, and the island has been occupied by Egyptians, Romans, Europeans, and Asians over its history. The strategic location and presence of resources including copper and lumber have heightened the island's significance and made Cyprus the object of invasion even in modern times.

Unfortunately, I was not there to sight-see; I would have to visit the Roman ruins, historic settlements, and beautiful beaches on another trip. Even more disappointing, I was not there to stay; my plans were to return to Maryland in a few days. In a week, I was scheduled to appear before a group of 1,200 honoring our selection as the Maryland Small Business of the Year, and a week later I was flying to the other side of the world to meet a Nauticos team returning to Honolulu from explorations at the site of the 1942 Battle of Midway. (A return to the site in September confirmed that we had discovered wreckage of the Japanese aircraft carrier *Kaga*, one of four sunk by U.S. forces during that battle, but at that time we had only tantalizing sonar targets.) One of the drawbacks of having two major expeditions going at the same time, along with the everyday challenges of business, was that I didn't feel I could devote full attention to either. Fortunately, I had full confidence in Tom Dettweiler to manage the *Dakar* expedition, and he was far more experienced in field operations than I. Similarly, Tom Bethge was managing Nauticos operations with the joint Navy project at Midway. My role was to stay in Maryland and make sure both teams were properly supported and the business itself didn't suffer with the strain.

And it was a thrill to receive the Small Business Administration award. As part of my short acknowledgment, I was very happy to applaud the team:

> It's easy to get recognition when you have such an exciting job and such a remarkable staff. A number are here today, including Joe Crabtree who helped get things started over twelve years ago, and Dave Wyatt, a ten-year veteran. Thanks for your help and encouragement.
>
> A couple of important folks couldn't be here, because they are involved in some exciting projects we are working on. Carla Bowling has been my business manager for nine years, and is an indispensable part of the organization. From nearby Odenton, she is currently manning our expedition in the Pacific to search for Japanese ships sunk at the Battle of Midway. You never know when you'll be sent to sea if you work at Nauticos! The only reason I'm not there is I had to come to this breakfast!
>
> But the real inspiration for this business has been Tom Dettweiler, who has been with me for ten years. He is leading our expedition in the Mediterranean to search for a submarine which disappeared mysteriously in 1968. A veteran of deep ocean exploration, he has visited the *Titanic* three times and has found shipwrecks as deep as 17,000 feet. To get a different perspective, Tom recently went skydiving from 17,000 feet up! With people like that to work with, it's easy to be inspired to do your best.
>
> I am especially thrilled to get this award because it supports my conviction that business is about much more than money. Businesses have a responsibility to community and to youth . . . to educate and inspire the next leaders; to create a professional environment for growth. To be a good neighbor and set an example for staff and associates to follow.
>
> At Nauticos, we have tried to do all these things in some measure, as well as making a profit. This award tells me we're on the right track!

Besides being professional and capable, my team had a sense of humor and a knack for practical jokes. Shortly after our *Dakar* contract award, I took a business trip down to Florida and spent a couple of days with Bruce Crawford, former head of Perry Technologies, and one of my trusted business advisors. When I arrived, he had a paper in his hand and a very worried look on his face. It was a fax from Kalman Lior at the Israeli procurement office in New York. The contents, terse and direct, informed me that the project had been delayed indefinitely, and that we were to cease all activities immediately! Having already spent tens of thousands of dollars, and signed contracts for ships and equipment, I immediately thought of years of work about to become worthless, and began to calculate how we were going to save the business. Then I noticed the date: April 1. And a more careful read showed the author to be Kalman "Filter" Lior, referring to a computer algorithm (the Kalman filter) that was the basis of our renavigation software. I am pretty sure Julie was the author of the prank, which may have spawned some extra gray bristles in my beard.

✡ ✡ ✡

Mobilizing for a deep-sea search is a chaotic, night and day event. It is noisy, hot, frantic, exhausting, stressful, and exciting, all at once. The first problem is establishing a team and a clear objective; fortunately, this is one of Tom's many strengths. The challenge lies in the mélange of skills, languages, cultures, and personalities that must be quickly blended to contribute to a common goal in a short time, and achieve this in a foreign country and an industrial environment so that the ship gets underway in time and nobody gets injured. In this case, we had a ship, the research vessel *Flying Enterprise*, provided by a Greek-Egyptian owner, operating from a Cypriot port, with a master from the U.K., and a crew from various places, including Rumania, South Africa, and Kenya. The Kenyans were a special challenge, as they were not able to speak any language we could understand. Our team was based in Maryland, and Williamson's group was from Seattle. Of course, our customer was Israeli. Besides some traditional language barriers, there were differences in the technical language of the engineers and the sometimes arcane jargon of the professional seaman. The equipment included ten-ton hydraulic winches that had to be welded directly to the ship's deck; delicate sonar electronics that had to withstand thousands of pounds per square inch of sea pressure; computers, displays and software; and miles of steel-armored cable for towing the sonar. Supplies, spare parts, food, and consumables for a month of operations had to be collected, inventoried, loaded, and stored.

An enormous spool held the cable, in itself a remarkable piece of machinery. It had to be strong enough to hold the half-ton sonar vehicle and pull it through the water; stronger yet to hold its own weight, thirteen tons for a ten-thousand-meter cable. It also had to carry power down to the vehicle through three copper conductors. And it had to bring telemetry signals back from the vehicle electronics. In the case of the sonar, this was carried by standard copper wires. For the robotic vehicle, with high-resolution cameras, a trio of fiber-optic strands allowed laser communications at very high data rates. When the cable is manufactured, it is "torsion balanced," a process that allows it to unwind smoothly without twisting or kinking. These unique devices are custom-built at great expense, with price tags over a quarter of a million dollars.

The cable is fed through a winch, operated by massive hydraulic motors operating with thousands of pounds-per-square-inch of hydraulic pressure. The taut cable is fed across a huge block suspended over the stern of the ship from a steel A-frame capable of withstanding the tremendous force of static weight, as well as dynamic loading from drag through the water and heaving of the deck in heavy seas. In spite of all of this force, the winch can delicately unspool or reel in the cable at very slow speeds, allowing the vehicle above the sea floor to be adjusted by mere inches at a time.

It would be impossible to gather, test, install, and stow everything if each piece was collected individually. To save time and to help ensure nothing is forgotten, most of the gear is loaded or integrated into shipping containers, which then serve as operating and maintenance huts on the ship. These standard containers will neatly fit on a cargo ship or semi-truck for transportation, and are placed right on the ship's deck and welded down for the mission. Inside the maintenance van is a collection of spare parts, tools, manuals, and consumables. The operations van is outfitted with consoles, computers, instruments, and controls to operate the vehicle, conduct navigation, and even perform analysis. The vans are prewired, air-conditioned (more for the electronics than the people), and reasonably comfortable. All is normally powered from the ship's generators; in this case, a separate turbine engine-powered generator joined the cluster of equipment on the aft deck to supplement the ship's marginal capability. As part of the mobilization setup, all navigation information coming into the ship's bridge, two decks above, is wired back to the control van, which also sports an independent GPS (global positioning satellite) navigation system. Since a lot can go wrong out in the ocean over the course of weeks, spare parts, redundancy, and talented technicians are essential.

The array of equipment on the *Enterprise* was designed to support the key piece of search technology, an AMS-60 side-scan sonar, capable of imaging a mile-wide swath of the ocean floor in sufficient detail to detect the hull of a *Dakar*-sized ship. This complex device is a ten-foot steel frame known as a sled (because of its shape), covered in bright yellow "syntactic" foam to render it close to neutrally buoyant. The special foam is made of tiny glass microspheres embedded in epoxy; this helps it resist collapse in the high-pressure water of the deep. Sensitive electronics are carried in a cylindrical tube fastened securely to the undercarriage. Sonar projectors are fastened to the sides, and connections are made with wires snaking through tubes filled with high-pressure mineral oil. The sled, which, thanks to the buoyant foam, tends not to sink or rise, trails behind a "depressor," essentially a steel slug that weighs down the system so it will sink near the bottom. In operation, the sled is towed at slow speeds (less than three knots) about two hundred feet off the bottom. Slowly, patiently, the sled builds an image of the bottom in long mile-wide swaths, a process called "mowing the lawn," for obvious reasons.

The intense activity surrounding preparations aboard the *Flying Enterprise* would be duplicated aboard another ship of the EDT fleet within days of the search ship's departure. This equally challenging process was managed by Tom's operations assistant, Bruce Brown. Bruce was a trained ocean engineer with decades of experience in the design and operation of robotic vehicles. He had helped develop this technology for the U.S. Navy, and in 1998 helped Tom coordinate the Discovery Channel *Titanic* live broadcast. He was also a veteran of recovery operations to locate flight recorders and other wreckage from the 1996 ValueJet Flight 592 crash in the Florida Everglades and the 1986 *Challenger* space shuttle accident, among others. Bruce would be accompanied by Yechiel's assistant, Rubin Rosenblat, looking out for our customer's interests.

While the *Flying Enterprise* was set up to acquire sonar data, EDT *Argonaut* was outfitted to carry the Phoenix robotic vehicle, Remora. Also known as a remotely operated vehicle, or ROV for short, Remora carried several still and video cameras, as well as a scanning sonar made by Simrad. The Simrad sonar would look ahead several hundred yards, allowing the ROV to be maneuvered toward contacts detected by the search sonar aboard the *Enterprise*. With lights and cameras, the sonar target would be seen and identified. The motion of the ROV was controlled in all directions by experienced pilots Casey Agee and Peter McKibbin using a joystick, receiving visual clues and readings through remote cameras and instruments on the vehicle. Hence, it is a remotely operated vehicle. A very expensive and realistic video game!

We could also count among our assets help from the U.S. Navy's Deep Submergence Unit, who had conducted the prior summer's search and were eager to do what they could. They detailed electronics technicians Richard Penny and Shawn Dann to us as ROV navigators. Shawn eventually joined Nauticos and manned future expeditions with us. The Oceanographer of the Navy, the Naval Meteorology and Oceanography Command, and the Navy Oceanographic Office also provided support to Nauticos through an official cooperative research agreement. This included some key equipment through a leasing arrangement, weather forecasting, and general well wishes. And we figured if we were attacked by pirates on the high seas, we could count on two navies to rescue us!

✡ ✡ ✡

I regretfully returned home at the beginning of May, just before the *Enterprise* cast off mooring lines and headed southwest to the *Dakar* search area. The mobilization included a host of technical problems that were solved one by one and did not delay departure. A lot of this was thanks to the cooperative spirit of the technical teams and the support of Darios and Yechiel, who made sure we had full support from the shipyard and no undue interference from local port authorities or customs officials. We received an e-mail from John Coombs during that time, outlining some work he was doing on a gyro problem, and describing his interface with the Williamson team, one individual in particular: "We have a Williamson female on board. She mainly works with the post-processing and mosaicking, but she picked up some mechanical abilities along the way. She was having difficulty with the cable cutter and I helped her with that. I also scavenged metal for the GPS antennas and helped run a lot of cable. In other words, I'm playing well with the other kids."

The "Williamson female" was Donna Johnson. Donna was a unique member of the team. For one thing, it is uncommon to see a woman as part of a sea-going ocean technology crew. Most women who enter the ocean field choose to pursue one of the traditional sciences, such as marine biology, and are usually found with academic research groups. More important to us, Donna was unique in her abilities. With a bachelor's degree in geological oceanography and a master's in geophysics, Donna specialized in digital sonar data processing and analysis, and was a veteran of over two dozen ocean expeditions supporting undersea telecommunications cable route surveys, offshore pipeline surveys, geophysical surveys, and even a few deep-ocean searches. She had years of experience in operating Williamson's AMS sonar system, and could produce detailed sonar mosaics, bathymetric maps, and target presentations. The state-of-the-art of desktop computers and software had advanced to where this task could proceed while at sea and allow Donna to help direct the search as it was in progress. In a 2005 interview, Donna describes her life's work:

> I work a twelve-hour watch, which meant twelve hours on and twelve off. It's what I do, and I really like what I do. Yes, it's looking at a screen for a lot of hours, but I enjoy it. To me, it's not just a screen. I take all the target information, compute the size, process the image, prepare a sheet on each target, and plot them all in AutoCad. I create a mosaic as we go along, and that's always fun. On the *Dakar* mission, there were times I was bored, but mostly not. There was basic harmony on board with a special breed of people who can go out to sea and do what we do. This was special in the case of my crew because we've been on a

lot of jobs together, and when you spend twenty-four hours a day with people, you see the best and the worst and learn to live with it. We're basically a good team, and we're good at what we do. The mix goes well together.

Our business thrives on people who have the patience to spend days on end in a harsh environment, the adaptability to work well with all kinds of shipmates, the intelligence to solve difficult problems to successful conclusion, and the creativity to make the job fun whenever possible. Donna is one of these unique individuals who expects little credit, but is one of the many critical elements to success.

I received a phone call from Tom on May 7, using the Inmarsat marine satellite communications network, after they had been underway for a few days and should have begun the search. The gist of the report was that they were having a lot of problems with the search system, which we discovered had suffered a series of accidents during its last voyage, including being dropped. This is sometimes referred to ruefully as a "percussion calibration." Apparently, it suffered damage that was not evident until operating at depth. However, they were getting problems solved one by one, and hoped to have an official test shortly. This was part of our contract, and it was possible for Israel to shut us down if they felt we were not performing and their money was in danger of being wasted.

A side benefit of this otherwise grim situation was that cameraman Dave Brown had ample opportunity to film the AMS being deployed, retrieved, and deployed again. There was an electrical ground in the system that appeared soon after the vehicle was dropped in salt water, and the Williamson team seemed at a loss to find or fix the problem. All hands on watch turned out to slide the massive yellow sled to the stern, where it was hooked on to a crane and swung outboard. Each time it slid beneath the waves, the sonar signal would degrade as the ground fed electrical noise into the system, so up it would come, in a frustrating, seemingly endless repetition.

Tom also cautioned me about communications security. No operational details were to be provided to the New York office or to the Naval Attaché in Washington; they would be informed through official channels. Communications in general would be strictly controlled: no more newsy e-mails, and downloads only once per day, possibly with a twelve-hour delay. (I assumed this meant we were being censored, which was fair in this case.) The critical sign-off sheets, validating that we had met our milestones and progress payments could be released, would be faxed. Clearly, tension was high between Tom and the Williamson team, as it was so critical to resolve these sonar issues immediately, but Mike himself was on board taking responsibility for all repairs. Darios was not on board, but he was available at all times on cell phone.

One interesting tidbit of information: Tom was told that Netanyahu was "against it," but overruled by President Ezer Weizman. I don't know if that meant he was against the mission, or the search in general, or if it was accurately reported or even true. But it was interesting to know that we were being discussed in the highest levels of the Israeli government. If we needed further motivation (we did not), this was the ultimate source.

But the best news was Tom's closing remark: "Yechiel says don't worry, we're OK."

I took solace in that bit of encouragement, and told Tom that all he could do was his best. That had always proven to be good enough.

✡ ✡ ✡

Chava Barkay was waiting, still, after all the years. The question of what happened to her Boomie and the other men, and where they were resting, was never far from her mind. Part of what sustained her was the continued commitment to search. She knew the Nauticos team was out there, and she willed it to succeed.

> I wanted very much that the search be continued every year, that they didn't stop until they found it. It was very strong feeling for me, that is necessary to find it, to know what happened. Even if it's in a deep place that they can't take it out. Let it be the grave of them, yes, but I want to know where they are and what happened.
>
> And I had a good feeling every time they sailed. We keep searching next season, next year, even if they're searching in other seas, in other places. I say okay. I knew that I could keep living, if I knew they are searching. I know now it was very, very necessary for my spirit, so I could keep on living. (2002 interview)

With the good wishes of Chava Barkay, the skill of the technicians, the patience of the Israelis, and some measure of good fortune, the sonar was pronounced operational, concluding what John Coombs described by e-mail as "week one of hell on Earth." On May 9, 1999, the first images of the *Dakar* search area began to appear on Donna Johnson's screen.

✡ ✡ ✡

Donna was looking for something that had the characteristics of a submarine hull, but how to recognize it if it appeared? The job required patience, above all. The sonar could image a swath of the ocean floor about a mile wide, including overlap with adjacent swaths to account for any errors in navigation. To cover the sixty by eight nautical-mile search area, counting the distance needed to turn around at the end of each pass, the *Enterprise* would travel around one thousand miles. At the slow speeds of less than three knots, it would take weeks of continuous scanning to cover the entire area. Working in a small van welded to the deck of a pitching ship for twelve-hour shifts was wearing, and it took real discipline to keep sharp and make sure nothing was missed.

Of course, Donna could not do it alone. Success in this endeavor required the careful choreography of people and equipment, always adapting to the ever-changing conditions of the sea and weather. First of all, the ship had to be run smoothly and had to precisely follow an imaginary line on the ocean's surface, guided by a blend of modern electronic navigation and the ancient art of the seafarer. The *Flying Enterprise* was captained by Master Duncan MacKenzie, a British citizen living in South Africa, possessed of a wry, sly sense of humor, a saving grace over long, tedious missions. A former Gulf of Mexico workboat that had serviced the offshore oil rigs for many years, the *Enterprise* was pretty old, but the owner and crew kept it up as well as can be expected, and it was quite seaworthy. At 170 feet long and 560 tons, the ship could accommodate a charter crew of eighteen in addition to the ship's crew of nine in common bunk rooms with shared bathroom (head) facilities. As the only woman on board, Donna was fortunate to have her own room, but she shared a bathroom with several other members of the expedition team. The vessel was strictly utilitarian, with a large, flat after-deck designed to accommodate as much as 450 tons of equipment with ample working space for towing operations. Her hull was painted the brilliant orange typical of search, salvage, and rescue equipment, which posed a problem for our video cameraman by imparting an orange cast to anyone standing too close to a bulkhead.

As on working ships everywhere, maintenance and painting is a continual process, in this case carried out by a team of perpetually smiling Kenyan deck hands. Within hours of leaving port, the grime of the Limassol mobilization had been scoured, scrubbed, and hosed away. Interior wooden paneling and furnishings were kept immaculately clean by Gigi, a dark, rail-thin man in his early twenties who relentlessly washed, polished, and shined the cabins and living spaces. Gigi's stocky older brother, Tamaso, was the cook, generally thought to be the most important member of a ship's crew for obvious reasons. No complaints were lodged against the cooking, so I gather Tamaso was excellent. The brothers were from Rumania, as was the gigantic, bearded chief mate, Damir Gasic.

Mike Williamson and his technicians Tom Stein and Wesley Lablanc had managed after days of around-the-clock effort to wrestle the AMS sonar into service, get it to the bottom, and start collecting images. But their work was far from done. The weak sonar echoes that were hoped to contain evidence of the *Dakar* were nearly overwhelmed by background noises, filling the ocean with the sounds of snapping shrimp, surface storms, passing ships, and other biological, natural, and man-made distractions. The bottom itself is far from featureless. If one can distinguish the noise from a real echo of the bottom, rocks, cliffs, sea mounts, and variations in soil all produce signals that can mimic or mask the real target. So the Williamson team constantly monitored and adjusted the sonar settings, trying to get the strongest signal back without being blanketed by noise.

Part of this was making sure the sensor was kept at just the right height above the bottom. This would be easy if the bottom was flat, and if the ship could travel the same speed at all times. But varying topography, water currents, and changing winds make that very difficult. Towing a sonar system like Williamson's AMS-60 is almost like flying a kite, where the kite is the sonar vehicle (or sled) on the end of a long string. The string to the kite does not form an absolutely straight line to the kite, but instead it droops slightly to form a curve called a catenary. The tow cable behaves the same way. With a kite, as you let out more string, the kite does not just go exactly one foot higher for each foot of string let out. Instead, it gets further away as it gets a little higher for each foot of string reeled out. Likewise, to get the sonar near the sea floor ten thousand feet below, you probably need to let out as much as twice as many feet of cable, depending on the speed. The faster the boat is going, the more the sonar will "kite" away from the sea floor; if you go slower, the sonar will descend toward the bottom, and plow into the sea floor if too much cable is reeled out, thus becoming a sled in another sense of the word. This unfortunate occurrence is sometimes referred to as "bottom sampling."

So the tow cable is constantly being reeled in and out by small amounts to keep the sled at just the right altitude for the sonar to work best. A forward-looking sonar scans the path ahead to detect any sharp rises or cliffs, so that the sled can be reeled in (and up) quickly, and "violent sampling" can be avoided. To handle all of this stress, the cable is wrapped with a couple of layers of high-strength steel armor strands that give it the necessary physical strength to carry its own weight and also tow the sonar vehicle. The armor strands make the cable look like a smooth wire rope to some extent, but with the electrical and data lines contained within it. The individual armor strands are a little thinner than spaghetti. Through normal wear and tear, these strands become stressed and will eventually fail. This can be worse if the cable is over stressed or if the same spot on the cable is allowed to run over a pulley or sheave for long periods. Progressive tow-cable failure begins when the armor strands start to fail, one at a time or a couple at a time, until the strength of the cable is reduced so much that it breaks. If it breaks under load, it can become a deadly and uncontrollable whip that can kill people in the vicinity. As the individual strands break, they can also become hopelessly tangled in the rest of the cable or in the winch. And a quarter-million-dollar tool becomes useless.

Yet another critical element of this process is keeping the ship on the right path. Survey lines are laid out on a chart ahead of time, but wind and weather call for adjustment if the ship cannot follow the planned path accurately and slowly. At less than three knots, it is hard to control a ship like the *Enterprise.* Ships with bow thrusters and more sophisticated positioning systems were not available or were too costly for this mission. And just staying near the path was not good enough. The sonar would follow the ship, so to be sure it was following the right path, miles behind the ship, the ship must plod steadily along without varying speed or "snaking" down the path. This task was the purview of navigators Glenn Chaffey and Mick Harvey, veterans of Williamson operations.

Tom and Dick Boyd stood alternate supervisor watches, and took overall responsibility for the operations and, above all, the safety of the crew. It is a testimony to Tom's thoroughness, skill, experience, and leadership that time and again successful missions are conducted under his direction without the slightest injury to anyone, in spite of the demanding and dangerous conditions aboard a research vessel, and the unforgiving presence of the sea.

Yechiel was everywhere, all of the time. Donna remembers him at the screen for most of the survey, and doesn't remember him ever sleeping.

✡ ✡ ✡

Donna continued to analyze the sonar data, looking at each target and considering its merits against the criteria Tom had established. One problem she faced was a special kind of "noise." Mariners have plied the Mediterranean Sea throughout seafaring history, and of course ships have been lost from the beginning. During the world wars, aircraft were added to the litter of thousands of forgotten hulks resting on the bottom. Although unburied wooden vessels are consumed over time by natural and biological processes, their cargos of ceramic vessels (called amphora), ballast stones, grinding wheels, and other durable items may remain for thousands of years. In the deep abyssal plains where our team was searching, rates of silting are so low that only millimeters might accumulate in a millennium.

Over the course of the *Dakar* search, 320 targets were noted, cataloged, and analyzed. How to pick the right one? Tom's criteria helped. He devised a ranking system to grade sonar "blips" and help focus attention on the most likely ones:

A. Contact near debris field or impact crater.
   Measurements match size of target.
   Contact has features of man-made target (shadowing, hard edges).
   Contact is abnormal to bottom environment.
B. 3 out of above 4
C. 2 out of above 4
D. 1 out of above 4

The contact logs show that among the hundreds of contacts, only five were rated A, and fourteen B. These were the primary focus of identification by the *Argonaut* and the ROV team led by Bruce Brown.

Donna could not watch the screen every minute; in fact, she did not watch the data as it evolved. Real-time monitoring was the job of John and Dave Brown, who stood the sonar operator watch. One way that we could afford to bring a cameraman along for the month's mission was to expect him to do double duty. Dave had limited experience as a sonar monitor, but had been to sea with Cousteau and was a quick learner. Dave and John, taking twelve-hour turns, would watch the sonar display on the screen like a waterfall. Newest information was produced at the top, and it would scroll down and eventually off the bottom of the screen. As the information scrolled, it was also recorded for Donna and Tom to analyze later. It was tedious, but also exciting, as their eyes were the first ones in history to see images of that part of the Mediterranean Sea floor, and they both hoped to be the first to see the *Dakar*. In the vast majority of cases, images developing on the waterfall image would begin to show the distinctive curve of a natural sea floor feature. However, there were many items that were potentially man-made. When Donna started her watch, she would scroll through the saved data, focusing on the contacts that Dave or John noted, sort of like fast forwarding a videotape to the good parts and skipping the commercials. This way she could scan, assess, and compile the information from an entire day during her half-day watch.

The days wore on. Area C was covered first, at the insistence of our Israeli customers, who had a hunch about it and were swayed by the tantalizing, but deceptive, Naval Oceanographic Office data. Over one hundred targets were logged, with a few As and Bs. John reported dead calm glassy seas, reflecting a waning gibbous moon. This pastoral image of the view from the ship's bridge was punctuated by the sounds of recorded music from a Greek barbershop quartet, apparently the first mate's favorite. As the ship moved into Area B, the weather shifted as well, and for days the ship trudged through heavy swells, tossing the crew around severely. John wondered if the ship was really seaworthy, and began to refer to his wallowing home as the *Flying Enterpoop*. Dave captured dramatic video of the swells cascading over the flat aft deck, washing the careening surface in two-foot-deep waves. Still, the cable dipped into the water, and, miles down, the AMS sonar chirped peacefully and patiently.

Then a new and serious problem developed, as the team began to notice that armor strands on the tow cable were failing. Mike Williamson would wrap the broken strands with duct tape to prevent them from unwinding and getting tangled in the rest of the cable or the winch. He did this at great personal risk, often on a ladder, sometimes at night, with the ship rolling and waves crashing over the stern. The tape did not stand up well, but the gooey adhesive would work into the strands and help hold the broken ones in place—for a while. The trick was repeated many times, adding to the multitude of unique uses for duct tape. But with each failing armor strand, the cable was weakening. Mike imposed a limit on the amount of cable we could deploy in order to prevent exposing the failing section. This meant they would need to slow down in the deeper areas to let the sonar "sink" to the proper altitude above the sea floor. But if they tried to go much slower, steering the ship would become unmanageable. It was beginning to look like the search would be cut short because of the tow cable problem. The sixty-mile lanes were taking over a day each to complete, plus six hours or more added time to turn around with such a long cable streaming behind.

The turn-around time is a frustrating reality in deep-ocean searches. With miles of cable trailing behind and below, and the sled at the end, the ship has to proceed past the end of the search area and then make a large sweeping turn to allow the cable and sonar sled to snake around behind. After some distance, the sled is stabilized on the adjacent track, hopefully before the boundary of the area is reached, and the search continues. There is no alternative to the hours that must be invested in this; it is just part of the overhead cost of the search. Fortunately, the long lanes of the *Dakar* search area reduced the number of turns needed.

Meanwhile, the companion *Argonaut* team was having their own problems getting the Phoenix Remora ready for operation. Bruce Brown had some capable shipmates, engineer Steve Abdalla, ace technician Shawn Dann, and Steve St. Amour of Phoenix, who had built the Remora. This was its first operational deployment, as it was never used on the prior year's *Titanic* expedition. Bruce Brown's mobilization log described problems with the ship's generator, concern with overloading of the deck with the winch system, and a host of damaged plugs, valves, and fittings on the ROV. It was hard to communicate with shipyard welders to get them to do exactly what was wanted, complicated by their being carted off to Immigration for several hours right in the middle of things. Finally, by May 15, the little ROV was sending video pictures through its fiber-optic cable to the consoles on the ship.

One of the first targets checked was designated B-129. One of the early targets seen in Area B, it was described as: "Very hard target, abnormal in bottom environment, no shadow, and probably too small. Impact crater." It was rated a "B." The *Argonaut* was sent to investigate and report. Soon, the word came back to Tom on the *Enterprise*: B-129 was just an old ship. Tom said, "Well, *how* old?" Answer: "*Very* old." So Tom climbed into a launch used to shuttle personnel between the ships to take a look for himself. What he found astonished him. A field of ceramic amphora, or clay jugs, two to three feet high, numbering in the thousands, lay peacefully in the shape of the cargo ship that was carrying them ages ago. It really *was* very old! He directed the team to spend twenty precious minutes mapping the site with a camera, sweeping the whole area for a panorama of the wreck. Although the wood of the ship was long gone, the cargo had settled where it was stacked, and had not moved since. The galley area was visible, with cookware and plates. Ballast stones and lead anchor stocks were lying exactly where one would expect. Remarkably, a bronze cauldron was resting upright, half full of silt, the world's oldest known sediment trap! Ten thousand feet down, nothing, not tides, currents, weather, dredging, fishing, nor divers, had ever disturbed this site.

It was later determined by archaeologists from the Institute of Nautical Archaeology at Texas A&M University that the ship was probably carrying a cargo mainly of wine, possibly from the ancient seaport on Kos, a Greek island near Rhodes. It was found on a direct route to Alexandria, Egypt, about halfway across the sea, 150 miles from land. It could date from as early as 200 BC, although I would like to think it was taking wine to Cleopatra, which would make it a little more recent!

Other targets were found that have yet to be identified. They probably are ships, but they didn't have characteristics that made them likely to be submarines so they were bypassed. Still, they may represent a collection of shipwrecks that lie along the ancient sea lanes, and that is something we are hoping to investigate in the future. So, we were lucky again, but I was happy that we had the foresight to write into our contract with Israel that we would be free to pursue these ancillary finds later.

Another interesting contact was identified as a 1930s-era steamer, just like the one Harrison Ford sailed on as Indiana Jones in the movie. Who knows where it was headed, what its cargo was, and how it sank?

Square miles of search area were being relentlessly covered and carefully inspected. Contacts that held promise were proving to be interesting, even fascinating, but nonetheless disappointing. None of them was the *Dakar*. Despite the problems with equipment, the changing weather, and the rigors of life at sea, the *Enterprise* worked its way south, lane by lane, as the remaining acreage of Area B continued to shrink. By May 23, there was little time, money, or area left. Still no *Dakar*.

Triple-A-Plus

The last week of May approached. Only a few days remained of the *Dakar* search, and only a few lanes of the sixty by eight nautical-mile search area remained. Area C had been completely covered, and every likely target inspected. No *Dakar*. Area B was divided into sixteen lanes, sixty nautical miles long, which would cover the area completely, twice. This redundancy was desirable because it ensured complete coverage and allowed two looks at every target from different directions. However, there was no time in the plan or budget for this luxury. Complete coverage could be obtained by covering the odd-numbered lanes numbered 3 to 15, seven lanes total. Even-numbered lanes were laid out on the search grid, but only provisionally. The search area was oriented with the long axis nearly east–west, and the lanes were numbered from the bottom (south edge). When the search team finished Area C, which took until May 13, they were on the northeast corner of Area B. Tom decided to sweep a long turn with the sonar snaking behind and run right down the center of area B, down lane B9. This was essentially the path that the *Dakar* planned to follow back in 1968.

Lots of target characteristics were logged, but almost all were ranked C's and D's, a few B's, no A's (see Chapter 13). Target B-129 provided some excitement, turning out to be the very old ancient wreck. But no *Dakar*.

What next? The sequence of lanes to cover was arbitrary, so Tom planned to arrange things to lessen the cost of turning at the end of each lane. It was easier and quicker to make a very wide turn and line up several lanes over than trying to narrow the maneuver and hit the adjacent lane. So it made sense to cover either lane 3 or lane 15 next, but there was no obvious reason to choose one over the other. Tom picked lane 15, to the north.

After lane 15, came lane 7, then lane 13, and so on. By 2:30 PM on the afternoon of May 23, the next to last lane was completed, and the *Enterprise* began its slow, deliberate turn onto lane 3, the last swath to be covered in Area B. Six hours later, the AMS sled had reversed direction, stabilized on its new lane, and was proceeding down the path. This was the last chance for the Nauticos team.

David Brown was manning the sonar display, called Isis. Over the preceding weeks, he had gained much experience, appreciation, and skill, and was developing an eye for a promising contact. More than eleven hours into his daily watch, halfway through the last lane, something caught his attention. David writes in his expedition journal:

> I am on watch, hunched in my seat, the glowing Isis screen showing miles of soft gray nothing, a frustrating reminder that the sea is vast, deep and beyond our ken. It's close to the change of watch, nearly midnight, and my butt aches from hours spent huddled in my chair. Out of the corner of my eye, a target begins to appear on screen, scrolling down slowly as the AMS passes across something hidden in the black, crushing depths far below us. I straighten. The target appears to be a solid object, a long, narrow form lying in two pieces, well away from any geological features that would suggest it's part of the bottom topography. There are numerous smaller, hard objects scattered about, and my hand is shaking as I pick up my sonar log and excitedly assign a "B" to the target. I haven't dared grant that high a grade since the last pile of rocks that I had flagged weeks before.
>
> Just then, Yechiel Ga'ash wanders in to the control van, the graying beard he has grown on the trip a painful reminder of the previous weeks of frustration. Looking over my shoulder, his tired eyes lock on to the target creeping slowly up the screen, then down to my log sheet.
>
> "I'd give it an A."
>
> "An A?"
>
> I look up at the face that had moments before been the very picture of discouragement, only to see a remarkable transformation has taken place. His eyes alert and alight, he elaborates:
>
> "Give it an A-plus."
>
> "A-plus ?!"
>
> "Triple A."
>
> After nearly two decades of searching, Yechiel Ga'ash believes he has found his Grail. Grabbing a bottle of "Whiteout," I hastily revise the grade to "A."
>
> I go off watch and hit the rack, exhaustion finally winning out over the excitement of a good target. Very few things happen quickly on a deep sea search, and I know too well that it could be a very long time before we further investigate our find. We systematically plod

northwest along the remainder of our 60-mile-long line, while the next watch analyzes the target, and the coordinates are radioed to the *Argonaut* for investigation by the ROV.

Target B-289 fell just about halfway along lane 3, the last lane fully covering the southern part of the area. The *Argonaut* was deliberately investigating Tom's list of contacts. B-289 was added to the list and given priority. The *Argonaut* wrapped up work on another site, recovered the ROV, and sped toward B-289.

Working an ROV at a depth of ten thousand feet, as I said, is a tedious and exhausting job requiring skill, patience, and teamwork. The idea is to position the ship directly over the target, two miles below, dangling the ROV on the end of its steel-armored fiber-optic cable. Once near the bottom, the ROV pilot scans the area with his Simrad sonar by slowly spinning the ROV, controlling its thrusters with a joystick. The ROV itself consists of a box-like aluminum frame that cradles electronics pressure bottles and holds thrusters, lights, cameras, robotic arms (called manipulators), and any other equipment needed for the mission. Atop this frame is a shaped block of syntactic foam, designed to compensate for the weight of the rest of the vehicle and make it neutrally buoyant. That way, the ROV is able to cruise along near the bottom without sinking or floating back up. The ducted propeller thrusters can move the vehicle up, down, forward, back, and sideways, as well as twirl it like a robot ballerina.

The main tools of an ROV are its video cameras, which are the pilot's windows on the undersea world and his main sensor for its control and operation. High-intensity lights push back a bit of the otherwise complete darkness of the ocean floor, allowing visual ranges of a few dozen feet in clear water. The pilot watches the video monitors, as well as scanning sonar, depth, speed, and heading sensors, to attempt to locate and approach a target for investigation.

The ROV is tethered to the cable, which is its power and data lifeline. The heavy cable cannot be pulled very far by the ROV, so the operation depends on holding the ship directly over the target. Moving the ship and the cable is a very slow exercise, hence the requirement for patience. But how to know the location of the target? The coordinates passed from the search ship are calculated from the known position of the ship (with its very accurate GPS navigation system) by adding a "layback" and "offset" to account for the location of the actual sonar, miles below and behind, and the range of the target from the sonar. This cannot be done with complete precision as it depends on a model of the shape of the cable, which in turn depends on speed, depth, and the amount of cable deployed. So, when the ROV descends on the coordinates of the target, the pilot knows it may be some distance from the position given, and he may have to search around a bit.

The presence of the cable makes for another complication. As the ship heaves and rolls in the seas, this motion is felt by the cable, which transmits it down to the ROV. The cable absorbs some of the motion by bending and stretching, but still the ROV will gently bob up and down, confounding the pilot's job of maneuvering. Also, the cameras display this motion, which is out of step with the motion of the ship. So, imagine being in an enclosed, windowless van on the pitching deck of a ship, with the only visual clue being the ROV monitors, which are showing a completely different motion! This is an excellent recipe for seasickness. Yet the ROV operators overcome this disorientation, keep track of a dozen instruments, and maneuver the ROV as needed. It can be a grueling task, but very rewarding when something compelling comes across the monitors.

The *Argonaut* deployed the Remora ROV, which started its two-hour descent to ten thousand feet. The sonar revealed nothing. Scanning in all directions, the pilot thrusted around in a limited search pattern, restrained by the heavy cable. Still nothing. B-289, a.k.a., Triple-A-Plus, had evaporated.

✡ ✡ ✡

Meanwhile, on the *Enterprise,* Tom came to the end of lane 3 and began the slow turn onto the adjacent lane 2, hoping to get another glimpse of the target. Beyond that hope, there was the grim prospect of going back over the even lanes of the search area, effectively covering it twice, assuming the Israeli customer would authorize the expense. There was a real chance that yet another search for the *Dakar* would come up empty. The unflappable Tom remained stoic. The emotional Dave Brown could hardly contain himself. After a few hours' sleep, Dave returned to his sonar station, eager to learn the results of the ROV investigation. He would have to wait. And wait. From his journal:

> The next day heavy swells roll in from the North, accompanied by a freshening wind, the first indication that the calm weather we have enjoyed over the last few days is leaving us. I eagerly seek out Tom Dettweiler prior to my watch to find out if *Argonaut* has visited the target site. The news is bewildering; they have, and found nothing. Although the exact position of an object nearly two miles below us is difficult to fix, every other set of coordinates we had sent to the ROV ship had yielded solid contacts, albeit with a tramp steamer, several wrecks from Roman times, and the occasional rock pile. What are the odds that our most promising target to date should be incorrectly plotted?
>
> Tom is difficult to read. He is far too experienced at deep water searches to be whooped into a frenzy over a single sonar trace.

Conversely, he is not about to give up on a likely hit after the first pass by the AMS and a miss by the ROV. I go on watch seething over the unflappability of the veterans of this arcane profession. I grumble to myself that if it were up to me we'd have swung around and taken a few more sonar pictures of the target after the first pass. Of course, I would have been similarly tempted upon discovery of our first target weeks ago. Days would have been wasted chasing false leads, and we would never have gotten even halfway through the search box in the allotted mission time. As I settle into my well-worn spot in front of the Isis screen, I reflect that it's just as well that I'm not in charge.

Another day trudging through heavy seas at 1-1/2 knots finds us at the western edge of our search area, and we begin the enormous swing that will bring us around to the next line down the grid, and hopefully yield a reverse angle on our elusive target. The wind and seas have kicked up hard, though, and it takes a full 11 hours to pull our 3-kilometer tow into position to run down the line. Within hours of attempting the line, it becomes apparent that King Neptune has other ideas. Seas pound us from the port quarter, pushing the stern to the South, and at this slow speed we cannot hold course with the precision needed to keep the AMS sonar on track. We cannot speed up, as this will pull the sonar too far off the bottom for good imaging. We decide to haul the device near the surface, speed up, steam down to the other end of the 60-mile box, then redeploy and come up our line heading into the seas, a tactic that should make it far easier to steer.

Another day passes, the anticipation of seeing our target again growing by the hour. The seas calm, and we begin the slow progression up the line from the eastern end of the box. A full 2-1/2 days after the first pass, I come on watch at noon to find the tiny van crammed with off-watch spectators, all anxiously waiting to get another look as we pass by our "Triple A" site.

The navigator calls out the time to contact.

"Five minutes."

No one moves. The small, claustrophobic room seems to contract to a single glowing computer screen, slowly scrolling data from the AMS creeping through the pitch-blackness beneath us.

"One minute."

The seconds tick by, the gray, featureless image on the screen a tantalizing prelude to the solid black targets we hope to see appear.

"We should be alongside now."

Nothing. No black, cigar-shaped object. No debris field. No crater. Incredulous, I scan the faces of my companions, certain that there must be some mistake. We're in the wrong place, or the original target was somehow plotted incorrectly. Tom displays his usual cryptic deadpan. Not so Yechiel; 31 years of a country's futile search for its lost sons appear in his tired eyes. He heads the dispirited procession out of the van.

The implacable Isis screen reveals nothing of interest for the next eleven hours, reinforcing the crushing knowledge that our search must continue. We have completed the primary grid, and once we close out the box there is a possibility that the mission will be extended to fill in the lines between the lines. This means another two weeks away from home, with 12-hour watches spent staring at the blandness of the Isis screen to look forward to.

Target B-289 remained elusive.

Tom remained patiently positive; he truly believes that every square of ground covered and eliminated from the search improves the chances that the quarry will be found in the remaining area. So, even lack of targets is progress. But B-289 should be there. Tom has one more card to play; he can try to tease something out of the data in the post-processing lab. And he has Donna Johnson to help. Together, they use the Isis to correct for the geometries of the sonar beams, adjust contrast, and apply other image processing algorithms designed to separate signal from noise, target from background. After a while, according to Dave, Tom had news for him:

> I am trying not to think about it, tiredly contemplating my bunk at close of watch, when Tom emerges from the analysis side of the van and drops a piece of paper on the desk in front of me. Etched clearly on the page is an elaborate ink-blot sonar trace that closely resembles the original "Triple A." Taken aback, I look at Tom's slyly smiling face.
>
> "What is it?"
>
> "It's our target. I ran some corrections on the data from earlier today. "
>
> "But all we saw was a blank screen."
>
> "We went right over the top of it. Would you like to come over to the *Argonaut*?"
>
> I scramble out of the van into the night, racing for my cameras. Fifteen minutes later I've assembled my gear, joining Tom and Yechiel on deck to watch the other EDT ship come alongside. Passing my gear across, we step onto *Argonaut*, and are underway for "Triple A" in minutes. It's good to see new faces after weeks aboard *Flying Enterprise*, and

after an hour of socializing I make my way to temporary quarters to grab a couple of hours of rest before the ROV deployment at sunrise.

Apparently, there was no problem with navigation. In fact, the track was so precise that the sonar tracked directly over the target! Because the sonar is towed several hundred feet above the bottom, signals from the ground below come back from a very steep angle, whereas those from the far range of detection come from a very shallow angle. When the raw data shows up on the Isis screen, the near field data is compressed, while the far field is stretched. This simple geometric effect can be compensated for on the computer by a "slant range correction," but still the compressed data from directly beneath the sonar is useless. This "shadow zone" is a serious problem in sonar coverage. Fortunately, it is small, and objects near the edge of the shadow zone can be teased out of the data if you know how to process it. Tom and Donna know how.

The new target that corresponded to B-289 was designated B-310. Every indication was that they were one and the same. The second look provided a better fix on position. It was time to find out exactly what Triple A was. From Dave Brown's journal:

Dawn breaks on a perfectly calm, blue sea. There is scarcely a ripple as the ROV is swung off the stern, then released to begin the long trip to the bottom. I picture the bright yellow robot descending from the brilliant sunshine into a dark world, the sunlight giving way to ever deepening shades of blue, then blackness. It will be a couple of tense hours before she is on bottom and can attempt to find our target using the sonar she carries.

Somehow the hours pass, and we find ourselves jammed into yet another metal cubicle, the control van for the ROV, eyes riveted to a bank of television monitors, computer screens, and a sonar display. The cameras at first reveal only the ancient ooze of the bottom, but the sonar screen makes immediate contact with what appears to be a large, metal object. The robot's thrusters engage, carrying her steadily across the featureless sea floor toward the sonar target.

The interior light is very dim so as not to distract the ROV pilots, but I do my best to film the faces around me, attempting to capture their intensity in the tiny, twilight world of the control van. We are riveted to the television screens as a dim object appears in the distance; even from afar the jagged outline is clearly not of natural origin.

The form looms large on screen; a twisted metal mass surrounding what appears at first inspection to be a rocket thruster or part of a jet engine. It's a large, silver cone, and if anyone in the van knows what it is, they are not telling. The silence deepens; the occasional murmured conversation between the pilots the only noise. The ROV has picked up another sonar signal, this one much larger, corresponding to the cigar-shaped object we had detected with the AMS system, and they move onto it.

Again, a flat, mud bottom. The hazy outline of a very large structure on the sea floor ahead becomes steadily clearer. A large, black ovoid shape fills the screens. It is the sonar dome that was mounted all the way forward, on the nose of all T-class submarines, and we now know that we have found *Dakar*. The distinctive black form looks for all the world like a tomb. The silence in the van is complete.

✡ ✡ ✡

But was it really the *Dakar*? The Mediterranean Sea floor was sprinkled with the hulks of World War II submarines, even more than a few British T-class boats. They had to be sure.

We were prepared for this question. The team had architectural drawings, including detailed descriptions of the special modifications that were unique to the ship. So by looking at key features they could distinguish between a British T-class submarine and that particular modified British T-class submarine.

Over the next few hours, the ROV imaged the sail (broken off, and lying on its side), and two major hull sections. The hull was broken aft of the sail, and many identifiable features were seen, such as capstans, periscopes, sonar domes, and anchors. The bridge gyro repeater was seen eerily laying face up, showing the southeasterly course set by the *Dakar* as she made her transit across the Mediterranean. But was it really the *Dakar*?

The ROV combed the wreckage in search of a Hebrew letter painted on a bulkhead, or any of a number of other distinctive clues, but to no avail. Aft of the sonar dome, the hull was mangled wreckage, clearly the result of a massive implosion. This chaos had obliterated all evidence. Finally, the ROV left the main body of the wreck, moving in reverse of the original path of discovery, out to the first chunk of wreckage found. There, the team found their proof. The chunk was the submarine conning tower, or bridge fin, separated from the hull during the long fall to the sea floor. Inside the detached piece was the odd metal cone, first seen, and thought to resemble a rocket engine. It actually was a custom-made enclosed ladder leading to the top of the conning tower, built for commando egress from the ten-man diving chamber. Finally, proof positive!

As soon as Yechiel was satisfied, he called headquarters in Haifa and notified the Admiral. In a few short hours, there appeared a sleek-looking gunboat bringing out Raz and his team to make the official determination. Most of them had been part of our original Committee, including Mike Kaisari. With them was Doron Amir, the man who was to have sailed on the *Dakar* in 1968, but was bumped for lack of space on board. Amir insisted that the team take a piece of paper, and without any emotions, write down what they were looking to find, any conclusive sign, that would prove the wreck to be the *Dakar*. Too much time, money, and effort had been spent to make a mistake, to allow the excitement of imminent discovery, after over three decades of frustration, to cloud their judgment. So, it was without emotion that the team came aboard, deliberately and carefully studied the images on the monitors, and saw that the wreck was, indeed, the *Dakar*. They took charge of ROV operations and spent quite a bit of time making a thorough identification. Then they called back to Navy Headquarters and said, "The *Dakar* is found!"

Admiral Raz describes that moment:

When I realized that what we saw on the video from the underwater vehicle was the *Dakar*, I had two different reactions. The first was the *Dakar* looked like a live submarine. The first impression—she was alive. It was like she was an hour ago, operational, and all the faces of the people came back to me. But as the camera moved to the aft, and we saw the mess of the piping and cables, and the parts of the hull— this was a very different impression. Everything changed. It was obvious that the submarine went through a terrible event. We hoped that what happened was very swift, and the people did not suffer long.

At the same time I had the feeling of achievement, after thirty years of looking and working hard, after all the rumors and a lot of false information, we found her at last.

This is actually the *Dakar* which we remembered as she was leaving Portsmouth, over thirty years ago.

✡ ✡ ✡

I was in contact with the search, but not frequently, and received only intermittent reports. There were frequent daily reports at first, but some concern was raised about the amount of information in them, and we were directed to cut that off. If there was a problem, they could ask for our assistance, but there was some very intense interest by the families and the press in what was going on, and the Israelis wanted to control the information. So, after a few days, we lost frequent contact; that was OK, though. We had a good team out there, and there was other business to be focused on.

For a couple of weeks, then, things were rather quiet from the Mediterranean. Most of our communication was limited to what we needed to know to conduct business, so when we reached a milestone we would get a paper that was signed off on the ship that would indicate we had achieved the next milestone in the contract. And that would trigger a payment to us, and then we would pay our contractors and we would move ahead. There was a lot going on, and we knew things were progressing, and I had to be more worried about paying the bills than exactly how things were going out at sea, as long as they weren't having problems. Ultimately, I had confidence in our plan and in our team. I believe it was Amelia Earhart who said, "Decide whether or not the goal is worth the risks involved. If it is, stop worrying." So I wasn't worrying.

Then, one day I got a phone call. It was the week of my daughter Bethany's high school graduation, and we were meeting her and another girl and her parents for a celebration lunch. I was just about to leave the office, but it was Yochay Ben-Joseph, the Israeli Naval Attaché calling, and I wasn't about to miss that one! He said he'd received a call from the Israeli chief of naval operations, and they probably had found the submarine, but they were working on a positive identification. I should wait to hear from Admiral Raz before saying anything, but he offered his congratulations.

I was stunned!

In a few short minutes, the phone rang again, and it was Tom, with essentially the same news.

It is not possible to prepare for that kind of news because you have to prepare yourself for the disappointment of *not* finding it, and that's not an event, it's a process. You don't all of a sudden *not* find something. You try and try and at some point you've exhausted your resources or your plan, but it's not a finality because you can always try again. But the awareness that you *have* succeeded occurs all at once. You don't really have a chance to prepare for that or get used to it—it just happens.

I'm sure I said something appropriate, but it was hard to express in a telephone call the gravity and excitement of the moment, which kind of built as I got used to it. How exciting it was to spend a moment absorbing the fact, and then walk out into the halls of the office, gather the staff together, and announce it—that was fun. Of course, I couldn't just walk away then. There were other people to call, some immediate plans to be made. I had to decide whether it made sense to go out to Israel at that moment. And I was late for lunch with my daughter. So I wrapped up things as quickly as I could and dashed out for lunch—and Bethany forgave me right away for my tardiness. She knew how important this was.

We got this news on a Friday preceding the Memorial Day holiday weekend, and it was a tradition among several of the Nauticos families to go out to a lake in western Maryland called Deep Creek and go camping together. We decided to go ahead, as there was nothing we could do to help the team in the

Mediterranean. Six or eight families spent the weekend together, and Friday night, sitting around the campfire, we got so noisy that the park ranger had to come three times to ask us to be quiet. "But you don't understand! We found the *Dakar*!" He didn't understand, but was patient enough to let us quiet down on our own.

✡ ✡ ✡

The position of the submarine was nearly in the center of the area originally proposed by Nauticos in 1997. Once again, the integrated, cross-trained team of operations experts, ocean engineers, and navigation analysts had come together and worked a tough problem to a successful discovery.

The Israelis immediately informed all the family members before the news was made public. Within hours, planes were flying overhead with press and photographers, and boats were on their way out to the site. The teams decided to leave the area immediately so not to reveal the *Dakar*'s position prematurely, and the ships returned to Cyprus to begin demobilization. Tom, Dick Boyd, and Dave Brown were whisked off to Tel Aviv for press conferences, interviews, and meetings with the grateful families of the *Dakar* crew. Included in the celebrations was a well-deserved promotion of Yechiel Ga'ash from project officer to commander. His personal eighteen-year quest was finally successful.

We cannot imagine how the family members must have felt. One woman, whose brother had been on the *Dakar*, took Dave Brown's hands in hers. She said that on the night of the day she received news of the discovery, it took her a long time to get to sleep. On awakening, she looked in the mirror to see a different person. She declared, "A dark cloud was lifted from my heart."

✡ ✡ ✡

I was sorry I missed it. There were two reasons I didn't go. One was the timing: I would have had to leave immediately and spend a fortune on a last-minute plane ticket. The other was that it was a team effort, with Tom leading the team, and I didn't want to steal the limelight from him at that special time. I didn't want to be seen as the boss who sat back at home and then showed up just in time to get the recognition. I made a conscious decision not to go. But I got a call from Yechiel just after the press conference. "I'm going to kill you!" he said. "You should have been here!" He said Tom would be a "hostage" of the Israeli Navy for the rest of the week. I asked him if we could report our success publicly; he said, "Shout it out loud, with pride!"

The first and most dramatic step in solving the mystery of the *Dakar* was taken. As with any other disaster at sea, the cause of the tragedy would soon be revealed by a careful forensic study of the wreck data, which required another visit to the site to check for specific damage, hatch positions, valve settings, and other details. At that point, however, no final determination could be made, and Nauticos discussed with the Israeli government the possibility of future forensic operations and, if desired, recovery of artifacts. Plans were soon made for a return to the site of discovery.

PRESS RELEASE
June 1, 1999
    For Immediate Release

    Maryland Company Locates Israeli Submarine

Hanover, Maryland—A 31 year search for the missing Israeli submarine DAKAR officially ended with the identification of wreckage from the vessel on Friday, May 28th. Nauticos Corporation, an ocean exploration company based in Hanover, Maryland, under contract to the Israeli Government, located the DAKAR in the Mediterranean Sea.

The DAKAR was a WWII "T-class" boat built by the British, and sold to the Israelis after modifications, upgrades, and sea trials. In 1968, the DAKAR was en route to Haifa via Gibraltar on its maiden voyage for delivery to the operational fleet. During this transit, communications inexplicably ceased and the submarine was never heard from again.

Nauticos Corporation committed a combination of advanced, proven equipment and a highly qualified team of search and operations experts to undertake this operation for the Israeli Navy. Thomas Dettweiler of Nauticos Corporation was the operations manager. He was assisted by Nauticos ocean experts, as well as experts from Williamson & Associates of Seattle, Washington, and personnel from Phoenix Marine, Inc. of Arlington, Virginia. Navigation support was provided by the U.S. Navy's Deep Submergence Unit. The Oceanographer of the Navy, the Naval Meteorology and Oceanography Command, and Naval Oceanographic Office also provided support to Nauticos through a cooperative research agreement (CRADA).

Williamson & Associates provided the AMS-60 search system used to locate the *Dakar*. Nauticos and Williamson personnel operated this system 24 hours per day during at-sea operations.

Once the search system provided a good sonar contact, the REMORA 6000, a remotely operated vehicle (ROV) equipped with both video and still cameras, was used to verify the sonar contacts and identify the *Dakar*. The REMORA 6000 was built by Steve St. Amour of Phoenix Marine, Inc. Both

Phoenix and Nauticos personnel operated this vehicle during target identification and verification operations.

Nauticos president, David Jourdan gave his thoughts regarding the discovery of the *Dakar*: "Our team is proud to work with the Israeli Navy and play a key role in this discovery. I hope that solving this mystery will provide some resolution for the families of the crew of the *Dakar*."

Sixty-Five Seconds

Chava Barkay:

It was Friday afternoon. The last few years, I was so sure that they were doing all they could. I knew they were searching; the time will come, when the sea's okay, when the time is okay. I was relaxed. I knew that they were doing the job.

And in the afternoon, Friday, I'm making dinner for my family, and I get a call from one of the officers from the Navy. He said that they are not sure but the camera saw something, that it could be the *Dakar*, and the next morning they are going to see if it is the boat. They couldn't promise me that this is the *Dakar*, but from the sound of the voice, I knew this happened. I knew.

I called my son, of course, and I felt excited. I say, "Oh, it's about time!"

But in the middle of the night, I get another phone call from my brother-in-law's house, and they said that he killed himself. He was very, very sick, with cancer. I asked what happened, and they say the Commander of the Navy told him also that they found the *Dakar*.

I don't know why he decided the same day to do it. I was so mixed with my feelings. I was sad, I cried. So we went over to a friend's house, and I was sitting up all night, and the day after they said this is the *Dakar*. So what to do? I mean, I went through a tough few hours. (2002 interview)

A young Chava Barkay had started down the path of tragedy on that day in 1968, and after so many years was nearing the end of her journey. But there was still a road ahead. Having found the *Dakar*, the mystery was far from solved. The family members now clamored for more information, and real answers. What could the wreck tell us about that day?

Few could address the topic of growing loss and acceptance better than the captain's son. For Oded Ra'anan, mourning was both personal and public, as there was so much controversy over the disappearance and whether his father had remained on course according to orders. It became a matter of honor. If Captain Ra'anan had gone off course for any reason, his memory would have been dishonored. The young man Oded persisted over the years in pushing the Navy to investigate—and it wasn't always rewarding. At one point, he felt that no one "is taking this story seriously." He thought the authorities withheld information from the families. He wanted to see all the search documentation and to convince the Israeli Navy, "You cannot investigate yourself." He felt they needed a neutral party, a think tank with a diverse membership.

After the discovery, it was immediately clear that Captain Ra'anan was on his planned course, and could not be criticized for disobeying orders. His father's name was cleared on that point. While that was a satisfying resolution, the mystery remained. Oded Ra'anan became interested in the process used to acquire and refurbish the *Dakar*, and wondered if the wreckage could offer clues as to why the ship sank. He still had letters from his father about problems with the ship, leaks in the torpedo room and with batteries. These letters haunted him.

Michael Marcovici, whose brother had been on the *Dakar*, was similarly elated and perplexed by the discovery. What did it really mean? What questions were answered, and what remained unknown? How could we learn more? Michael was one of the leaders of the family association, unwilling to be satisfied with the bare fact of discovery.

I am now fifty years old, and I'm looking back. All the places where I chose to live in Haifa were always with the view to the sea, so that if one morning she will come, at least I will be able to see her.

I think that the first time that I realized that this is the end, was when Alex Tal called me and told me, "We found her." This was the first time that I knew she is not going to come home anymore. Until that time, I always had the doubt of one, or 0.11—or 0.00001 percent, that maybe . . . maybe they are really in one of the gulags in Russia.

And by the end, we found that she is here. So there was no place anymore to hide. We had to come to face the reality.

There were parents that died with this feeling that maybe something happened, and they are somewhere, and they will come back. Finding the submarine was really to close a circle, because from that moment we realized that it's finished. This is also why, for most of the families, it is important to try to bring the whole submarine to Israel. I know that this is not an easy task. I know that it would cost a lot of money.

But I think that if there is a possibility to do this, it is "a must" to try anything possible to do it. I don't want to say that we have to risk any lives to bring the submarine out. If I would know that this is the situation, definitely, I will be against it. But if there are any other possibilities to bring her, then I think that we should do this.

I think that we will find in the submarine a lot of things—and I don't speak about remaining bodies, if they are at all—but all the personal things that are there. A shoe, or a watch, or sunglasses, or a ring. Every soldier has his chain with his numbers. All these things are there. For us, this is what's left from our beloved ones.

And you know that in the Israeli Army, we never leave any wounded in the field. We are trying not to leave any bodies there. This is the duty. And I don't speak as a religious man. But it's a moral obligation

I can't tell you that this is the feeling of the whole families. But I think that most of them would like to see this happen. (2002 interview)

✡ ✡ ✡

Nauticos and the discovery team had been forced to leave the site as helicopters were flying over with cameramen hanging out the hatches; there was no time for a thorough investigation. Anyway, a proper marine forensic investigation required planning and preparation, none of which could begin until after discovery. There was a lot of work ahead; but what would we be expected to do? The options ranged from recovery of the entire ship—a task we knew was all but impossible in view of the mangled state of the hull—to leaving well enough alone.

After some months of debate and consideration in Israel, it began to look like we could count on a return to the site, with Nauticos in charge of operations. This was only logical, but we were happy we didn't have to prove ourselves all over to a new crop of officials. In August 1999, Tom and I returned to Israel to discuss plans for a forensic mission. Lynn and our son Eric joined us and got a chance to see some of the wonderful places I had toured in 1997. A plan was beginning to take shape.

It seemed we would be tasked with three major objectives. First, we had to conduct a marine forensic investigation in an attempt to determine the cause of the disaster. To lead this effort, we proposed Robin Williams from the United Kingdom. Robin is a civil engineer specializing in naval architecture, and is credited with the most comprehensive commercial deep ocean forensic analysis ever completed, the 1980 loss of the bulk carrier M/V *Derbyshire* off the coast of Japan. The *Derbyshire* was a 200,000-ton monster of a ship, and its mysterious sinking in a storm caused great concern about the safety of other ships in its class. Robin led an analysis team that studied data collected from the wreck site, lying at a depth of nearly 14,000 feet. New technologies and practices were pioneered during this significant forensic study, many of which would be applied directly to studying the *Dakar*. Robin sports an "OBE" (Order of the British Empire) after his name, in recognition of his scientific and technical contributions.

The second task was to conduct a human forensics investigation to determine whether any remains of the crew were present in the wreck, and to recover them if possible. We were more than mildly surprised to discover someone who specializes in this arcane discipline: Dr. Marcella (Marci) Sorg, a member of the faculty of the University of Maine School of Nursing, and forensic anthropology consultant. Marci uses the science of taphonomy, which is concerned with the processes responsible for any organism becoming part of the fossil record, to support scientific research as well as practical matters such as crime-scene investigations. She can help estimate how long a body has been in seawater, and work backwards to the time of death. Marci gave a gruesome but very interesting slideshow on this topic, and convinced us she knew her business.

The third task was to recover certain artifacts to support the investigations, but what is more important, to contribute to a memorial for the crew of the *Dakar*. On top of this list was the four-ton sail, or conning tower, or bridge fin, as it was variously called, that had separated from the wreck during the sinking.

So Nauticos and our team set about to develop plans for the prospective return to the *Dakar*.

Robin Williams worked with colleagues in the United Kingdom (including former T-Class submariner Commander Jonty Powis), Nauticos engineers, and key specialists from Israel to work out the details of all loss scenarios that could be imagined. The approach was to then identify as many clues as possible that could support or refute each scenario. For example, if a collision with a passing ship was the cause (a scenario favored by many in Israel), one would expect to see evidence of impact damage, paint scrapings, and other effects distinct from the implosion event and crash on the sea floor. On the other hand, flooding, fire, battery explosion, or other casualty would be expected to leave different clues. After everything the team of experts could think of was listed, organized, and described, an operations plan was devised to look for these clues in the actual wreck site.

The matrix of scenarios included general categories of: snorkeling (snorting) casualty, collision, flooding, propulsion casualty, planes (ship control) casualty, issues relating to high speeds, gaseous poisoning, high sea state (weather) issues, explosion, fire, hostile activity, morale issues (including mutiny), electrical failure, environmental problems, structural problems, and human error. These general categories were expanded to "direct cause" and "detailed cause" to be investigated. No likelihood was considered for any of these causes. Even though the idea of a crew mutiny was an incredible (in many minds, impossible) consideration, it was not discounted in the investigation. In all, over 280 detailed causes were tabulated in the matrix of ship loss scenarios.

The primary tool for the underwater marine forensics investigation would be the video and still cameras on the Remora ROV; these would be upgraded and reconfigured to collect enough images to make a complete mosaic of the wreck site. Also, a small camera was mounted on a pole to allow limited penetration into the hull itself, and get a peek inside.

Marci Sorg and her colleagues in Maine spent some time making predictions about the state of remains on the sea floor in these conditions. We knew that under unusual circumstances bones from ancient Roman times have been found; however, this usually involves nearshore sites where land processes create special water conditions and silting has buried remains, protecting them to a degree from deterioration. In the deep ocean, however, biological and chemical processes tend to consume remains rather quickly, and it was doubtful that there would be any traces of preserved bodies in or about the submarine. Still, it was important to find out for sure, and be prepared for any result. Marci prepared formal protocols for visual assessment of potential remains, for handling medial specimens, for collecting chemical samples, and for collecting soil samples. The chemistry of the water in confined spaces could hint at processes involved in the decay of remains, and give some indication that they might be lurking in spots protected from general deterioration. Detailed procedures were devised for calibrating equipment and using the penetration device for sampling inside enclosed spaces. We couldn't have been better prepared for our tasks.

The recovery of objects was a job we were familiar with, and we were fortunate that a sizable piece of the wreck was detached from the hull. Video from the discovery mission showed us that the piece was structurally intact, and there were "strong points" that could be used to attach custom-built lifting clamps to attach a lift line securely. Although technically demanding, the task was straightforward to plan.

But in the fall of 1999, it was still quite uncertain that we would get a chance to do any of this. There were those in the Israeli government and Navy who felt that their job was done, and spending more on the project was of little value. It was hard to justify performing a marine forensics study, as it would be unlikely to learn anything about the thirty-year-old wreck of a fifty-five-year-old submarine that would have any bearing on modern ship design or operations. Of course, failing to do such a study would fuel speculation that the Navy was trying to hide something. Admiral Tal was more interested in the human remains issue, and the idea of recovery for a memorial was appealing.

Meanwhile, Nauticos was inundated by international press coverage. The vast majority of this was extremely positive, although every now and then someone suggested that it was wrong for an American company to make money from an Israeli tragedy. Then there was our short-lived colleague, Professor Gitay, who had quit the Committee in frustration that we did not give enough attention to his "Lagoon theory." He continued to question the discovery, and does so to this day. According to him, the Egyptians sank the *Dakar* near their coast and later on towed her to her final resting place in a lagoon. He doubts she was found at all, and that the sail and other alleged debris are genuine. In a 2005 lecture, he suggested that the ship was found, in the lagoon where he predicted, but towed out to sea and resunk, so it could be "discovered" along its intended route.

Despite these curiosities, public relations regarding our *Dakar* discovery was hugely complimentary, and we were eager to strike a deal to turn our raw film into a documentary. As a business, we certainly wanted to make a profit on the endeavor, but we all believed that the story was a positive and inspirational one. We sought permission from Israel to release the information as specified in our contract, while trying to sort out opportunities, culling the empty promises from the real prospects. Frustratingly, stateside documentary broadcasting companies showed little interest in this "non-American" story, but we received many inquiries from Israeli sources and from BBC affiliates. When we met with Admiral Tal in Israel in August, he was sympathetic, but concerned about newspapers looking to vilify anyone making money from the tragedy. He held release for the time being.

We returned from Israel both encouraged and frustrated. It seemed certain that we would be tasked to do something, but exactly what, when, and how much was a roll of the dice.

I had a pleasant distraction from all of this in September of 1999, when I went to sea with our Midway team and the Navy Oceanographic Office, which led to verification that we had, indeed, found the wreckage of the Japanese aircraft carrier *Kaga* during our sonar survey earlier in the year. It was rewarding to relive war history, stay for a couple of days on Midway Island, and see the first videos of the great ship sunk by gallant Navy pilots almost six decades earlier.

Nauticos' successes were mounting, and we were eager to keep going! But there was no good word from Israel; in fact, some rumors were discouraging. In October, we were told it was "back on track" (not being aware it had been "derailed"). Tom returned to Israel in November to participate in a touching memorial service, where all of the family members were invited to sail to the site, perform ceremonies, and drop wreaths over the resting place of their lost sons, brothers, and fathers. Still, he could not return with a positive indication of future missions.

Another pleasant surprise was announced by John Coombs: he and Donna's professional relationship during the *Dakar* search had blossomed. Says Donna:

> About our romance, this is the story of that: I was the only woman on either boat and wasn't in any significant relationship at the time. At sea we were always very professional, so there's no story on the boat. John and I were coworkers who overlapped for maybe 6 hours on a watch. He had a different watch, but in the same twenty-foot container. I was at one end, he on the other, and it was just friendly banter. I thought he was awfully cute, but I don't fraternize on the boat, so nothing happened.
>
> I wanted to take four days off when we landed at Cyprus so I could see the island. John planned for one day off. We started going around the island, saw the ruins, probably talked more than on the boat, non-work stuff about our families and other interests. When John had to leave a little earlier than I did, he still hadn't asked me out. He just left.
>
> It was much fun going around the island, and it's said that Aphrodite was supposed to be born there or went ashore there. So it's known as her island, and that might have had something to do with us getting together. We corresponded by e-mail, and John asked me to come back east for a visit. Strangely enough, I accepted. We did bicoastal meetings back and forth for about a year and then John took a job with Nauticos in California. So for another year we were in the same time zone, and then we got engaged and I moved to California and the rest is history. We got married, had a baby, and now we're back near my home in Washington State. (2005 interview)

We were all very happy for both of them, and counted it as one more positive outcome of the *Dakar* project.

Little happened over the holidays, but in March 2000 we received an urgent call from Israel. On March 27, an F-16 jet fighter had crashed in the sea off the Israeli coast, and the Air Force was looking to recover the wreckage as soon as possible. The urgency was increased by the identity of one of the two crewmen: Major Yonatan Begin, former Prime Minister Menachem Begin's grandson. Although there was no hope of survival of the crew, time was of the essence as the squadron was grounded until the cause could be found. And, of course, Israel wanted to recover the remains of the aviators. Nauticos was called on the day after the accident, and we were asked if we could begin search and recovery operations on April 9, in eleven days! As the location was well known, and this was primarily an ROV operation, it seemed best to let Phoenix take the lead, and Nauticos provide support. Together, we successfully recovered wreckage from the plane, which was reduced to small pieces due to the violence of the crash, and managed to recover the helmets of the crew.

In spite of these successes, time and uncertainty marched on. In July, we started hearing rumors of attempting a recovery of the entire submarine, an undertaking that we did not recommend due to the condition of the wreck and the cost versus benefit. I was enjoying giving talks of our exciting discovery to various groups, and even discovered the U.S. Naval Academy Jewish Midshipman's Club and Rabbi Irving Elson along the way. We were getting some movement on documentary prospects, having been contacted by Arnon Manor, son of the *Dakar* crewman Dan Manor, only twenty-four years old when he went down with the submarine. Arnon was a talented special-effects artist in the film business, and his British father-in-law, Tony Klinger, was keen to make a documentary in the United Kingdom about the *Dakar* and Arnon's quest to find his father. But still no word on a *Dakar* mission.

Finally, in August, we got positive word that a mission would proceed, and in September we were given a schedule for operations in October. *Dakar* II was finally underway.

✡ ✡ ✡

As seems to be an unavoidable norm in ocean operations, once we finally had the agreement to go ahead, there was little time to mobilize. As winter was approaching, with stormy weather and high seas impending, we could not afford further delays. We had, as always, some tense times. For one thing, after the gear was shipped out to Cyprus and was in the process of mobilization, the robotic vehicle failed. There were problems with power on the ship, some of the chemistry equipment hadn't arrived yet, and we were still negotiating our agreement with Klinger for filming. One of our engineers jury-rigged a replacement part for the ROV while we were waiting for new ones to come from California. In the end the repair part was used for operations and worked fine, and the new one was kept as a spare. Because of these setbacks and potential delays, there was a lot of tension about performance and payments, and we had the added complexity of organizing filming.

In spite of it all, the EDT ship *EAS* arrived on site on Saturday, October 7, 2000. The Nauticos team, supported by Phoenix and the ROV pilots, was joined by Robin Williams and Commander Jonty Powis, Royal Navy, and an Israeli contingent including Lieutenant Commander Eyal Israeli, Commander

Doron Amir, and Dr. Barak Herut. Our three mission goals were confirmed: to try to determine the cause of the loss, to locate and recover remains, if any, and to recover the bridge fin and other artifacts. Because the weather was good and there was no guarantee how long that happy circumstance would last, Tom decided to start on the most difficult and delicate task first: the recovery of the bridge fin.

Using the ROV Remora cameras, the bridge fin was inspected in detail to be sure nothing had changed in the eighteen months since the discovery mission. Once everyone was satisfied, the ROV was recovered and rigged with lifting equipment. Additional lifting gear was loaded into a recovery basket, including a four-kilometer length of Dyneema rope, an incredibly strong, slender, and positively buoyant synthetic line. Since the line was only for lifting and did not need to carry power or telemetry, it did not have the weight of copper and steel and did not add to the lifting load. The rope was attached to a ten-ton crane, in turn attached to a motion compensating device that would help reduce the surge and heave of the line due to sea motion.

The ROV was launched over the port side, and the recovery basket over the stern. Descent to the bottom was tricky, as entanglement of equipment was a real concern. Two hours later, the basket successfully landed on the bottom, and the ROV began rigging the bridge fin for the lift. This involved using the robotic arms to attach clamps and screw them tightly to strong points on the fin. In the middle of this delicate work, a hydraulic leak developed on the ROV, which had to be recovered, repaired, and redeployed. All the while, the *EAS*, equipped with a dynamic positioning system allowing it to "hover" on one spot over the ocean floor, held its position. Back on the bottom, the task was completed, and the ROV returned to the lift basket, pulled out the end of the Dyneema lift line, and attached it to the clamps.

After forty-eight hours of tedious work, all done remotely through video screens and joysticks two miles up on the surface, all was ready for the lift. At 7:15 PM on October 9, the *Dakar* bridge fin began to slowly rise from the ocean floor. The dramatic moment was captured by the cameras of the Remora ROV, and watched breathlessly by the team, crammed snugly into the control van high above.

Nine tense hours ensued. The weather held. Finally, at 4:30 AM, the four-ton bridge fin broke the surface, was lifted over the stern, and secured to the deck. When Tom climbed the ladder to attach the lines that would secure it for its ride home to Haifa, he realized he was the first to stand on the bridge of the *Dakar* in thirty-two years. He stood where Boomie Barkay was last seen saluting, gesturing thumbs up, as the *Dakar* left Portsmouth. They sped to Haifa, Israeli flag flying from the bridge once again, to meet Chava and the family members and end their long wait for the *Dakar*'s return. Chava remembers that moment:

> Oh, this is perfect! When I first saw the bridge, in Haifa, I couldn't move for maybe ten or fifteen minutes. I just stood in one place. Because this is the bridge which I went up.
>
> I realized, suddenly, that I may be one of few people left, who went on this bridge. This is the bridge which I was so proud to look at, and it was so beautiful. And the bridge that my husband was on when he saluted to the captain. This was the *Dakar*.
>
> I'm waiting for the bridge to be placed as a memory of *Dakar*. (2002 interview)

The *Dakar*'s interrupted voyage was finally over.

But the operations team had no time to savor the moment. The budget clock was ticking, and every hour gone meant more costs for ship, equipment, and people. After a mere three hours in port, the *EAS* was heading back west. Arriving on the site, the ROV was deployed to begin forensic investigations. Two days were spent on the bottom, scanning the entire hull to make a side-view visual mosaic, photographing specific points on the wreck and collecting chemical samples. Once finished with this work, the vehicle was recovered and reconfigured to carry the specially designed penetration camera and other sampling gear. A day was spent continuing the image collection, sampling, and collecting small objects for recovery.

The small items from the debris field were placed in the recovery basket and brought to the surface, where they were photographed, inspected, cataloged, and preserved for shipping to Israel. There were dozens of items thought to be of technical interest; but one in particular was of special significance. An item wrapped in a clear plastic bag was seen and picked up carefully by the ROV and placed in the basket. Upon recovery, with great care, the contents of the bag were removed and found to be an Israeli sailor's uniform, vintage 1968. The plastic had preserved the wool tunic and pants, neatly arrayed on a hanger with a blue nylon wind breaker—a dress uniform, ready to be worn proudly at the ceremonies planned for the *Dakar*'s triumphant arrival. Much of it had been protected from the natural elements and was in good condition. On the left side of the shirt, still attached, was found an Israeli submarine qualification badge, in excellent condition.

Traditionally, these qualification badges are numbered, and each bearer is recorded in "The Submariner Book." The back of the badge was engraved with the number "420." Later, back at submarine headquarters, the book was consulted, and number 420 was found to belong to Yosef Suisa-Almog, graduate in the class of 1967. Twenty-two members of this class were lost on the *Dakar*.

The uniform was restored and presented to Yosef's family. According to their wishes, it is now on display at the naval museum in Haifa.

The ROV and its patient team of operators still had work to do. The vehicle was again reconfigured, this time to collect a complete vertical-view mosaic. Another day was spent with this task. Finally, the remaining items of interest were recovered. The last item found in the extensive debris field was the emergency buoy basket. A piece of the mystery fell into place as the ROV cameras peered inside to discover the basket—empty! No reel, no wire, no horn. We can never prove it for sure, but my theory that the buoy, that "orange herring," floated around the Mediterranean just submerged, trailing the wreckage of its wire and reel, was largely confirmed by that find.

✡ ✡ ✡

The delivery of the final report of findings was anticlimactic. In fact, we didn't even go to Israel to present it. The situation in the region had deteriorated for visiting, and there was not a large budget for such activities. So a detailed and extensive written report was produced, complete with CDs containing the final photographic mosaic, all digital still images, chemistry files, and artifact reports. Tom, Robin, and Marci gave their briefings to the camera, and their filmed presentations were shipped with the report to Israel. It was unfortunate that we didn't have more of a ceremonial presentation, but the circumstances didn't favor it.

Still, the *Dakar* II mission was a complete success. The dramatic arrival of the bridge fin to shore and its subsequent unveiling as a memorial to the sixty-nine sailors was the most visible outcome of the work. But the forensic results were of even greater interest to many family members, who really wanted to know what happened, why, and was there anything left of their loved ones to bring back.

Marci Sorg's detailed analysis of video and chemistry was quite conclusive. The summary of her report stated:

> We conclude the bodies had a variety of postmortem histories and ultimate fates depending on their primary position in the vessel and subsequent exposure to currents and scavenging animals. It is very likely that the remains of most, probably all, of the men who died aboard the *Dakar* were lost, with no hope of postmortem recovery, at the time of the accident or soon thereafter, due to the implosion-explosion of the submarine while it was far above the sea floor. If any remains were initially preserved, shielded by the wreckage or by burial, these were very likely rare and incomplete. They would have been virtually impossible to locate in 1968 within the very large debris field

several kilometers in diameter. Now, after more than 30 years of exposure to biological and physical processes, it is very likely all of the remains have been re-incorporated into the natural environment, regardless of their immediate postmortem location or circumstances.

In less scientific terms, Marci was saying that today there is not a scrap of evidence that any physical remains are present. There was no direct or indirect evidence of human remains surrounding the submarine, within the debris field, or just inside the hull breaks. There was no indication of any sediment-covered masses that might include human remains. In fact, there was no evidence of any animal skeletal remains, human or nonhuman. On the other hand, there was lots of evidence that all remains had been consumed by the sea and its biological and chemical processes. Further, she believes that the bodies of the *Dakar* crewmen were shattered and dispersed by the energy of the implosion of the hull at the time of the sinking, and that recovery of any meaningful remains would have been unlikely even immediately after the sinking.

What about that hull implosion? Robin described the process, which is by no means fully understood. What we do know is that because the hull was designed to withstand fairly high pressures, which at a crush depth of around 650 feet approached 300 PSI, a huge amount of energy was built up and released all at once. In a matter of milliseconds, the interior space in the submarine hull was compressed to a fraction of its original volume, and the pressure instantly rose to, and past, the pressure of the water. In fact, the momentum of this pressure surge generated an overpressure, at least ten times the ambient sea pressure! Quicker than a blink, the atmospheric pressure inside the ship rose from normal conditions to many thousands of PSI, more than inside a fully charged scuba bottle! As with any compression of gas, the temperature rose, possibly to over 1,000 degrees Fahrenheit. A tremendous pressure shock wave rocketed through the hull, shattering metal and men, reducing a well-ordered technological wonder of a machine and her highly trained crew to a mess of twisted wreckage and broken bodies.

Just as quickly as the implosion crushed the hull, the massive overpressure was relieved in an equally energetic explosion, spewing the debris of the wreck out of the hull breaks and into the surrounding water. With energies equivalent to the detonation of tons of TNT, the rate of rise of strain and heat in the hull was so great as to cause random and erratic failures of both brittle and ductile nature. That is, the two-inch thick hull steel was twisted and extruded like taffy in some spots, and shattered like glass in others.

The evidence of such an event was clear from the photographic mosaic of the *Dakar* wreckage. Most of the 220-foot-long pressure hull was crushed beyond recognition. At the time of implosion, failures occurred at weak points along the top of the hull, where the sail, hatches, hull penetrations, and other superstructure elements were attached. These points buckled inward, then blasted back out, rotating hull plates and equipment in unexpected ways. A section of hull appeared to have an unusual large pipe attached to it. This mystery was resolved when it was realized that the hull steel itself had been extruded into that pipe-like shape! The tail cone aft of the pressure hull separated completely, as did the forward section of the bridge fin, sliding neatly off the attack periscope and leaving it protruding naked from the rest of the wreckage of the control room. The bridge fin was probably ejected by a separate implosion-explosion of the ten-man diving chamber, of which no pieces could be found.

This event occurred high up in the water column, at less than one thousand feet, so the wreckage and its cloud of debris had another nine thousand feet or more to fall to the ocean floor. The heavy main hull section probably fell quickest, landing on what was left of its keel, gouging a crater and surrounded by clouds of billowing silt. The tail cone with its rudder, stern planes, and twin propellers landed askew next to the main hull, the pointed stern end aimed at what was left of the sail. The sail itself, less the four-ton forward piece containing the bridge, was twisted over on its side, still attached to the control room wreckage by a cluster bent antenna and mast tubes. The forward part of the bridge fin came to rest about two hundred yards from the main hull, surrounded by other bits of debris that rained down over the area.

A large motor-generator set, ejected from the stern section, landed neatly on the bow deck, looking as though it had been installed there deliberately.

Curiously, but most important, a significant length, over eighty feet, of the forward part of the pressure hull was completely undamaged. Including the bow sonar dome, anchors, and forward deck, this was the first part of the wreckage seen in 1999, giving the impression to Admiral Raz that the ship was still alive. Bow tanks, torpedo room, torpedo storage, and the front half of the accommodation compartment were completely whole and unscathed. Abruptly, at frame 59 (out of 132), the carnage of implosion-explosion began, and continued aft for the remainder of the pressure hull. The only explanation for this was that at the time of hull collapse those compartments were already full of water, and completely pressure compensated. This could only point to a massive flooding casualty in the bow of the ship.

Despite the state of the wreck, Robin and the team did their best to seek the clues they were looking for to support or refute the loss scenarios. Snorkel induction valves, exhaust valves, fan duct dampers, hatches, engine controls, battery vents, clutch positions, and many other specific pieces of equipment were sought and their condition noted. Many could not be found or seen clearly enough in the tangled mass of pipes, wires, and twisted metal. Nothing was in its place, and some items that were supposed to be at the bottom of the hull were found near the top of the pile. But enough was discovered to be quite certain that the ship was submerged and snorkeling (snorting), and was likely in the process of securing from snorkeling, that is, preparing to dive deep. Robin concluded in his report:

It is disappointing to have to report that, due to the utter devastation of the control and engine rooms and the ravages of time which show as virtually total galvanic degradation of the aluminum structures still attached to the steelwork of the hull, the survey was unable to gain answers which might have given conclusive evidence as to the vessel's mode of operation and any emergency procedures in hand at the time of the loss.

No firm conclusions can be given as to the sequence and cause of the loss.

The following conclusions are therefore presented on the basis of an opinion as to the balance of probabilities:

The vessel was proceeding unhindered on her course to the Port of Haifa.

The vessel was most likely to be "snorting" or in the process of "stop snorting."

The vessel was subjected to a rapid and large volume of ingressed water perhaps into the torpedo storage space forward. This exceeded the buoyancy reserves.

The vessel pitched forward in a steep and rapid dive which could not be controlled by planes, propulsion, blowing tanks, or combinations of these.

Despite the best efforts of the crew the vessel exceeded her crush depth and the hull imploded-exploded catastrophically.

Robin added a footnote: "For the crew of the *Dakar* those last seconds before the hull collapsed would have been very busy with all together working as a team to try to save the vessel. When the end came it was instantaneous as if someone just turned off the light. TO THE UNDYING MEMORY OF THE MEN OF INS DAKAR."

Despite Robin's careful wording and unwillingness to speculate in an official capacity, the evidence of the *Dakar* II mission was quite clear. The ship did not suffer a collision, and was not attacked or damaged by hostile forces. There was certainly a massive hull breach in the forward part of the pressure hull, leading to uncontrollable and catastrophic flooding of the bow spaces. This probably occurred at the time the ship was securing from snorkeling and beginning a deep dive from periscope depth.

We don't know the speed of the ship at the time of the emergency, but it is safe to say that Captain Ra'anan was running fast most of the time. At an initial speed of eight knots at periscope depth, and assuming the tremendous weight of water flooding the forward compartments defeated any attempts to arrest an uncontrolled nosedive, the ship could have exceeded a collapse depth of around 650 feet in sixty-five seconds. There was no way to stop or even slow the descent. The *Dakar* crew had little time to realize what was happening, take immediate action, and combat the casualty before it was all over.

The source of the flooding is unknown; however, it had to be massive enough to fill over eighty feet of pressure hull in barely more than a minute. By the time collapse depth was reached, over ten thousand cubic feet of water had entered the hull, weighing close to four hundred tons. All of this weight was in the front of the ship, and nothing could have overcome the downward force, pitching the ship into a steep dive. To take in such a huge amount of water, there had to be a huge hole, probably the equivalent of eighteen inches or more in diameter, something like an open torpedo tube or failure of a major hull fitting. No such hole could be seen in the bow, although much of that section, including the torpedo tubes, was below the mud line.

A hole that size, under the pressure of seawater at the keel depth while snorkeling, would allow a massive slug of water to rush in the hull at a speed of thirty-five miles per hour. Over six thousand pounds of water would enter the ship in the first second, and the rate would increase as the ship dove deeper and the sea pressure rose. Any unfortunate crewman in that space would face the equivalent of being in the middle of a head-on collision between two automobiles, recurring again and again each second! No one in the torpedo room would survive such an onslaught, and crewmen in the accommodations section would probably have been knocked senseless by the shock of this deluge before they knew anything was happening.

The officer of the deck would have ordered immediate actions for combating a flooding casualty, including full rise on all planes and blowing of all ballast, but these measures would have been ineffective. As Robin Williams so aptly stated, after a matter of seconds, the lights switched off.

✡ ✡ ✡

I have told the story of the *Dakar* as I know and lived it, as accurately as I could. For many of you, the story should end here. But many may want to know more. What exactly happened in those final moments, and how did the men of the *Dakar* cope with their fate? Of course, we can never know for sure. But we can drape the bare facts with possibilities, based on experience and a little imagination.

There are those who are uncomfortable with any discussion beyond the facts, including the Israeli Navy, so I must make it perfectly clear that what follows is purely my own invention. However, it does not require a flight of fancy or wild speculation to imagine what must have been happening to Captain Ra'anan, Isaac Marcovici, Boomie Barkay, and the rest of the sixty-nine crewmen in those final sixty-five seconds of the voyage of the INS *Dakar*. For those who care to join me, I invite you to continue.

The Final Deep Dive of the INS *Dakar*

Two more days! Isaac Marcovici was having trouble containing his excitement. Well, it would really be four days before he would go ashore, touch the soil of his homeland after so long, and see his parents and brother Michael again. But in two days they would be in Israeli waters, and it would feel like home.

It had been a grueling transit, especially for the mechanics. The captain had pushed the machinery hard, and the people harder. Isaac was tired. Much of the time had been spent in snorting condition, with the diesels running full tilt, making best possible speed skimming just below the surface. Half of the crew was needed to run the ship in this situation, so everyone spent four hours on watch and only four off. Isaac was responsible for equipment maintenance and repairs when not on watch, and several minor, but nagging problems had cut seriously into his bunk time. But no matter, with only a few days left it was hard to sleep anyway. Two hours earlier, when his "hot bunk" mate had come to rouse him to go to his watch station so he could take over the bunk, Isaac was already awake.

Now halfway through the watch, Isaac was getting ready. Some repair work would keep him very busy for the next couple of hours, and he had to focus on the task at hand. At age twenty, he was already feeling experienced. He took a great deal of pride in his work, and felt almost paternal with his machines. He had suggested that the diesels be shut down for a short while to repair a leaky fitting, and Chief Engineer Ran Shimon and the captain agreed. Isaac was pleased that they would take the advice of a twenty-year-old mechanic.

Captain Yaacov Ra'anan, however, was not pleased. Only two days' transit left and headquarters would have him wait, after two years, to bring his ship and crew home. Two wasted days! He was counting on the admiral to grant permission for early arrival, if he could make good time crossing the Mediterranean. He had done his part. Still, they would make him wait.

He hid his frustration from the crew as he sat in the wardroom, sipping coffee, considering options. Well, he would press on, arrive early anyway, and maybe headquarters would yet reconsider. Meanwhile, there were matters needing attention, including some diesel maintenance. That would involve shutting down the engines and running on the electric motor under battery power for a while. Although that would reduce speed considerably, it would offer yet another opportunity to practice a deep dive, and a few hours of fully submerged transit would give the crew a rest. It had been a strain making maximum speed for hours on end, keeping the four-on and four-off watches, always on the lookout for shipping that might unwittingly cross the *Dakar*'s path. And always keeping depth just low enough to stay underwater, but high enough to keep the periscope and diesel intake above the waves. Ra'anan knew it was not easy, but he was proud of his crew and how well they had handled the long voyage. Soon they would be home, getting some real rest. Ra'anan sent a messenger to the control room, giving the order to Boomie Barkay, the officer of the watch, to "stop snorting" and commence a deep dive.

Barkay's job was probably the hardest on the ship. The captain had the ultimate responsibility, and it weighed heavily. But the first officer was the "enforcer," the one who must support and execute the captain's orders, no matter how unpopular, no matter what his own opinion might be. Sometimes it meant meting out discipline, or setting up an unpleasantly rigorous work schedule. On top of that, Boomie had to stand regular watches, and was responsible for ship's administration. It was a tough life, but the reward would be the pinnacle of his career: command of his own submarine. Just thirty-one years old, Barkay had done well, and was certainly on his way to further successes.

Chava and Guy would be so happy to see him again in Haifa, and he knew they would be proud of him. As soon as he could get free, he would take them to Jerusalem. So much to look forward to! With these happy thoughts in mind, Barkay was about to take the first step in a chain of events that would dash the hopes and expectations of the crew of the *Dakar*, their families, and their nation.

Barkay gave the order: "Stop snorting . . . secure from snorting. Half-ahead port and starboard motors." The helmsman repeated the order, and set the engine order telegraph handle to "Half ahead." The steady hammering of the huge diesel engines quieted. The hydraulic clutch was released, allowing the propellers to be turned by the electric motors, drawing power from the batteries. Isaac Marcovici removed his earplugs and drank in the relative silence of the humming pumps and other machinery, as he followed the steps to secure the engines and prepare them to be restarted, just in case.

The engine room reported, "Snorting stopped. Main suction and exhaust hull valves shut!" These valves sealed the large openings in the hull that allowed air to flow in to the diesel, and exhaust to leave the ship.

Barkay continued, "Make your depth one-five-zero feet. Lower the snorting mast."

The diving officer ordered a 5-degree down-angle on the ship, beginning a controlled dive to a safe depth. Barkay took a last look around through the periscope before it slipped beneath the waves. No contacts in sight. The next minute would be the most dangerous to the submarine, as it was shallow enough to risk collision with a big cargo ship, but too deep to use the periscope to see and avoid such a vessel. Once steady at a depth of 150 feet, she could slip safely below the keel of even the largest ship seen in those waters. His sonar could help him "see" other ships, but the torturous path of sound echoes near the surface made that technique undependable. Because of this, he must give the transitions from periscope depth to deep cruising and back his utmost attention in order to avoid trouble, and be ready should it happen.

Captain Ra'anan felt the ship's angle shift by degrees, and didn't give it a second thought. He knew Boomie was in charge, and the ship was under control. As the ship began to nose down and descend, trouble struck.

It happened too fast for anyone to sense it, even Ra'anan or those on watch. A hull weld in the torpedo compartment, weakened over twenty years of service and undetected by any inspections, with no sign of imminent failure, cracked under the change in sea pressure. A huge hole suddenly opened into the pressure hull, admitting a slug of water at high speed. The noise was horrific and the shock wave immediately overwhelmed everyone in the compartment. They had not a moment to sense the impending disaster, and were unable to take any action to stem the flooding. Tons of water rushed in the ship every second.

In the control room, Barkay felt the impact and immediately assumed there had been a collision. "Klaxon! Klaxon!" he shouted, ordering the ship's alarm to be sounded. "Both motors full astern! Hydroplanes to full dive!" These measures were designed to back the ship away from and below the object of the collision, to avoid another impact. Boomie was trained to stabilize the situation and assess damage.

"Report to Damage Control!" Watch-standers in the control room immediately shut the watertight doors to the adjacent compartments. Everyone started taking the immediate actions for a collision. Back in the engine room, Marcovici instantly began preparations to restart the diesels, as soon as the snorting mast could be raised. Watertight doors were shut. Watch-standing supervisors began reporting from each compartment "Engine room secured," "Control Room secured." Barely ten seconds had passed.

"Sonar, contacts?" Sonar could hear nothing but the roar coming from the forward bulkhead. Barkay realized he had received no reports from the forward part of the ship, and the horrible noise was still shaking the bow. Flooding! In seconds, Barkay grasped the seriousness of the situation and ordered the immediate actions for flooding in the torpedo room: Full rise on all planes, engines ahead full. If he could bring the bow up, the angle of the ship could carry a great deal of weight of water, and he could drive to the surface. This would reduce the sea pressure and thus the flooding, allow him to start the diesels and put on more speed, and take control of repairs.

But the ship was not responding. Another ten seconds had passed. The ship's angle was not reducing; in fact, it seemed to be getting steeper. Depth was ninety feet. The planesman reported a loss of indication of the bow planes angle. Things were getting worse. Still no report from the forward compartments, and the terrible noise went on. Before another second passed, Barkay expended his last and most drastic measure:

"Emergency blow all main ballast tanks!"

This would admit high-pressure air into the external tanks, adding tons of buoyancy to the ship. The submarine should pop to the surface like a cork. This uncontrolled surfacing was not desirable, especially if there had been a collision and a ship's hull was right above them. But Boomie saw no alternative.

Twenty-five seconds had passed. The diving officer reported that the aft ballast tanks were blowing, but the forward tanks were not. Depth was 130 feet, and the ship's down angle was increasing fast. At 30 degrees pitch, everyone in the control room was hanging on.

The roaring din emanating from the forward bulkhead suddenly stopped.

Captain Ra'anan in the accommodations compartment came to his senses, to pandemonium. The noise in his head that had been drowning out all thought had stopped, as quickly as it started. But everything was wrong: the ship was at a steep angle, people, mattresses, and gear were tumbling forward, and his head was in a vice. Pressure was rising as the compartments, sealed from the aft part of the ship, were filling with seawater. The crack in the hull was completely covered now, smothering the horrible roar of water rushing into air. But the water was still rushing in; nearly one hundred tons already.

The *Dakar* was doomed, and Ra'anan was beginning to realize it.

No one had been able to shut the watertight door to the torpedo compartments, the source of the flooding. As the ship continued to pitch forward, the swirling maelstrom could be seen below through the open door, bathed in the eerie glow of emergency lighting, a surreal scene. Crewmen in accommodations, many of whom had been asleep when disaster struck, were beginning to wake up, clearing their painful ears as the air pressure continued to rise. Ra'anan struggled to think, to assess the situation, to take some action.

As the men began to regain their ability to function, training told them what to do. The immediate response to a flooding casualty had been drilled into every crew member: shut watertight doors, isolate the source of flooding, and report to the control room. Those who had regained their faculties began to make their way to the hatch, through obstacles strewn about the passage-way that continued to tumble forward as the deck canted to nearly 45 degrees. Disoriented by the chaos around him, Ra'anan lost seconds finding the internal communications phone, and finally reported to control the dreaded news that Boomie had already surmised.

"Flooding in the torpedo room! Accommodations is NOT rigged for flood-ing. Shutting watertight door now. This is the Captain. Take immediate action for flooding!"

Forty-five seconds had passed since the hull failed. Water was gushing over the sill of the hatch to the torpedo room; crewmen were struggling to shut the heavy door, discovering that it is practically impossible to pull it upward with the ship at such a steep angle. No one was alive on the other side to help.

In the control room, Boomie and his watch-standers were still focused, trying to ignore the sliding clipboards, smashing coffee cups, and other small debris falling from crazily canted surfaces. He acknowledged the captain. "Sir, all immediate action for flooding taken. Trying to bring the bow up. Sir, you MUST get the watertight doors shut!"

There was no response from accommodations.

In the engine room, Isaac and the other engineers had done all they could. The electric motors were spinning at full speed; the battery amp-hour meter clicked over the discharge rate faster than anyone had seen before. Men were watching all of their gauges intently. Off-duty crew had responded as trained to look for leakage in their assigned space. Anyone not specifically engaged was assigned to recheck stowage. All of this became more difficult as the decks turned into sliding boards. But everyone had something to do, partly because things needed to be done, and partly to help the men avoid panic. Cool heads and trained responses were the only means of survival. Isaac checked and rechecked the diesel, hanging onto railings with one hand. Everything was as ready as he could make it—they just had to get to the surface.

Depth three hundred feet. This was "test depth" for the ship, the deep-est designed for normal operations. Still, Boomie knew they had a way to go before the ship would fail. He knew that World War II submarines were leg-endary for diving deeper than designed or imagined, and surviving to tell the tale. As depth increased, the hull made popping and cracking sounds as steel frames were compressed and welded joints were stressed. A certain amount of hull shrinkage would be normal, and he was used to noises that sound to the uninitiated like a collapsing hull. And he knew that if the hull collapsed, no one would feel it.

Boomie reviewed his actions. He was sure he had done everything, and there was no second guessing now. He had ordered the bilge pumps to take suc-tion on the torpedo room and pump to sea, but that was akin to drinking from a fire hydrant with a soda straw. The pumps could drain no more than one thousand pounds per minute—less as the depth (and outside pressure) increased. By now, thousands of pounds per second were rushing in the hull breach. Over two hundred tons so far. This exceeded the entire reserve buoyancy of the ship; there was no hope of recovery.

But Boomie didn't know all the numbers; he only knew what he had to do. Speed was increasing, and so was the force on his stern hydroplanes. If he could just get the bow to come up before the ship exceeded crush depth, he might yet save the day. All of his thoughts were focused on this, willing the angle to decrease.

Another ten seconds. All was quiet in the control room, except for the depth reports from the helmsman: 450 feet, increasing. Boomie felt the down angle stabilizing. He didn't know the number since the gauge was pegged at 45 degrees. He stopped listening to the depth reports and focused on the angle gauge.

Sixty seconds. Depth 550 feet. Over three hundred tons of icy seawater filled the torpedo compartments, and was rising in accommodations.

Boomie watched the angle gauge. It didn't move.

Sixty-five seconds. The lights went out.

✡ ✡ ✡

The undamaged bow of the submarine *Dakar*, still looking alive, as if it will rise from the bottom and sail home with Isaac Marcovici, Abraham Barkay, Captain Yaacov Ra'anan, and the rest of the crew, rests quietly at the bottom of the Mediterranean, ten thousand feet below the storms and conflicts of man and nature. There it will likely remain for one hundred years or more, as it slowly dissolves into the sea. On the bow rests a plaque, fashioned at sea by the discovery crew, placed gently and ceremoniously, as the team members solemnly watched. The plaque will dissolve as well in time, but the sentiment will remain. It reads:

> The Men of INS *Dakar*
> Never Forgotten!

Postscript

Israel, June 2, 1999
From the Families of the Submarine *Dakar*
With Love and Appreciation

Dear Friends,

We are here today to thank you and to give you our love with a big hug for the wonderful job you have done.

By finding *Dakar* you accomplished a holy mission that was a dream to us. Some people thought it was a "Mission Impossible." You made it possible.

Thank you!

For the last 31 years we've been living our lives in the shadow of the tragedy of *Dakar,* raising families and growing older under the dark cloud of the mystery. How painful it was!

We were great troublemakers; we didn't let go, we didn't give up. Sometimes we lost our tempers, but we never lost hope.

We believed.

In our tradition, we do not leave our soldiers behind, dead or alive. No matter how long it takes, we dream to bring them back home.

You made this dream come true; you brought them home; even deep in the sea, still it's home to us. Thank you!

Our lives changed the moment you cried out "We found!" From now on, we are able to look up to the world with a brighter look, with a happier smile—because of you!

We are grateful to you for every single day of hard work, for every sleepless night you went through, for every moment of courage and determination.

We love you very much!! May God bless you!!

Epilogue

I felt the story of the loss of the *Dakar* could not end with a description of the forensic investigation and carefully worded reports of findings. Right or wrong, I felt that the memory of the men who went down with the ship would be best served by an attempt to describe what might have been happening to them in their final moments.

One of the reasons for this was my experience of being asked by a family member what it was like for their loved one at the end. I could state with conviction that the end was quick, and during the brief time the crewmen were wrestling with disaster they could rely on training and procedure to help them manage their fears. This was of some comfort, but when I thought about it further I couldn't help wondering about the details.

Up to the last chapter in the story, I tried my very best to stick to the facts, and describe everything as accurately as I could know it. But to imagine what happened on the last deep dive of the *Dakar*, I had to go a bit beyond facts, and make some assumptions. There were technical assumptions about how the water flooded into the ship and what effect that would have on the machine itself. Much of this could be calculated from the details of the forensic study, although the exact source of the flooding will never be known. I also chose to invent a scenario describing the actions and experiences of Isaac, Boomie, and Captain Ra'anan. This, of course, is my own pure speculation, although I tried my best to describe what they would have done in that situation.

I hope I have shown that, indeed, the crew of the *Dakar* had little time, and there was nothing they could have done. Even if my estimate of sixty-five seconds is off, it certainly did not take as much as two minutes. So much water entered the ship so quickly that no action could have saved them. I note that it took me over eight minutes to read aloud the passage describing the final sixty-five seconds.

Commander Bar-Yam told me that I should admit that there are many possible causes to the flooding, and that the failure of the hull itself was very unlikely. I agree with him completely. . . but I contend that it probably was a very unlikely event that caused the demise of the ship. Otherwise, the *Dakar* would have come home safely.

No one should read into that last chapter any justification for cause or blame. If any family member is offended by those words, I apologize. It was my intent to honor the memory of the men of the *Dakar* . . . never forgotten!

Appendix: The Crew of the INS *Dakar*

The list below is from the official book of the *Dakar*, published in 1968 by the Israeli Ministry of Defense. The sixty-nine names, with their respective ages, are sorted according to the Hebrew alphabet, as in the original list (but with English spellings). If the original family name was not Hebrew, it is given in parentheses. Note that English spelling of Israeli names can vary.

Aharon Aharon (Duga), 22
Shlomo Ofek (Opotchinski), 35
Josef Almog (Suissa), 20
Noshe Ereel (Angle), 21
Avraham Baz (Bozna), 21
Eliezer Ben-Zvi (Bjejinski), 19
David Ben-Shalom (Yidlovker), 21
Chaim Bar-Zeev (Reichberger), 21
Josef Barnea, 21
Avraham (Boomi) Barkai (Bursuck), 30
Michael Gal (Hafner), 20
Reuven Gal (Gelman), 22
Noshe Gadish, 20
Yehuda Galili (Gelula), 21
Josef Debie, 20
Menachem Degani, 21
Azriel Dror (Donius), 33
Nimrod Drori, 20
Michael Hadar, 24
Zvi Har-Even (Harivan), 22
Shlomo Vardi, 21
Zvi Zahavi (Goldstein), 21
Josef Zohar, 22
Zvi Tal (Teitler), 37
Mordechai Tarshi, 21
Yeshayahu Yochai, 20
David Yanai, 19

Meir Yarom, 20
Nissim Cohen, 33
Israel Karmi (Weinstein), 22
Josef Lahav (Sikurel), 26
Dr. Shabi-Yaacov Maor, 29
Oded Madmon, 21
Yehezkel Mizrachi, 25
Yaacov Mizrachi, 21
Benyamin Meimon, 42
Dan Manor (Maness), 24
Josef Netzer (Wallberg), 21
Menachem Narkis (Nargus), 20
Gideon Segal, 24
Reuven Snapir (Shnaper), 22
Meir Safran, 20
Yizhack Ogen (Marcovici), 20
Betzlel Ozeri, 20
Avraham Atari, 29
Amnon Paz (Piza), 20
Arieh Paz (Feingold), 22
Zvi Paz (Pomera), 21
Zvi Parag, 24
Josef Farchi, 21
Eli Kadosh, 19
Zeev Kol (Kalvari), 23
Avraham Ron, 20
Amnon Ron (Ringvald), 25

Yaacov Ron (Shukrun), 27
Yehuda Ronen (Shtein), 22
Yaacov Ronen (Vaknin), 20
Yaacov Ra'anan (Frish), 34
Refael Refaeli (Fadida), 29
Avraham Shachar (Shpitler), 23
Yossi Shalev (Friedman), 20
Ran Shimon, 34

Chaim Shani (Shneorson), 19
Yuval Shmueli, 20
Alexander Sharoni (Kendel), 20
Eliezer Sharoni, 21
Yehezkel Sasson, 22
Bennie Shaked (Mendel), 21
Amnon Tamir (Kaplan), 24

Index

About the Author

David W. Jourdan is the co-founder and president of Nauticos, a company devoted to the exploration of the deep ocean. He studied physics and engineering at the U.S. Naval Academy and Johns Hopkins University, and served as a U.S. Navy submarine officer during the Cold War. As a physicist at the Johns Hopkins University Applied Physics Laboratory, and as leader of Nauticos, he became an expert in the exploitation of undersea environmental data and has supported many scientific, archaeological, and military programs. He has written about diverse technical topics including underwater navigation, oceanographic survey, remote sensing, underwater vehicles, ocean exploration, and ocean renewable energy applications.

Jourdan and his Nauticos team managed ocean operations for the Discovery Channel during the live broadcast from the wreck of the *Titanic* in 1998. He is responsible for the discovery of the Japanese aircraft carrier *Kaga*, sunk at the World War II Battle of Midway in the Pacific, and the Japanese World War II submarine *I-52* in the Atlantic, both at depths exceeding 17,000 feet. His team discovered the missing Israeli submarine *Dakar* in the Mediterranean at 10,000 feet, and he has led two deep ocean expeditions in search of Amelia Earhart's lost Lockheed Electra airplane. He has spoken to military, business, and scientific organizations across the country about his major discoveries and has appeared on the National Geographic Channel, the Discovery Channel, and the *Today Show*.

Jourdan was named Maryland Small Business Person of the Year in 1999 and is an International Fellow of the Explorer's Club. He has been active in many humanitarian programs, including Rotary International since 1994, and has traveled to Africa to support initiatives to combat AIDS and provide fresh water to rural communities. Jourdan lives with his wife Lynn in the coastal Maine village of Cape Porpoise.

The Naval Institute Press is the book-publishing arm of the U.S. Naval Institute, a private, nonprofit, membership society for sea service professionals and others who share an interest in naval and maritime affairs. Established in 1873 at the U.S. Naval Academy in Annapolis, Maryland, where its offices remain today, the Naval Institute has members worldwide.

Members of the Naval Institute support the education programs of the society and receive the influential monthly magazine *Proceedings* or the colorful bimonthly magazine *Naval History* and discounts on fine nautical prints and on ship and aircraft photos. They also have access to the transcripts of the Institute's Oral History Program and get discounted admission to any of the Institute-sponsored seminars offered around the country.

The Naval Institute's book-publishing program, begun in 1898 with basic guides to naval practices, has broadened its scope to include books of more general interest. Now the Naval Institute Press publishes about seventy titles each year, ranging from how-to books on boating and navigation to battle histories, biographies, ship and aircraft guides, and novels. Institute members receive significant discounts on the Press's more than eight hundred books in print.

Full-time students are eligible for special half-price membership rates. Life memberships are also available.

For a free catalog describing Naval Institute Press books currently available, and for further information about joining the U.S. Naval Institute, please write to:

Member Services
U.S. Naval Institute
291 Wood Road
Annapolis, MD 21402-5034
Telephone: (800) 233-8764
Fax: (410) 571-1703
Web address: www.usni.org